Object-Oriented
Software

Object-Oriented Software

- **Ann L. Winblad**

- **Samuel D. Edwards**

- **David R. King**

 Addison-Wesley Publishing Company, Inc.

Reading, Massachusetts • Menlo Park, California • New York
Don Mills, Ontario • Wokingham, England • Amsterdam
Bonn • Sydney • Singapore • Tokyo • Madrid • San Juan

Library of Congress Cataloging-in-Publication Data

Winblad, Ann L.
    Object-oriented software / by Ann L. Winblad, Samuel D. Edwards,
    David R. King.
        p.   cm.
    Includes bibliographical references.
    ISBN 0-201-50736-6
    1. Object-oriented programming (Computer science)   I. Edwards,
    Samuel D.   II. King, David, 1949–   III. Title.
    QA76.64.W56   1990
    005.1—dc20   90-31928
                                                             CIP
Reprinted with corrections September, 1990

    4 5 6 7 8 9 10 AL 95949392

Preface and Introduction

- **Introduction**

- **Why Object Orientation Now?**

- **Who Should Read This Book?**

- **How Should You Use This Book?**

- **Acknowledgments**

In this preface we set forth this book's goals. We shall explain how the book is organized and suggest ways that readers with different backgrounds and objectives might best proceed. Finally, we shall acknowledge those who have influenced us in our explorations of object orientation.

Read the preface for a thumbnail sketch of the book.

Introduction

At the onset of the 1990s, software lags behind hardware capabilities by at least two processor generations, and the lag is increasing. There is general agreement that conventional software tools, techniques, and abstractions are rapidly becoming inadequate as software systems grow larger and increasingly more complex. This presents a major dilemma for commercial and corporate software developers. No "silver bullet" (Brooks 1987) is forecast for the near future, but a concensus is building that the new paradigm of object orientation may help control complexity and harness the expanding system environment into more useful and exciting applications.

In the 1990s, applications will need to satisfy more sophisticated requirements, use more complex data structures and architectures, and be delivered to an increasingly broad base of users. All these factors are driving the need for a quantum leap in the capacity of software devel-

> Programmers have become part historian, part detective, and part clairvoyant.
> *Corbi, 1989*

opers to build, extend, and maintain complex, large-scale systems. More-over, delivery to a broader base of users requires that software be more flexible and easier to use.

As we enter the 1990s, software development remains virtually in the dark ages. Although universities and advanced research and development organizations have made a great deal of progress on the tools and techniques used for software construction, little of this progress has pervaded the everyday tasks of the typical software developer. Much of today's software development processes remain preindustrial, with programmers still functioning like craftsmen. They build unique, noninterchangeable components and assemble them by hand, and then they struggle over time to understand the code created by their predecessors and to extend and refine the software product. Because software products fail to adapt to changing environments, such as enhancements in computing hardware and operating systems or the increasing expectations of users, they rarely survive ten years. The issue is clearly not hardware performance in this "MIPS to the moon" era; it is software capability that lags several processor generations behind. As powerful computers pervade the lives of more and more people, the inability to deliver and maintain equally powerful software is an increasingly visible problem.

Object orientation provides a new paradigm for software construction. In this new paradigm, objects and classes are the building blocks, while methods, messages, and inheritance produce the primary mechanisms. Historically, creating a software program involved defining processes that act on a separate set of data. As we will thoroughly discuss in this book, object orientation changes the focus of the programming process from procedures to *objects*—self-contained modules that include both the data and the procedures that act on the data. The procedures contained within the object take on a new name, *methods.* Unlike the passive data in conventional programs, objects can act and are activated by *messages* from other objects. Objects that have a common use are grouped together in a *class,* and new classes can be created that *inherit* the procedures and data from classes already built, enabling the programmer to reuse existing classes and to program only the differences. The paradigm is one that offers a new level of abstraction, with prebuilt libraries of classes and even prebuilt application-specific class libraries or *frameworks.*

Object orientation may well be the new and established view of software in the 1990s, with both programmers and end users potentially benefitting from the implementation of this new paradigm. Although the shift from designing and programming around process to designing and programming around objects may seem extreme, object-oriented programming is a more natural form of software design and modeling. With full implementation of object-orientation, end users may be able to extend their ability to modify and perhaps program their own applications. Programmers may be able to design more complex applications in parts that are modular and interchangeable.

Is it exaggeration to state that object-oriented software will be an established computing model in the 1990s? Certainly the computer software industry is prone to hyperbole. Great groundswells of promise are created before new technologies are commercialized and broadly understood. This overenthusiasm is not necessarily bad; it has been a driving force for both acceptance and rejection of new technologies. However, the primary question remains: When and how will the benefits of object-oriented software arrive for the developer, the user, and for the software industry as a whole?

Those software developers who have had years of experience with the paradigm of object orientation would say that part of this dilemma is due to resistance to change by programmers who are familiar and comfortable with their traditional languages, tools, databases, and overall development paradigms. Yet we would argue that such resistance is being acknowledged and is gradually being overcome, as existing tools, languages, and databases that incorporate object-oriented mechanisms allow the software developer to straddle the old and the new and to experience the benefits that object orientation brings to software construction.

Object orientation is an important paradigm for the software development challenges of the 1990s. Its promises will be delivered incrementally and across a broad range of technologies and will permeate the next generation of software architectures. The paradigm will improve the software development process and will cause new and better applications to evolve. The potential is already being demonstrated and embraced by leading software developers who have object architectures, the foundation upon which future applications will reside, under construction. Thus, although object orientation is not yet fully embodied in the software development tools and applications used today, the fundamental building blocks for object-oriented development environments are in the hands of premier developers, and they are already yielding demonstrable benefits in terms of development time, programming resources required, and ability to construct new generations of existing software.

Why Object Orientation Now?

Object orientation is not a brand new concept. In fact, it is at least 15 years old. Its roots can be traced to Norway in the late 1960s in connection with a language called Simula67, developed by Kristen Nygaard and Ole-Johan Dahl at the Norwegian Computing Centre (Millikin 1989). Simula67 first introduced the concepts of classes, coroutines, and subclasses, much like today's object-oriented languages.

Then, in the mid-1970s, scientists at the Xerox Palo Alto Research Center (Xerox PARC) created the language Smalltalk, the first complete and robust object-oriented language. In Smalltalk, every element of the language was implemented as an object (Goldberg and Robson 1983). With Smalltalk, every aspect of the language, the programming environment, and the culture that surrounded it was object-oriented. Even today, Smalltalk is considered the purest of the object-oriented languages. The Simula and Smalltalk developments launched much of the work occurring now. Simula67 demonstrated the modeling power of a class-based programming language as well as the idea that data and operations should be stored together. It became recognized that programming effort could be saved if common properties of objects could be preprogrammed.

Until recently, object orientation was slow to penetrate the mainstream computing community. This slow migration was due to a number of factors. Although well known in university circles, Simula67 and Smalltalk were relatively inaccessible to the mainstream software community until the 1980s. The pioneering work in Smalltalk, for example, was not widely publicized outside Xerox PARC until the August 1981 issue of *Byte* magazine. Requirements for specialized computing platforms also made the use of these early languages economically unattractive to corporate and commercial software developers. Many developers, when first introduced to Smalltalk, thought of it more as a windowing system than as a revolutionary programming paradigm. The failure to appreciate the object-oriented programming paradigm in Smalltalk is exemplified by the subsequent development of many interfaces that use windows and icons without allowing users to modify these objects (Thomas 1989).

In the 1980s, C became a popular development language, not just on microcomputers but across most computing architectures and environments. In the early 1980s, Bjarne Stroustrup of AT&T Bell Laboratories extended the C language to create C++, a language that supports object-oriented programming (Stroustrup 1986). Subsequent tool enhancements and commercial releases of the C++ language by AT&T,

as well as a number of other vendors, account for much of the widespread attention to object-oriented programming in the general software community. With C++, programmers were able to learn the object-oriented paradigm in a familiar, popular lexicon, without having to invest in a new and different computing language and environment.

Price/performance obstacles that prevented the widespread use of object-oriented technology have also dropped by the wayside. The configurations of today's powerful personal computers have satisfied the basic requirements for higher-performance workstations, higher-quality graphic displays, and fully supported, tool-rich, development environments; and the introduction of integrated object-oriented environments, specifically the Macintosh in 1984 and the NeXT machine in 1988, were significant milestones in moving object orientation into mainstream computing.

Increasing technological complexity, however, is the underlying accelerator for the use of the object-oriented paradigm. Object orientation provides a better way of dealing with technological complexity. Programmers using current development tools to build applications indicate that without layers of abstraction, application development chokes. Object orientation allows programming at increasingly higher levels of abstraction—from the object to the class to the class library, and ultimately to entire application frameworks.

Finally, the software industry is eager to try a better approach to software development. The software industry has become stalled (some have described it as "beached") by a lack of better processes. Object orientation promises to deliver to commercial software developers the capability for accelerated product development, extendable code, and products that can be marketed to a broader base of customers.

Who Should Read This Book?

This book provides a framework for people interested in understanding the nature of object-oriented software, its influence on software construction, and the place of object orientation in the future evolution of the software industry. It will outline the key concepts and trace the history of the object-oriented paradigm. It will also show how object-oriented tools and techniques are used by software developers and how the object-oriented paradigm drives the functionality of application software.

You don't have to be a programmer to read this book, although having computing experience will add depth to your understanding of its examples and terms. For readers who are programmers or students of computer science, the book provides the big picture of object orientation and provides a useful overview as a prelude to selected technical readings. Procedural programmers who have experienced computer programs only as a sequenced set of instructions may find a path to a different view. When you finish this book, you will not be an object-oriented programmer, but you will know

- the benefits of object orientation from the points of view of both a user and a software developer;

- the meaning of terms and techniques most frequently used to describe object-oriented software construction;

- the influence of object orientation on fundamental software building blocks, including languages, databases, and user interfaces;

- the influence of object orientation on new and existing software applications; and

- the books, articles, and other resources available for further study of the many subtopics that constitute object orientation.

How Should You Use This Book?

Object orientation may at first appear to be a complex subject. After reading this book, you should find object orientation intuitive and compelling.

We realize that members of our audience have a variety of backgrounds and motivations for reading this book. For non-programmers, we provide an overview of object orientation, how it applies to the overall system environment, and how it will affect applications. For programmers, we provide and explain the basics of object-oriented software design and construction. And for all readers, we offer perspective on how object-oriented technology will affect the software marketplace.

To accommodate different kinds of readers, we recommend three alternate paths:

Path 1: If you are a generalist, consultant, or manager and have no computer experience, then Path 1 is for you. Path 1 focuses on basic terms, benefits, and applications. It also provides you with an overview of the use of object orientation in both the developer's and user's environment. Figure 1 shows the route you should take.

Path 2: If you have some programming experience and you want to see some code, this path is for you. Path 2 reviews basic terms, benefits, and applications. It also examines the implications of object orientation on computing languages, databases, and interfaces. This path provides both a general overview and technical detail. Figure 2 illustrates the route you should take.

Path 3: If you are a serious programmer who wants a broad introduction to object-oriented technology, our book will be a primer.

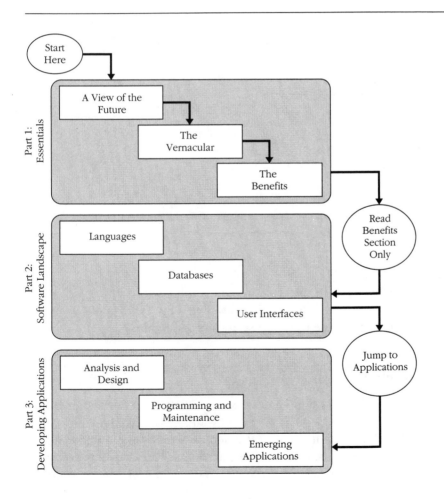

Figure 1
Path 1 for the Generalist, Consultant, or Manager

Figure 2
Path 2 for Those
with Some Program-
ming Experience

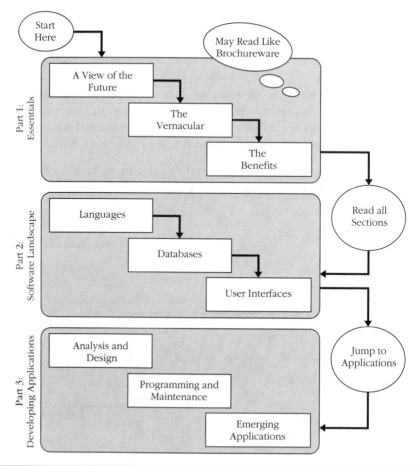

Path 3 begins with the software landscape, reviews object-oriented
software development, and finishes with a review of applications.
Figure 3 shows the route for serious programmers.

Acknowledgments

We began writing this book in the spring of 1989, and we launched the
project with a series of what we called "object-oriented dinners." Capi-
talizing on the fact that many of the people associated with object orientation live and work where we do, in the San Francisco Bay area, we
invited scientists, engineers, programmers, product managers, venture

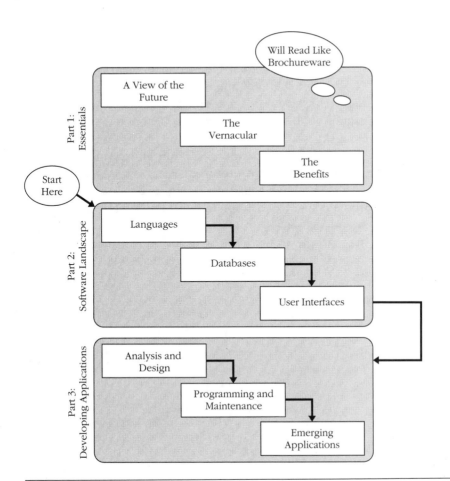

Figure 3
Path 3 for the Serious Programmer

capitalists, and a few CEOs to talk with us about object-oriented technology and how it would benefit programmers and users. Both skeptics and believers were included in these soirees. Our conversations focused on three key questions:

What is the essence of object orientation?

What will the benefits be for programmers?

What will the benefits be for users?

Our guests did not always agree when answering these questions. From the discussions that ensued, we began to forge our ideas into the chapters of our book. We thank our guests for accelerating our understanding of the issues and opinions surrounding object orientation. Table 1 lists those who came to dinner.

We thank Addison-Wesley Publishing Company and especially our editor, Peter Gordon, for their continuing support, encouragement, and critiques to help us to stay on task and on track.

Our colleagues at the Price Waterhouse Technology Centre provided encouragement as well as computing and library support. Special thanks to Tom Orsi, managing partner; Paul Turner, executive director; and Linda Veenker, information center manager.

We also wish to thank the many researchers and pioneers who have created the products that we mention in our book and the authors who have followed and written on the topic of object orientation. We acknowledge these people in the Further Readings and References sections at the end of each chapter. These are the experts whose knowledge this book has, we hope, inherited.

Table 1.
"Object-Oriented Dinner" Attendees

Name	Affiliation	Name	Affiliation
Brad Beitel	IBM	Gregor Kiczales	Xerox PARC
Danny Bobrow	Xerox PARC	Jaron Lanier	VPL Research
Mark Boyd	ServioLogic	Dave Liddle	Metaphor Computer Systems
Phill Christensen	ServioLogic	Bill Parkhurst	NeXT Computers
Bill Crow	Hewlett-Packard	Harry Reinstein	AION
Peter Deutsch	ParcPlace Systems	Daniel Sagalowicz	Consultant
Hal Elgie	VPL Research	Mike Seashols	Object Sciences
Bob Epstein	Sybase	Dan Shafer	Writer
RuAnn Ernst	Hewlett-Packard	John Shoch	Asset Management
Bob Field	Objectivity	Lee Sigler	Sun Microsystems
Paul Gavanni	Apple Computer, Inc.	Hal Steiger	Oracle
Chris Goad	Silma	Paul Turner	Price Waterhouse Technology Centre
Adele Goldberg	ParcPlace Systems	Scott Wallace	Apple Computer, Inc.
Bill Joy	Sun Microsystems	Tony Wasserman	Interactive Development Environments
Gerald Kaplan	Go Corporation		

Finally, we acknowledge the patience and encouragement of our families and friends. Susan King played a special role as consulting wordsmith as did Joe McGuckin as a technical editor in the final months of the manuscript's preparation. Rachael Edwards, born during the writing of the book, napped in accordance with her father's writing schedule. Mary-Suzanne King filed articles and built a Hypercard stack for our references. Our multitude of friends and colleagues listened and commented on our obsessive concern with the topics of object. Special thanks to John Hummer who uncomplainingly helped lug books and manuscripts to 25 U.S. cities while successfully raising the funds for Hummer Winblad Venture Partners.

Key Points

- Object orientation represents a major shift from traditional methods of software construction.

- Traditional methods apply active procedures to passive data. Object-oriented methods encapsulate procedures and data.

- Object orientation applies to most major software components, including languages, databases, and interfaces. The result will be software that is easier to extend and maintain and applications that are richer, easier to use, and more flexible.

- Object orientation is important today because of the increasing complexity of software and the need for better software construction processes.

- This book is designed for readers who have different backgrounds and objectives. Choose an appropriate path for you.

- We appreciate the support of our publisher, colleagues, friends, and family who all helped us to write this book.

For Further Study

Peterson, G. E., ed. 1987. *Tutorial: Object-Oriented Computing, Volume 1: Concepts.* Washington, D.C.: Computer Society Press of the IEEE.

Peterson, G. E., ed. 1987. *Tutorial: Object-Oriented Computing, Volume 2: Implementations.* Washington, D.C.: Computer Society Press of the IEEE.

These volumes provide a systematic survey of object orientation with articles reprinted from a variety of sources.

References

Brooks, F. P. 1987. "No silver bullet: Essence and accidents of software engineering." *Computer,* 20 (4): 10–19.

Corbi, T.A. 1989. "Program understanding: Challenge for the 1990s." *IBM Systems Journal,* 28 (2).

Goldberg, A. and Robson, D. 1983. *Smalltalk-80: The Language and its Implementation.* Reading, Mass.: Addison-Wesley.

Millikin, M. D. 1989. "Object orientation: What it can do for you; from operating systems to user interfaces, commercial viability is near." *Computerworld,* March 13.

Stroustrup, B. 1986. *The C+ + Programming Language.* Reading, Mass.: Addison-Wesley.

Thomas, D. 1989. "What's in an object?" *Byte,* March.

Contents

■ Part Three: Developing Object-Oriented Applications

Chapter 7   Analysis and Design   175

Chapter 8   Programming and Maintenance   207

Chapter 9   Emerging Applications   237

■ **Part Four: Appendices**

A   Glossary   261

B   Collected References   281

Part 1

The Essentials of
Object Orientation

- **A View of the Future**

- **The Vernacular**

- **The Benefits**

Chapter 1
A View of the Future

- **Introduction**

- **The Driving Forces**
    Multimedia Information
    End-User Computing
    Distributed Processing

- **The Future**

- **The Recent Progress**
    The Apple Macintosh
    The NeXT Computer

- **The Object Architecture of the 1990s**

- **Summary**

This chapter provides a glimpse into the object-oriented software landscape of the 1990s. We shall identify the forces that are propelling object-oriented technology into mainstream computing. We shall discuss the progress of object-oriented languages, databases, user interfaces, operating systems, and applications. These forces include the needs of multimedia information, end-user computing, and distributed systems.

Read this chapter to understand the basis for the excitement surrounding object orientation.

Introduction

> Programmers have become part historian, part detective, and part clairvoyant.
> *Corbi, 1989*

After years of relative obscurity, object orientation appears to be entering the mainstream of commercial computing for both software developers and end users. A shift to object orientation is occurring simultaneously across a wide range of software components, including languages, user interfaces, databases, and operating systems. While object-oriented programming is no panacea, it has already demonstrated that it can help manage the growing complexity and increasing costs of software development.

Object orientation, as it is integrated into the fundamental components of the software landscape, is to the 1990s what structured programming was to the 1970s: a new and important paradigm for improving software construction, maintenance, and use. Object orientation will change the way programmers work, and it will increase the speed with which they produce next generation applications. It may also expand the programming capability of the end user. Object orientation will expand the functionality that can be built into applications, and object-oriented approaches will enable end users to gain access to current and expanded types of data across heterogeneous computing platforms.

Object-oriented systems have been used in the research community for over 15 years. Unlike many new techniques that remain of interest to academics and advanced research and development groups, object orientation is well on its way to the mainstream. Already thousands of programmers in the top commercial software companies are using object-oriented languages and programming tools.

> If we had object-oriented applications, there would be a different application ecology. It would mean the end of the era of monolithic applications.
> *Kapor, 1988*

Some of the force of object orientation has already been felt. Object-oriented language standards are beginning to crystalize with object extensions to popular programming languages such as Pascal, C, and COBOL. Object-oriented development tools, the true supporting components for languages, are quickly being adopted to facilitate object-oriented design, coding, and debugging. Development environments for constructing object-oriented user interfaces are also already in use. Built atop standard windowing systems, these user interface environments permit the more rapid creation of interactive applications from preexisting object libraries.

Not all components of the object-oriented architecture that will evolve in the 1990s are currently in use. Total commercial success will depend on a convergence and integration of systems software, languages, tools, databases, and prebuilt object libraries (class libraries) to

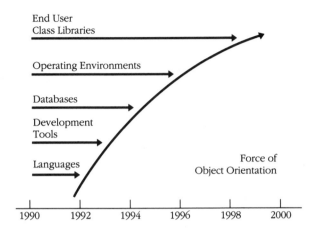

End User
Class Libraries

Operating Environments

Databases

Development
Tools

Languages

Force of
Object Orientation

| 1990 | 1992 | 1994 | 1996 | 1998 | 2000 |

Figure 1.1
Full Object Orientation Arrives

support the creation and implementation of full-scale systems with object architectures. At the time this book was published, for example, no object-oriented database had achieved commercial popularity. In fact, few object-oriented databases were available. Object-oriented file systems and operating systems were also not currently supported on popular computer configurations. While programmers were already benefitting from object-oriented programming environments, few tools were available to facilitate end-user programming. Lastly, there were few standards for object-oriented software in place, the evolution of which will determine the overall speed at which the technology envelope is extended. Figure 1.1 shows a timetable for total integration of object orientation.

The Driving Forces

Object-oriented programming and the accompanying object orientation of tools and architectures are rapidly changing the programming world. Acceptance is being driven by many forces. Increasing complexity, diversity, and interconnectedness are characteristics of most major systems of the 1990s. Enterprise-wide systems will accommodate many different types of information, with such information coming from many points within a network. Development tools, system environment, and applications that support multimedia information, end-user computing, and distributed processing are the driving forces for object orientation.

Multimedia Information

Today's systems continue to increase in complexity. Complexity is increasing in a number of dimensions, not only in terms of requirements for extended functionality but also in terms of diverse data types. Systems of the future will most likely process image, voice, and video in addition to text and numbers. As Figure 1.2 shows, improving performance and increasing capacity were the challenges for software of the past, while managing increasing complexity is the challenge of the future.

Computing has moved beyond record orientation to accommodate richer and more complex data types. Application areas such as computer integrated manufacturing (CIM), computer aided design (CAD), computer aided software engineering (CASE), and computer aided publishing (CAP) have already stretched the capability of current programming and systems software architecture with their requirements for simulation, real-world representation, manipulation, and complex interrelationships among a variety of data types. Figure 1.3 shows this shift in the data components of a typical system.

The requirement to support complex data types is rapidly extending into many other general application areas as well. Even the personal computer hardware of the 1990s will undergo changes to provide the capability for integrated multimedia support as part of the basic computer configuration. By 1992, a basic personal computer should be available that includes standard multimedia support (Alsop 1989). Features will most likely include digital signal processing (DSP) to allow the manipulation of audio data for either voice or music applications, integrated CD/ROM device, full-motion video, expanded memory, and enhanced color graphics. Software tools to support these rich combi-

Figure 1.2
The Growing Complexity of Software

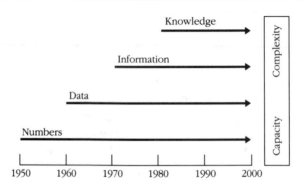

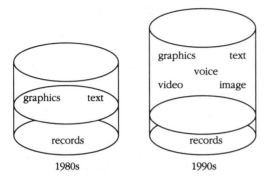

Figure 1.3
Record Orientation
Is a Minor Part of
1990s System
Architecture

nations of data will also likely evolve from the hypercard tools of today to an integrated object-oriented multimedia toolkit. As early as late 1989, with the release of the NeXT machine, many of these features reached the marketplace. Table 1.1 shows the typical configurations of the multimedia personal computer of the 1990s.

Not only does this forecast of a multimedia computer suggest a requirement to accommodate multiple data types, but it also implies that special developers and tools will be required to support the multimedia production system. Animators, sound engineers, musicians, and graphics

Table 1.1
Basic Multimedia
Computer
Configurations

	1990	1992	1994
Memory	>1M bytes	>4M bytes	>8M bytes
Graphics	512 × 512 pixels 4 bits of color	1024 × 1024 pixels 8 bits of color Limited motion video	1024 × 1024 pixels 32 bites of color Full-motion, full-screen digital video
Digital Signal Processing	No digital signal processing	Digital signal processing Audio data	Digital signal processing Audio data
Storage	CD/ROM Optional, unintegrated	CD/ROM Integrated	CD/ROM Integrated
Graphical User Interface	Window interface	Window interface	Object-oriented window interface
Tools	Limited multimedia tools	Hypercardlike authoring system	Integrated, object-oriented multimedia toolkit

artists will commonly be members of application development teams in the 1990s. Multimedia computing will demand development environments that support components from distinct programming work groups that must be integrated into a total application. It will require that programs respond diversely, for example, with sound or animation, as opposed to simply displaying textual or graphic information.

The computer of the 1990s will make it possible to immerse users in a virtual reality in which the computer generates an encompassing audio-visual environment. This ability to simulate rather than simply run a program will give users the opportunity to touch and walk among the objects in the application. Object-oriented CAD applications are already adding this simulation capability through virtual reality systems which allow three-dimensional objects to be manipulated by users wearing special glasses and sensory gloves. With such capabilities, architects and clients could virtually walk through computer-simulated buildings, and potential car buyers could simulate a test drive.

As we shall more fully describe in later chapters, object orientation provides the capability to support diverse work groups who build their own objects. It is a programming paradigm that allows different objects to respond to the same request or message differently. For example, display for some objects may activate motion, whereas for others, it may activate sound as well. Object orientation also allows extensions to be added to the applications as multimedia computing capabilities expand.

End-User Computing

Not only are applications becoming increasingly complex, but users are asking for more and more control over what applications can do. Demand is accelerating for improved prototyping tools and development paradigms that allow users themselves to build maintainable extensions to application frameworks. There has been some progress. Improved prototyping tools, such as fourth-generation languages (4GLs); macro languages, such as those incorporated with spreadsheets; and visual programming environments, such as Apple Computer's Hypercard, have incrementally improved the overall satisfaction of users with their ultimate applications.

Almost all companies, however, acknowledge a backlog of unfilled user requests for large-scale system development. Some companies admit an even greater hidden demand: Users no longer bother to ask for new or improved applications because they are well aware of the overwhelming load on their developers. This software backlog is also compounded by changes in hardware and diversity of operating environments. The backlog trench is getting deeper and deeper. With the current development approaches there will never be enough programmers to satisfy the more than thirty million users who will enter the 1990s with stand-alone or connected computers on their desktops.

The challenge of the 1990s is to exploit the opportunities for rich applications, while at the same time hiding complexity from all those involved with the software, including the user, the application developer, and the maintenance programmer. This has not been the case to date. Although graphical user interfaces, such as that of the Apple Macintosh, have made major improvements in hiding complexity from users and making applications easier to use, the requirement to support these graphically rich interfaces and their complex development environments has increased the burden of the programming and maintenance task.

First for software developers and ultimately for users, object-oriented programming will provide the opportunity to build substantial applications based on the work of others. User interfaces can be developed more quickly in an object-oriented development environment because the developer, and ultimately the user, begins with a palette of preexisting objects (e.g., an interface kit with prepackaged objects such as scroll bars, menus, dialog boxes, buttons) with which to construct an application. Objects created for one application can serve as building blocks for other applications. When one developer creates a clever word processor, it can be reused in building an electronic mail editor, in the same way that scroll bars, menus, and dialog objects are reused for different user interfaces. When another developer creates an object-oriented voice driver, it can be reused for voice mail. Object-oriented architectures will ease the task of integrating applications. This will reduce the number of basic applications (objects) that need to be delivered to make the computing environment extremely useful and extensible to both developers and users. With only a few key object-oriented applications, the user's palette for application creation will be extremely robust.

In the past, user programming was virtually an oxymoron. The popularity of user programming tools, such as Apple's Hypercard (more object-like than purely object-oriented) demonstrates that nonprogrammers can and will create systems if the right environment is provided. Beyond Hypercard, full object-oriented applications will also shed their monolithic nature. The notion that one application should do everything will be replaced; future applications will be composed of modules that snap together and assume their functions through the message-based mechanisms of object-oriented systems.

Distributed Processing

With the shift to distributed architectures that support multivendor platforms, users are demanding connectivity, interoperability, and tools for communication across the layers of system software, data formats, and applications. And as workstations have decreased reliance on shared processors, increasingly complex organizations and enterprises have also made it more important than ever to share data.

In the 1990s, local area networks (LANs) will increasingly lose their stand-alone nature and will have gateways to larger corporatewide area networks (WANs). The robustness of the backbone architectures of LANs will also improve, including the emergence of a fiber-distributed data interface (FDDI) to support multimedia data transmission as a backbone network protocol. These networks will evolve further from three-tiered hierarchies with each layer offering increased sophistication in communications, applications, and management, toward flatter, peer-to-peer networks.

These enterprisewide networks will also be supported by more robust backbone architectures. Integrated services digital network (ISDN) will provide end-to-end connectivity to carry every form of digital communication service, data exchange, electronic mail, fax, and videophone to provide seamless communication of information between computing devices.

One of the greatest challenges of the 1990s will be to provide ways for noncooperative programs to communicate, not just in one well-defined environment, but across an enterprisewide network of heterogeneous computing environments. An object-oriented architecture with industry, as opposed to vendor-specific, standards holds strong potential as a solution to this problem.

Monolithic systems play no role in an object-oriented architecture. Layered systems achieve a new dimension with object orientation. Form is reexpressed as a collection of objects communicating with each other through messages; applications are dynamically assembled, even across architectures, from these objects when messages are sent. Object architectures will support systems that can be mailed in their entirety electronically and be shared by more than one user. As such, object-oriented architectures will incorporate such issues as distribution of objects and reconfiguration of objects to enhance application use over truly distributed systems.

The Future

Object-oriented techniques will provide the clarity and flexibility essential to the successful development of complex systems. Today's applications do not offer the consistency and flexibility needed to make the computing environment more productive for users. Object-oriented software promises to change this with much more than the familiar point-and-click window interface. Application interoperability will extend far beyond today's clipboard. Object orientation will provide environments in which users can communicate among applications and navigate easily over distributed, heterogeneous architectures.

In the near future object orientation will deliver the most benefits to three categories of programmers: power users, general business programmers, and systems-level developers. The most dramatic near-term benefits will be for system developers who both require and embrace this development approach and its evolving tools to implement the increasingly complex and potentially innovative software of the 1990s.

Over time, object-oriented technology will begin to have increasing impact on general business programmers and power users. Carefully designed object libraries will become available to support less sophisticated programmers who want to assemble applications quickly from prefabricated parts. Figure 1.4 illustrates the impact of object orientation across the user community. As shown, the availability of prebuilt objects will be the enabling mechanism for ultimate user programmability.

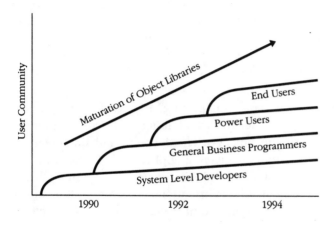

Figure 1.4
User Community
Broadens as Object
Libraries Mature

Some inertia will exist. Programmer ego, unlearning of traditional approaches, and the economics of purchasing new software and hardware have historically combined to maintain the process and problems of handcrafted software. The process of building software that will evolve with object orientation will present a challenge to those programmers who have always worked alone using their own tools and style. This will be but one of the changes that will impact the software craftsman. The programming community may indeed restructure itself, dividing into object producers and object consumers. Object producers will provide object libraries in specialized areas. Object consumers will assemble existing object libraries, with a few objects of their own creation, to build custom applications.

Current software conventions may well be rapidly eclipsed. Graphic metaphors familiar to many users will remain, but passive icons will be supplemented with active icons. These active icons will be referred to as intelligent agents that perform functions such as routing electronic mail or filling out timesheets. Such agents will work behind the scenes in many applications. Future object libraries will allow custom applications to be built easily from existing building blocks. Today much of the click art, buttons, procedures, and text contained in current libraries is static and cannot be modified. The user programmability of systems like Apple Computer's Hypercard and Lotus's Macros, although limited compared to the future offerings, provides a sneak preview of how users will build their own integrated applications, given the appropriate environment. In the future, objectlike extensions, such as Hypercard, will rapidly look like mere dashboards for users as compared to the full object-oriented construction sets of the future.

Interfaces of the future will encourage users to think of all visual elements (icons) as objects to be manipulated directly with the mouse and keyboard and supported completely by an underlying object system. Such applications exist as prototypes in research laboratories such as Carnegie-Mellon University's Andrew system (Palay 1989). In an object-oriented environment, interoperability will be streamlined. Preparing a compound document today consists of a multistep process: opening special-purpose applications, "cutting" to clipboard, closing one application, opening another, and "pasting" the result. A graph is updated by revising the spreadsheet on which it is based, recutting, and repasting the result. With the object-oriented compound document, drawings may be inserted without juggling applications. Updates to a spreadsheet will be reflected automatically in the graph that remains in the word processing document. Object-oriented file systems will lie under the applications and provide transparent management of all objects.

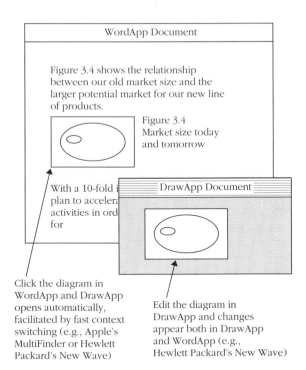

Figure 1.5
Evolving Interoperability: Beyond Basic Cut and Paste

Figure 1.5 shows an example of object management as available in early objectlike systems. In the example, the user edits a manuscript with a word processing application. In order to modify an embedded diagram, the user merely selects the diagram for editing. A window opens into the appropriate drawing application where manipulation of a graphic object changes characteristics of the object in both applications. Currently available commercial products, such as Hewlett-Packard's NewWave, facilitate this type of interoperability. Moving among programs, however, is still not transparent to the user.

Figure 1.6 illustrates the same application with greater application transparency facilitated by an object-oriented file system. An object, in this example the DrawApp object, carries its functionality with it. The user no longer needs to launch and exit programs. Functionality appears when it is needed. And, as in the previous example, changes to the diagram are saved automatically for all of its other occurrences.

An object-oriented system's visual objects will support this type of *ad hoc* or direct modification and appear to be significantly application independent. This is a major departure from traditional systems. Today, programmers or users must enter and exit files to achieve such inter-

Figure 1.6
Two Object Specific
Editors

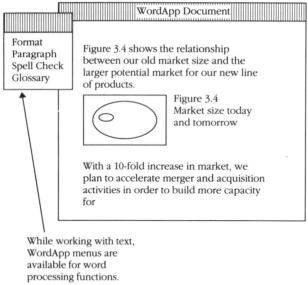

WordApp Document

Format
Paragraph
Spell Check
Glossary

Figure 3.4 shows the relationship between our old market size and the larger potential market for our new line of products.

Figure 3.4
Market size today
and tomorrow

With a 10-fold increase in market, we plan to accelerate merger and acquisition activities in order to build more capacity for

While working with text,
WordApp menus are
available for word
processing functions.

(a)

WordApp Document

Edit
Align
Select
Gridlines

Figure 3.4 shows the relationship between our old market size and the larger potential market for our new line of products.

Figure 3.4
Market size today
and tomorrow

With a 10-fold increase in market, we plan to accelerate merger and acquisition activities in order to build more capacity for

While working with
graphics, DrawApp
menus appear.

(b)

operability. Programmers must hard-code interfaces to accommodate application-specific formats. Users must open files, select the information, occasionally reformat it, and then transport it to the next application.

In an object-oriented system, the rule is, "Ask, don't touch." Complex data are treated as a single object managed automatically by the underlying operating environment. Users can link, combine, and manipulate complex data such as text, graphics, scanned images, and full-motion video. A facility is provided to browse or view complex objects without actually running an application. In our example, the word processing application would be accessed only for less generalized tasks such as page layout. Encapsulated procedures (i.e., the complexity) are completely hidden from the requestor. Beyond this streamlined interoperability, object-oriented application frameworks will encourage users to begin to think of objects as software robots that users themselves can program. Users will also be able to record and play their own scripts that prototype the actions of software robots.

Standards will be important, as with all system software components. Some *de facto* standards are emerging in the language area, but issues of standard setting will loom large with this major shift in development paradigms and system architecture. Object-orientation standards may also force a restructuring of the software industry. The king of the software industry will be the company who controls the application program interfaces (APIs) for communication of messages to objects. Application vendors will market objects in libraries and will engage in their own object wars to lay claim to domain-specific libraries of application components.

Along with the establishment of standards, major milestones in the software industry itself will need to take place. A major software concern, one which can establish standards, must establish object-oriented architecture standards. Application vendor specific implementations of object-oriented architectures will not suffice. Key competitors in the software industry must share standards to provide the interoperability among the objects that will be the applications of tomorrow.

Commercial developers, a notoriously independent group, will need to accept these standards, including perhaps key visual objects incorporated into everyone's object library. Commercial value must be established for object libraries, and critical mass in breadth of these libraries must be established to provide the building blocks for developer and user programmability. The reality of the currently complex challenge of interapplication communication will depend upon acceptance of these standards. Surrounding all this, incremental enhancements are needed in the robustness of languages and databases to exploit object orientation fully.

This vision of the future extends beyond the arrival of object-oriented system components, development tools, and standards. In the future users will have the power and flexibility to design their own "killer apps" just by snapping together the necessary objects. User-built objects could be traded like baseball cards. With objects, building applications will be a process of tailoring and linking reusable modules. Users will find applications easier to use and repetitive tasks easier to automate. Software robots, created by users, will control multiple applications from multiple vendors, as well as controlling their own activities.

Programming wizards of the future will do what they do best: hone the fundamental objects rather than dream up the killer apps. Ultimately, users may no longer need to post wishlists of enhancements that cause programmers to tear apart and rebuild an application; they may finally have the tools to construct what they need for themselves.

The Recent Progress

Expectations of greatly improved applications and development tools facilitated by object orientation are not simply imaginary. Throughout this book, we describe products and evolving product strategies that reveal the mainstreaming of object-oriented software and the attainment of the final goal: an integrated object architecture with languages, tools, file systems, and operating systems all working together. Considerable progress has already been made toward this goal.

The Apple Macintosh

The first commercial system with an integrated objectlike architecture was the Apple Macintosh released in 1984. In 1985, Apple released for Macintosh software developers the first version of MacApp, its object-oriented application framework, and Object Pascal, an object-oriented language.

The Macintosh MacApp environment was the first commercial object-oriented development environment. MacApp, however, represented a somewhat primitive version of an object-oriented development environment. Developers using MacApp were guaranteed conformance to the Macintosh interface, and users of applications developed in this environment were guaranteed an object-oriented interface of sorts.

Some object libraries were included with MacApp. MacApp provided objects to handle the construction of the Macintosh's standard user-interface features. This approach helped to enforce Apple's compatibility guidelines. The process of application construction conformed to an object-oriented approach. MacApp provided the standards, and the programmer built or tailored the application. The application was then implemented as a set of objects responding to standard MacApp messages.

MacApp itself was not a complete development framework. To build an interface or an application, a developer needed to learn both MacApp and an object-oriented language, such as Apple's Object Pascal. Once the look of the user interface was defined, the developer could leave the MacApp development framework and move into Object Pascal to build the events in the application.

The initial Macintosh Programmer's Workbench (MPW) also did not support a familiar object-oriented language, such as C + +. Debugging object-oriented code is a different process than debugging procedural code, and the initial environment was bereft of tools to browse and debug objects. The incompleteness of the object-oriented architecture provided some, but not all, of the benefits of an object-oriented environment to the developer and few to the user. User programmability was certainly not within reach with the initial Macintosh environment.

Development of the actual application underlying the user interface was only as object oriented as the developer who designed it; no object-oriented framework was provided with the Macintosh for this purpose. The Macintosh object architecture provided an object-oriented interface but limited application interoperability. Because the Macintosh architecture did not support objects in the file system, the objects were passive. A fast context-switching mechanism (Finder or MultiFinder) moved users from one application to the next. Objects were no longer active once clipped into another application and required opening from the appropriate application to be reactivated. For the user, the "point and click" or "drag to" functionality was object-oriented; however, in a fully object-oriented environment the user interface would support a "point and perform" (as shown in Figure 1.6), not just a "cut and paste" style of direct object manipulation. Table 1.2 summarizes the Macintosh object architecture.

The NeXT Computer

In October of 1988, the NeXT machine was announced. NeXT introduced a better integration of object orientation and a more complete model of how an object-oriented architecture might eventually fit to-

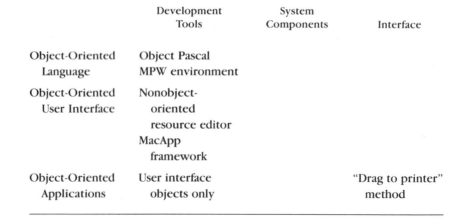

Table 1.2 Macintosh Object Architecture (Circa 1984–88)		Development Tools	System Components	Interface
	Object-Oriented Language	Object Pascal MPW environment		
	Object-Oriented User Interface	Nonobject-oriented resource editor MacApp framework		
	Object-Oriented Applications	User interface objects only		"Drag to printer" method

gether on all computing environments. NeXT's integration of object orientation into its systems framework was certainly the incremental commercial step toward a fully object-oriented architecture. The NeXT object-oriented architecture went a step beyond the object-oriented interface level of the Macintosh by providing further functionality, tools, and object libraries to facilitate not just an object-oriented user interface but also the development of object-oriented applications themselves. The completeness of the integration of the object-oriented development environment of the NeXT machine jump-started the software industry into the reality and feasibility of integrating discrete components into an integrated object-oriented architecture.

Several other commercial milestones for object orientation had also occurred by the time the NeXT machine was introduced. By late 1988, more developers were familiar with the object-oriented development process due to the success of object-oriented languages such as Smalltalk, C++, and Object Pascal. Significantly improved object-oriented development environments for user interfaces were also in the marketplace, for example, Whitewater's Actor.

NeXT's most significant innovation was an object-oriented onscreen interface development kit, NeXTStep. NeXTStep was particularly innovative in the eyes of developers who had struggled with MacApp. The NeXT machine still presented a complicated application environment: a multitasking Mach UNIX kernel and the complicated event-driven user interface that created the programming sinkhole for the Macintosh and other user interfaces, such as Microsoft's Windows. Yet with the NeXTStep Interface Builder, many of the difficult programming challenges of graphically rich applications were overcome. Developers could point the mouse toward visual representations (objects) in the NeXTStep object library, graphically link them together in a logical way, and then ask the Interface Builder to generate both the interface objects and the accompanying code to produce the desired result.

With the NeXT tools, programmers viewed and modified the original object library. Unlike with the Macintosh, it was rare that additional code was programmed directly, using an object-oriented language. In contrast to the Macintosh, the NeXT Interface Builder constructed the user interface and established how the objects communicated with one another. Intricate event-handling code that managed the user interface was encapsulated in NeXT objects. Message routes were usually established automatically, making the connection between the user interface and application code easier to build.

In addition to its true object-oriented Interface Builder, the NeXT machine also incorporated many more of the object-oriented features expected in systems of the 1990s. Objects in the application kit were arranged in a hierarchy, and the machinery of inheritance allowed programmers or object constructors to borrow behavior from existing objects when constructing new application frameworks. The NeXT environment allowed direct manipulation of the windows and window elements while building the user interface.

The NeXT machine was still clearly an early implementation of the future of object orientation. The application framework for the user was limited. The environment was not language-independent and requires premature acceptance of a language standard, Objective-C. Moreover, the NeXT system was based on a UNIX-based operating system. Table 1.3 summarizes the NeXT object architecture.

Software giants Microsoft and IBM have both followed the NeXT example and announced that object-oriented technology will be incorporated in their future system components, with goals of establishing and achieving the benefits of object-oriented architectures in the early 1990s. Apple has also extended the original object-oriented functionality. MacApp now includes more active objects on the desktop (e.g., not only does "drag to trash" delete a file, but also "drag to printer" prints), user interface design tools, and improved interprocess communication between objects from different application sources, albeit still solely within the Macintosh architecture. In 1987, Apple also released HyperCard, its object-oriented user development language. In 1989, Apple added support for the C + + object-oriented language.

	Development Tools	System Components	Interface
Object-Oriented Language	Objective C (preprocessor) Public domain C compiler and debugger		
Object-Oriented User Interface	Interface Builder visual prototyper Application framework	Standard visual objects in application kit	
Object-Oriented Applications			Limited support, configuration file per directory

Table 1.3
NeXT Object
Architecture
(Circa 1989)

The Object Architecture of the 1990s

Due to the pioneering commercialization of object-oriented technology, as exemplified by Apple and NeXT, it is easier to envision more robust system environments when forecasting the future of objects in programming languages, user interfaces, databases, applications, and operating systems. As object architectures become established in the 1990s, development tools for object-oriented software will improve dramatically. Standards will also be established, and industry leaders will comply with these standards.

Object-oriented systems of the 1990s will continue to pivot upon powerful development tools assembled as a complete application-building workbench. Microsoft refers to this future vision as an "object-oriented application factory" (Whitten 1989). More development tools will be packaged in powerful visual programming environments, much like the NeXTStep environment. These tools will support the construction of objects to build not only user interfaces but also complete applications. The factory will support the creation, browsing, and debugging of object-oriented systems. This complete support of object-program construction should simplify and organize the new method of programming and allow many types of developers to build applications from existing class libraries.

All of this will be supported by the basic paradigm of looking at applications and data files as objects. Any data file would become the system object and the application the set of methods that deal with the object. Object-oriented operating systems would perform actions (update, read, etc.) on objects rather than on data files. This abstraction—dealing with objects rather than discrete types of files—will provide a great deal of flexibility in both application construction and applications use. Applications will function based on the selection and integration of objects, not according to a predefined set of functions. Tools will allow this paradigm to be implemented fairly unobtrusively. Already tools such as Hewlett Packard's NewWave, an object-oriented application environment parked atop existing operating systems (e.g., Microsoft's MS-DOS), allow encapsulation of existing nonobject-oriented applications to facilitate some object behavior.

Object-oriented file systems will be an important foundation for managing the complexity, not only for applications but also for the computing environment as a whole. Object-oriented file systems and standard messaging approaches between objects will manage the distribution of objects across a network of computers and will work in conjunction with the client/server architectures of the 1990s.

When environments are entirely object oriented, the software-development life cycle will also change. Prototyping will be replaced by simulation, a simpler approach to application development. Users or programmers will build models that simulate their application in real time. They will modify the application models until they behave correctly and then simply request a snapshot (or realization), which is the final solution. Maintaining or enhancing applications will not involve rewriting intricate code segments; instead, it will involve building new objects derived from existing objects and then adding them to the application.

Components of a complete object-oriented environment will also include a variety of standard object-oriented languages that manipulate existing applications as well as data and objects. Some of the languages will be new, but many will be extensions to currently used languages, such as C, Pascal, BASIC, and COBOL. There will also be object libraries, for both particular development tasks and particular application frameworks. The environment will be one in which users can think about their tasks and information, while the system worries about applications, files, and operating systems.

Specific tools for developers should also improve. An application-builder tool will provide functions for manipulating, combining, and viewing objects. For the user, the builder will be a powerful visual-simulation tool for constructing many object groups, including application objects and user-interface objects. The builder will simplify object construction and classification. The builder will not be an abrupt change from current programming environments. Instead, like NewWave, it will also serve as a shell for other tools and provide interfaces to editors for traditional programming, as well as providing the enhanced tool requirements for object orientation such as browsers and object drawing tools.

From the application builder will evolve application frameworks for users that will include runtime object libraries, all managed by a common set of system components for object management and application services. With delivery of key object libraries, users will require less skill but gain more capability. The object richness of the application services will also provide much improved multivendor interoperability.

There will be an especially critical need for standards to insure cooperative processing among heterogeneous hardware and software platforms. The establishment of a well-defined set of object protocols or

Table 1.4
System Object
Architecture
(Circa 1994)

	Development Tools	System Components	Interface
Object-Oriented Language	Standard object-oriented languages such as C^{++}, BASIC, and PASCAL Robust object-oriented development and debugging tools		
Object-Oriented User Interface	Visual object development kit Application building tools (Application Factory)	Standard visual objects Object-oriented graphics	Direct manipulation
Object-Oriented Applications	Application frameworks	System object manager Standard application protocols External control language Object-oriented file system	System object browser Standard protocols for application invocation Object file management

message interaction with objects will be a major requirement for creating the object architectures that move past the 1990s. Table 1.4 identifies the typical components of object-oriented architectures of the 1990s.

Over the next decade, the difference between the old and the new will become increasingly obvious to both programmers and users. When the object-oriented future is fully delivered, this natural, intuitive paradigm will be strongly embraced and will provide benefits to programmers and users alike.

Summary

Object-oriented software architectures will be dominant in the 1990s. The transition to these new architectures is underway, marked by the arrival of object-oriented languages, databases, interfaces, operating systems, and development environments. New types of data, distributed processing, multimedia applications, and end-user computing are driving forces in the implementation of the object-oriented software landscape.

Recent progress in implementing object-oriented systems is dramatic. Today's graphical interfaces have acquainted users with object manipulation. Among object-oriented languages, C + + has become the *de facto* standard. Object-oriented extensions are also being implemented in most popular commercial languages. Integrated object-oriented development environments such as NeXT's NeXTStep provide clear examples of object-oriented programming and applications. Operating systems are also being extended to support interoperability among object-based applications. Finally, the 1990s should bring object-oriented programming not only to the developer but also to the end user. Robust class libraries and object-oriented application frameworks are prerequisites to the ultimate goal of user programmability.

Key Points

- Software currently lags hardware capability by at least two processor generations. The need for improved software-development tools and techniques is demonstrable.

- Object orientation represents an important advance for both software development and use.

- New data types, multimedia applications, end-user computing, and distributed processing are driving forces for object orientation.

- Commercial integration of object-oriented techniques is well underway. Full integration will occur in the 1990s.

- User interfaces and languages have already incorporated object-oriented functionality.

- Databases and operating systems are beginning to incorporate object-oriented functionality.

- Environments such as the Macintosh and NeXT computers have introduced object orientation to many programmers.

- Future success of object orientation depends on programmer acceptance, the establishment of standards, availability of object libraries, and object-oriented development environments.

For Further Study

Gibson, W. 1988. *Mona Lisa Overdrive.* New York: Bantam Books.
Gibson's science fiction view of the technology of the 1990s takes the reader well past the time frame of this book and into the world of cyberspace, the ultimate reality simulation.

Jeffcoate, J., Hales, K. and Downes, V. 1989. *Object-Oriented Systems: The Commercial Benefits.* London: Ovum Ltd.
This publication reviews the technical and market strategies of anticipated worldwide participants in the market for object-oriented systems. An overview of terms and technologies is also presented.

OOPSLA, the annual Object-Oriented Programming Systems, Languages, and Applications conference.
Sponsored by the Association for Computing Machinery (ACM), the annual OOPSLA conference provides access to many of the technologies and vendors relevant to object orientation.

References

Alsop, S. 1989. *P.C. Letter.* 5 (7), April 16.

Corbi, T. A. 1989. "Program understanding: Challenge for the 1990s." *IBM Systems Journal,* 28 (2).

Kapor, M. 1988. Dinner speech. *Conference on Object-Oriented Programming: Systems, Languages, and Applications 1988* (OOPSLA '88), San Diego, CA.

Palay, A. 1989. "The Andrew toolkit: The present and the future." *Object orientation: Defining the end-user platform for the 1990s.* Patricia Seybold's Third Annual Technology Forum, Boston, Mass.

Whitten, G. F. 1989. "Using object-oriented programming." Comments presented at the annual Microsoft System Software Seminar, Microsoft Corporation, Redmond, Wa.

Chapter 2

The Vernacular

- **Basic Mechanisms**
    - **Objects**
    - **Messages and Methods**
    - **Classes, Subclasses and Objects**
    - **Inheritance**

- **Key Concepts**
    - **Encapsulation**
    - **Abstraction**
    - **Polymorphism**
    - **Persistence**

- **Related Technical Terms**
    - **Dynamic Binding**
    - **Visual Programming**
    - **Blob**

- **The Traditional Approach versus Object Orientation**

- **Summary**

This chapter introduces and defines the basic mechanisms and central concepts associated with all object-oriented systems. We shall review terms that are specific to a particular implementation, such as language or database.

Due to the lack of standards and the newness of commercial use, not all object-oriented terms are refined, consistent, or parsimonious. In this chapter we shall sort out much of the jargon that obfuscates discussions of object-oriented systems.

Read this chapter for nontechnical definitions of terms used throughout the book.

For the nonprogrammer, object orientation means something quite familiar: thinking about the world as a set of entities or objects that are related to to one another and that communicate with one another. This is the way people ordinarily think about the world, so thinking this way inherently makes sense. For the system developer, object orientation is a level of computer abstraction beyond that of procedures and data. Object orientation encourages the system developer to concentrate on the important issues and to ignore the rest.

The focus on objects, however intuitive, marks a significant shift from the previous programming paradigms. Programmers of the 1980s have been steeped in a procedural approach to problem solving. Ada guru Grady Booch sums up the fundamental difference between procedural and object-oriented programming like this:

> Read the specification of the software you want to build. Underline the verbs if you are after procedural code, the nouns if you aim for an object-oriented program. (Booch 1989)

Booch's description implies that the object-oriented approach, with its emphasis on objects rather than on processes, is as different from procedural orientation as nouns are different from verbs. Beyond this analogy, there is no single, precise rule for describing or identifying object orientation. Rather, a collection of concepts together describe the new paradigm. Grasping individual concepts is not difficult, but understanding how to implement them requires the same level of diligence that is needed to learn about other significant technical innovations.

The chapter begins with a description of fundamental object-oriented mechanisms. Upon this foundation, more complex concepts are identified and defined. Finally, terms not central to object orientation, but which are frequently used in its context are discussed. The number of terms associated with object-oriented programming is disconcertingly large. This chapter sorts out which terms are fundamental, which are derivative, and how terms relate to one another.

Figure 2.1 shows the building blocks of object orientation that are covered in this chapter.

Basic Mechanisms

The basic mechanisms of object orientation are *objects, messages* and *methods, classes* and *instances,* and *inheritance.* All systems deserving the description object-oriented contain these essential mechanisms, al-

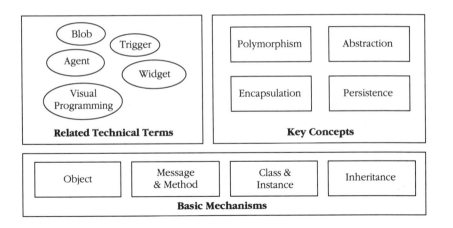

Figure 2.1
The Building Blocks
of Object
Orientation

though the mechanisms may not be implemented (or named) in exactly the same way. In this chapter, nontechnical definitions and examples will be provided for each mechanism. In subsequent chapters, these terms will be revisited and additional levels of technical detail will be provided.

Objects

A traditional program consists of procedures and data. An object-oriented program consists only of objects that contain both procedures and data. To put it another way, *objects* are modules that contain both data and the instructions that operate upon those data. Thus, within objects reside the data of conventional computing languages, such as numbers, arrays, strings, and records, as well as any functions, instructions, or subroutines that operate on them. Objects, then, are entities that have particular attributes (data) and ways of behaving (procedures).

Objects carry the names of elements of interest from the application domain. For example, in a word processing application, it is likely that one object will be named paragraph. In an accounting application, the balance sheet for June is a likely object. From the user's perspective, objects provide desired behavior. A paragraph can accept revision and realign its margins. June's balance sheet can be printed or consolidated with those of other months to form a quarterly report. From the programmer's perspective, objects are modules of an application that work together to provide overall functionality.

Applications may consist of different kinds of objects. A *passive object* is one that acts only upon request. Apple's Hypercard buttons are passive objects that must be pressed into action. *Active objects* monitor events occurring in an application and take action autonomously. Sometimes called *agents,* active objects initiate actions such as alerting a user to inconsistency in a balance sheet or reminding a writer to save results after a threshold number of changes have occurred.

Messages and Methods

Unlike the passive data items in traditional systems, objects have the ability to act. Action occurs when an object receives a *message,* that is, a request asking the object to behave in some way. When object-oriented programs execute, objects are receiving, interpreting, and responding to messages from objects. For example, when a user requests that an object called document print itself, the document may send a message to the object printer requesting a place in the queue, the printer may send a message back to the document requesting formatting information, and so on. Messages may contain information to clarify a request; for example, the message requesting that an object print itself might include the name of the printer. Finally, the sender of the message need not know how the receiving object will carry out the request. In other words, when the object document receives the message print, document itself knows exactly what to do. The object sending the message neither knows nor cares how printing is implemented, only that it happens.

The set of messages to which an object can respond is called the object's *protocol.* The protocol for an icon may consist of messages invoked by the click of a mouse button when the user locates a pointer on an icon.

Procedures called *methods* reside in the object and determine how the object acts when it receives a message. In addition, *instance variables* store information or data local to the object. Methods execute in response to messages and manipulate the values of the instance variables. In fact, methods provide the only mechanism for changing values of instance variables. Methods may also send messages to other objects requesting action or information. Figure 2.2 shows the anatomy of an object.

Like engineering "black boxes," the inner structure of an object is hidden from users and programmers. Messages that the object receives are its only conduits that connect the object to the outside world. Data

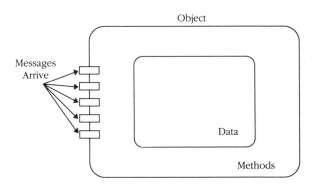

Figure 2.2
Anatomy of an
Object

within an object are available for manipulation only by an object's own methods. These characteristics of objects give object orientation its advantage: Object orientation encourages modularity by making boundaries among objects clear, communication among objects explicit, and implementation details hidden.

When an object-oriented program is running, three events are occurring. First, objects are created as needed. (The mechanism for creating objects will be discussed in the next section.) Second, messages move from one object to another (or from the user to an object) as the program processes information internally or responds to input from the user. Finally, when objects are no longer necessary they are deleted and memory is reclaimed.

Classes, Subclasses, and Objects

Many different objects may act in very similar ways. A *class* is a description of a set of nearly identical objects. A class consists of methods and data that summarize common characteristics of a set of objects. The ability to abstract common methods and data descriptions from a set of objects and store them in a class is central to the power of object orientation. Defining classes means placing reusable code in a common repository rather than expressing it over and over. In other words, classes contain the blueprints for creating objects. Finally, the definition of a class helps to clarify the definition of an object: An object is an *instance* of a class.

Objects are created when a message requesting creation is received by the parent class. The new object takes its methods and data from its parent class. Data are of two forms, class variables and instance variables.

Figure 2.3
Class paragraph
with Three
Instances

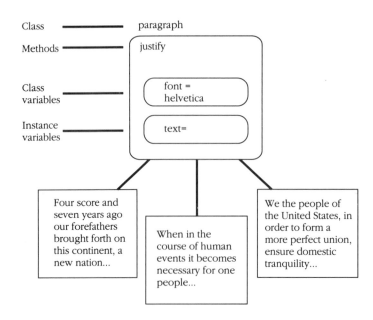

Class variables have values stored in a class; *instance variables* have values associated uniquely with each instance or object created from a class.

As an example, consider how a programmer might design a word processing application in an object-oriented manner. First the programmer identifies entities of interest. Paragraphs, for example, are potential objects. As Figure 2.3 illustrates, paragraphs are commonly justified and typeset text in a particular font. Justify is a method common to all paragraphs. Font is a class variable with the value helvetica. Finally, text is an instance variable with unique values for each object. It is useful to create a class called paragraph to hold this common information. The class paragraph then provides a blueprint for constructing objects. While specific data in each object (i.e., the words in the paragraph, the font, line spacing) may vary, all objects of class paragraph share common methods and class variables.

A class can also summarize common elements for a set of *subclasses*. In the case of the word processing example, the programmer may next consider table to be another class in addition to paragraph. With further thought, the programmer realizes that paragraph and table share some properties with a more abstract class, text. In a similar fashion, text and graphic may turn out to be subclasses of an even more general class,

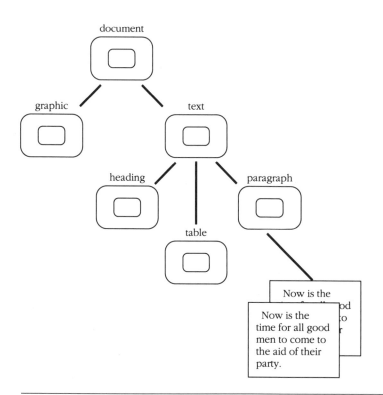

Figure 2.4
Subclasses of the
Class document

document. Figure 2.4 illustrates this hierarchy of document-processing classes. By using subclasses, object-oriented programmers describe applications as collections of general, or *abstract,* modules. Common methods and data are elevated as high as possible so that they are accessible to all relevant subclasses.

Subclasses are sometimes referred to as *derived classes.* On other occasions the terms *parent* and *child* are used to indicate the relationship between a class and a subclass. *Parent classes* are located above *child classes* in the hierarchy. Classes higher in the hierarchy are referred to as the *superclasses.* In Figure 2.4 for example, text is a superclass of table.

So far, this description of an object-oriented design has been "bottom-up." That is, the description emphasizes how common components (objects) are abstracted to become classes and superclasses. In fact, the term "top-down" more accurately describes the approach taken by many object-oriented programmers. They ordinarily begin work with a *class library* that contains generally useful programming modules. Using predefined classes as a starting point, programmers write new sub-classes that tailor the general-purpose classes in the library to the particular functional requirements of the application.

An application-specific class library is called a *framework*. Frameworks differ from class libraries only by degree: A framework is a class library tuned especially for a particular category of application, for example, an interface-building framework. Building and tailoring applications from frameworks is faster and easier than starting with generic class libraries. At the same time, a framework will not be as generally useful outside the application domain because it contains application-specific classes.

Inheritance

Inheritance is the mechanism for automatically sharing methods and data among classes, subclasses, and objects. A powerful mechanism not found in procedural systems, inheritance allows programmers to create new classes by programming only the difference from the parent class. When a programmer declares that paragraph is a subclass of text, for example, then all methods and instance variables associated with text are automatically inherited by paragraph. If the class text contains methods that are inappropriate to subclass paragraph, then the programmer can override these methods by writing new methods and storing them as a part of class paragraph. Figure 2.5 shows the relationship of an instance of class paragraph to its parent classes.

Due to inheritance, object-oriented programs consist of taxonomies, trees, or hierarchies of classes which, through subclassing, become more specific. Classes provide the blueprints for subclasses or for objects relevant to an application.

Single and multiple inheritance are two types of inheritance mechanisms commonly used in object-oriented programming. With *single inheritance* a subclass may inherit data and methods from a single class as well as adding or subtracting behavior on its own. *Multiple inheritance* refers to the ability of a subclass to acquire data and methods from more than one class. Multiple inheritance is useful in building composite behavior from more than one branch of a class hierarchy.

In summary, the basic mechanisms of object orientation lead to a particular view about modeling the world. Elements and their behavior are identified as objects. Behavior is implemented with methods and data stored in the object. Messages elicit an object's behavior by invoking a method in the object.

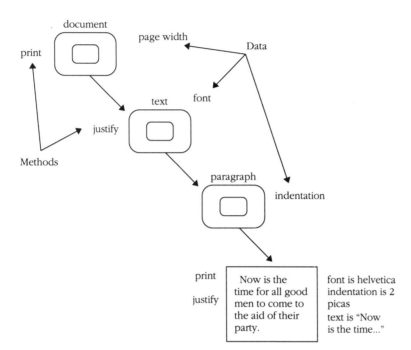

Figure 2.5
An Instance Inherits
from its Parent
Classes

Objects with common methods and instance variables are collected together in a class. Classes are organized in hierarchies, and inheritance mechanisms automatically provide each subclass with the methods and data from parent classes. Subclasses are created by programming the differences between available classes in a library and the particular requirements of the application.

Key Concepts

The basic mechanisms outlined above form the foundation for the object-oriented paradigm. Four key concepts that summarize the advantages of the object-oriented approach are encapsulation, abstraction, polymorphism, and persistence.

Encapsulation

Encapsulation is the formal term that describes the bundling of methods and data together within an object so that access to data is permitted only through the object's own methods. No other parts of an object-oriented program can operate directly on an object's data. Communication among a set of objects occurs exclusively through explicit messages.

Abstraction

Object orientation encourages programmers and users to think about applications in abstract terms. Beginning with a set of objects, programmers are encouraged to factor common behavior and locate it in abstract superclasses. Class libraries provide a repository for common, reusable elements. Inheritance machinery automatically maintains relationships among classes arranged hierarchically in a class library. Frameworks contain domain-specific class libraries. Each level of abstraction makes the job of programming easier because there is more reusable code available.

Polymorphism

Objects act in response to the messages they receive. The same message can result in completely different actions when received by different objects. This phenomenon is referred to as *polymorphism*. With polymorphism a user can send a generic message and leave the exact implementation details up to the receiving object. The message print, for example, when sent to a figure or diagram will call upon different printing methods than when the same print message is sent to a textual document.

Polymorphism is encouraged by inheritance machinery. It is common to store protocols for utility functions like "print" as high in the class hierarchy as possible. Necessary variations in "print" behavior are stored farther down in the hierarchy to overwrite the more general methods when appropriate. In this way, objects are ready and able to respond appropriately to utility messages like "print" while the method implementing the print function may exist at the object's immediate class or several levels above the object's class.

Persistence

Persistence refers to the permanence of an object, that is, the amount of time for which it is allocated space and remains accessible in the computer's memory. In most object-oriented languages, instances of classes are created as the program executes. Some of these instances are needed only for a brief period of time. When an object is no longer needed, it is destroyed and the memory space allocated to it is reclaimed. The automatic reclamation of memory space is ordinarily called garbage collection.

After an object-oriented program has executed, the assembled objects are not ordinarily stored; that is, the objects are no longer persistent. An object-oriented database maintains a distinction between objects created only for the duration of execution and those intended for permanent storage. Objects stored permanently are termed *persistent.*

Related Technical Terms

New technologies spawn new terminology at a feverish pace, and object orientation is no exception. Mechanisms and concepts considered fundamental have been identified and defined. Related technical terms fall into one of two categories: specialized concepts that are applicable to subareas of object orientation and objectlike terms that bridge between conventional and object-oriented techniques. Here are selected related technical terms.

Dynamic Binding

Dynamic binding is a common (but not necessary) characteristic of object-oriented languages. Binding is the process of weaving a computer program together so that all the proper connections exist among its components. For conventional programming languages, binding ordinarily occurs during the compilation process. With early or *static binding,* all connections are resolved before the program begins to run. Object-oriented languages often employ an alternative strategy called late, or dynamic, binding. The binding process is the same, but binding occurs late, while the program is running.

Late binding is an implementation consequence of polymorphism. As an object-oriented program runs, messages are received by objects. Often the method for handling a message is stored high up in a class hierarchy. The method is located dynamically when it is needed. Binding then occurs as the connections are made between the method and the data local to the object. That is, binding occurs at the last possible moment.

Visual Programming

Visual programming is often associated with object orientation. One simple example of visual programming is a drawing package in which objects can be stretched on the screen, not by changing numerical data in a table of dimensions but by manipulating the image itself. Application-building software like Hypercard provides "cut and paste" facilities that replicate the action linked to an image as well as the image itself. These examples and others form a loose category of applications called visual programming.

While it is true that some visual-programming applications provide object-oriented functionality to the user, a couple of other possible conclusions do *not* follow:

- First, visual programming is not inherently object oriented. An image or icon on the screen is neither a necessary nor a sufficient criterion to deem an application object oriented.

- Second, visual-programming applications are not necessarily constructed with object-oriented languages. In fact, the majority of existing products were constructed with traditional procedural tools.

Blob

Blob is an acronym for "*B*inary *L*arge *OB*ject." The term commonly refers to a data type useful for storing large chunks of data. Blob is frequently used in comparing relational and object-oriented databases. In most cases (and in contrast to our definition of object), the database does not interpret the contents of a blob (or its methods) but rather treats it only as an unusually large and undifferentiated chunk of data. A blob becomes object oriented only if methods are encapsulated with data, message handling capability exists, and the blob is part of a class hierarchy.

The Traditional Approach versus Object Orientation

From a traditional programmer's point of view, some object-oriented techniques appear to be traditional concepts with different names. And, indeed, some object-oriented concepts are analogous to conventional programming approaches. Here are contrasts between conventional and object-oriented terms and concepts.

- A method is like a procedure because both contain processing instructions. Class and instance variables correspond to data in traditional programming. Methods and data are different because procedures are usually not encapsulated with the data they manipulate.

Object-Oriented Techniques	Traditional Techniques	
Methods	Procedures, functions, or subroutines	**Table 2.1** A Comparison of Object-Oriented and Traditional Programming Concepts
Instance variables	Data	
Messages	Procedure calls or function calls	
Classes	Abstract data types	
Inheritance	(No similar technique)	
Calls under system's control	Calls under programmer's control	

- A class is like an abstract data type, although for object-oriented programs, the data typing process is not revealed outside the class.

- Inheritance has no immediate analog to conventional programming.

- Message passing replaces function calls as the primary method of control in object-oriented systems. With function calls, values are returned and control handed back to the calling function. In contrast, objects are set into motion by messages, and control is distributed.

Although traditional programmers will quickly see similarities with their current techniques, they will need to change their view of a computer program from being a sequence of instructions to that of a system of interactive objects. Table 2.1 summarizes the differences between the object-oriented and conventional perspectives.

Summary

The object-oriented approach promises to provide a higher level of abstraction than the approach supported by traditional views of procedures and data. In object orientation, procedures and data are melded together to form an entity called an object. Unlike the passive data of traditional systems, objects can act. Actions are prompted by messages sent to an object and then processed by internal procedures called methods.

Objects can be quite similar in their capabilities. The description of a collection of similar objects is a class. An instance of a class is an actual object described by a class. Further abstraction is encouraged through the use of class hierarchies. To reuse previously defined methods, class hierarchies rely on the unique object-oriented mechanism of inheritance.

Absorbing object-oriented ideas means learning the differences as well as the similarities between this approach and conventional programming.

Key Points

- Object orientation is defined by a set of mechanisms: objects, classes and instances, methods and messages, and inheritance.

- These mechanisms give rise to key concepts inherent in object-oriented systems: encapsulation, abstraction, polymorphism.

- The mechanisms and concepts of object orientation essentially lead programmers to write code at a higher level of abstraction.

- Absorbing object-oriented ideas means learning the differences as well as the similarities between this approach and conventional programming.

For Further Study

Beck, K., and Cunningham, W. 1989. "A laboratory for teaching object-oriented thinking." *Proceedings of Object-Oriented Programming: Systems, Languages, and Applications 1989* (OOPSLA '89). *SIGPLAN Notices,* Vol. 24, No. 10, October, pp. 1–6.

Beck and Cunningham have created an exercise in object-oriented design that is not only language independent but also computer independent. They use index cards to represent objects and annotate the cards to describe the object's methods and data. Try the exercise on a problem domain that is interesting to you.

OOPSLA '89 was the fourth annual meeting for an Association of Computing Machinery (ACM) special interest group concerned with all aspects of object orientation. The the convention offers tutorials as well as technical papers and a trade show. The *Proceedings* is a good choice for your library.

Cox, B. J. 1986. *Object-Oriented Programming: An Evolutionary Approach.* Reading, Mass.: Addison-Wesley.

> Cox's book was the first popular treatment of object orientation for commercial programmers. In addition to introducing Objective-C, Cox identifies the major strengths of object-oriented programming with interesting analogies. The most famous is the the analogy between a class and an integrated circuit (IC), which leads Cox to suggest that class libraries contain plug-compatible elements or software ICs.

Thomas, D. 1989. "What's in an object?" *Byte,* March.

> *Byte* magazine has monitored object orientation nearly from its inception. Thomas' article introduces object-oriented concepts in an issue dedicated to object orientation.

References

Booch, G. 1989. "What is and isn't object-oriented design." *American Programmer,* special issue on object orientation, Vol. 2, Nos. 7–8, Summer.

Chapter 3

The Benefits

- **Managing Complexity**
  Flexibility in Software Development
  Reusability

- **Increasing Productivity**
  Extensibility and Maintainability
  Programming by the User

- **Summary**

This chapter provides an overview of the primary benefits delivered to developers and users with the implementation of the object-oriented paradigm. We shall identify and discuss benefits associated with object-oriented analysis, design, and programming. We shall also review the benefits of object orientation when implemented in languages, databases, interfaces, and operating systems. Each of these topics will be explored in greater depth in Part 2: The Object-Oriented Software Landscape.

Read this chapter to learn what primary benefits will be derived from understanding and applying object orientation.

Many experts agree that object-oriented programming offers a tremendous opportunity for improving software productivity in the 1990s. The primary benefits of the object-oriented approach lie in its ability to cope with the two main issues in software engineering: managing complexity and improving productivity in the software development process. Object-oriented programming addresses these issues by encouraging the following software development strategies:

- writing reusable code,

- writing maintainable code,

- polishing existing code modules, and

- sharing code with others.

Complexity is reduced and productivity is enhanced when high-quality code is available for reuse. Object-oriented mechanisms, particularly inheritance, actively encourage reuse. Rather than copying and modifying modules, programmers can utilize class libraries containing refined and tested code. Frameworks are or will soon be available for thorny and complex areas such as graphical user interface (GUI) construction. Inheritance alone supports a quantum improvement in the developer's ability to build, extend, and maintain systems.

Object orientation offers its initial benefits to the software developer. Over time these benefits will be available to the power user, and ultimately all users will benefit. For the developer, whose current tools have not kept pace with the expanding complexity of the computing environment, the object-oriented approach provides a programming methodology supported by new languages and tools to improve productivity. For the end user, object-oriented systems will provide the consistency and flexibility needed to make applications easier to use and tailor for unique requirements.

Object orientation represents a fundamental change in the way software is developed and used. When software modules become interchangeable, the software industry will shift from its current preindustrial state. Software reuse implies that classes can be mixed and matched and easily modified to build new applications. Encapsulating data and procedures changes the entire nature of the programming process.

The historical programming division between data and functions imposes a tremendous burden on software development. Data structures often require modification. Control functions must then be reexamined to make sure that they are aligned with the data. Keeping data structures and functions properly aligned consumes a good deal of resource and introduces significant opportunities for error. The object-oriented approach of encapsulating both data and procedures in the object simplifies the process, streamlines maintenance, and lessens the likelihood of errors in the programming process.

In return for these benefits, developers must make substantial changes in the way they analyze problems and the way they translate problems into programs. The object-oriented paradigm is clearly different. Practitioners of the paradigm claim, "Object-oriented programs are easier to write." Still, the concepts are more abstract than the traditional approach and can be difficult to grasp at first. Often when novices make a change to object-oriented code, they say, "It just works, and I don't know why." There is a learning curve that is initially steep, with an "aha" coming at an unpredictable time.

In the object-oriented approach, design goals shift from modeling the behavior of the world to modeling the objects that exist in the world and their individual behaviors. If object-oriented techniques are correctly practiced, the architecture of an application follows the structure of the problem much more closely. This makes the development, use, and maintenance of an application smoother, easier, and faster.

Objects are relatively easy to define, implement, and maintain, because objects reflect the natural modularity of an application. With the enforcement of modularity and through the use of inheritance mechanisms, software objects can be reused in future applications and thus substantially reduce the amount of new code that must be written. A conventional application might use thousands of flat data records squeezed into predefined data types, but an object-oriented application can be created from a much smaller number of objects.

Object-oriented code can be general enough to reuse without modification. Because each object knows how to respond to requests in its own appropriate way, the same instructions can operate on many different objects.

A well-designed object-oriented system uses abstraction for efficiency. Abstract class libraries and application frameworks form scaffolding with which less skilled programmers can assemble applications more quickly and easily.

Managing Complexity

Breaking down an application into entities and relationships that are meaningful to users is a conventional analysis and design technique. With object-oriented programming this decomposition process is extended into the implementation phase as well. It is easier to design and implement object-oriented applications because the objects in the application domain correspond directly to objects in the software domain. This one-to-one correspondence eliminates the need to translate a design to a less natural programming language representation, even though most programmers have been trained to do this translation.

Flexibility in Software Development

Once objects are defined and class libraries extended, the programming process can become incrementally easier. The process of subclassing through the mechanism of inheritance allows programming to become the process of programming only the differences between the subclass and superclass or parent class.

The functionality of inheritance affects not only the efficiency and quality of program construction but also the allocation and use of programmers. Because the functionality of inheritance allows objects to be added or subtracted without deeply changing an application's logic, large projects can be divided among the members of a development team. Although the division of labor among programming teams is not a new concept, the object-oriented programming approach facilitates the independent workings of a large programming team. The actual implementation of each object and its methods can proceed independently without constant integration problems.

Here is how it works. A team of developers agree on an abstract set of classes and their corresponding methods and make this set of classes their application framework. Abstract classes function as templates that clarify the behavior the programming team must implement. Then, working individually, developers create appropriate new subclasses that respond to a single set of messages and are easily integrated into the total application. Talent on the programming team is optimized when some members implement code that coordinates the sending of messages, while other members define and implement new subclasses.

Each object is created and polished without forcing other team members to rethink or recode their portions of the system. Thus, work proceeds on a number of separate paths with consistency provided by common, parent classes. Object-oriented development tools also facilitate the debugging process that occurs when independent components are being developed as well as integrated into an entire system. These graphically rich environments include new tools such as browsers that enable faster and more effective debugging. And, as discussed in detail in Chapter 4, "Languages," object-oriented languages and constructs eliminate many of the common coding errors. In addition, the increasing existence of development environments accompanied by robust class libraries will substantially decrease the actual amount of code to be created, debugged, and integrated into large-scale systems.

Object-oriented systems provide the performance, flexibility, and functionality required for practical implementations. Programming can be done with extensions to standard, commercial languages, such as C, and object-oriented techniques can, to some extent, even be used in conjunction with current procedural languages. Because programming tools for object-oriented systems are more sophisticated than current programming aids, they further enhance the programmer's ability to manage and modify systems while they are being developed.

Object-oriented programming also expands the variety of applications that can be programmed because it unlocks the constraint of predefined data types. Object-oriented programming accommodates complex and heterogeneous data structures. New data types can be added without modifying existing code. In addition, object-oriented environments, such as Hewlett-Packard's NewWave, encapsulate disparate applications to provide an object-oriented bridge.

Reusability

Object-oriented techniques offer an alternative to writing the same programs over and over again. The object-oriented programmer modifies a program's functionality by replacing old elements or objects with new objects or by simply plugging new objects into the application. General instructions (messages) require no modification because specific implementation details (methods and data) reside within the object. That is, each object knows how to carry out its own behavior. This notion is in sharp contrast to procedural programming where operations and rules act on separate sets of data. In the procedural approach, programmers focus their attention on language issues, whereas in the object-oriented environment, the important issue is cultivating a robust class library or sets of objects that can be used in a variety of circumstances. A class library is a high-leverage, preexisting repository of code that has been written, tested, and debugged to provide high-quality application building blocks. Classes provide not only modularity and information hiding but also reusability enhanced by inheritance and polymorphism.

Conventional techniques for reusing software are not replaced by object-oriented techniques. In fact, conventional techniques often have object-oriented counterparts. For example, the concept of program skeletons is subsumed by the concept of abstract classes. When a conventional programmer might reuse code by copying and editing, an object-oriented programmer can accomplish this automatically by creating a subclass and overriding some of its methods.

Object-oriented environments for developing graphical user interfaces provide a current example of code reusability. When the graphical user interface became popular, it made computing easier for a broad class of users, and, correspondingly, it made programming more difficult for the programmers. Object-oriented environments such as Whitewater's Actor and Glockenspiel's CommonView, introduced in the late 1980s, allowed programmers to create graphical user environments in much less time and with much less difficulty by providing prebuilt, well-tested class libraries.

Software reuse does not occur by accident, however—even with object-oriented programming languages. System designers must keep the advantages of reusability in mind, planning ahead to reuse what already exists and designing reusability into the new components they create. This requires that programmers adopt new programming behavior, values, and ethics. Borrowing classes created by others must be considered more desirable than implementing a new class. Reviewing existing code to identify opportunities for reuse must have priority over writing new code. Finally, programmers must create simple, reusable classes rather than complex, inscrutable classes. Simplicity is a major tenet of the general philosophy of object orientation.

The tools available in the programming environment also play a critical role in making reuse attainable. For example, in Smalltalk, a browser is provided to locate code in the system of hierarchically organized classes. Many object-oriented languages also encourage reuse by providing robust libraries of prebuilt classes, browsers for locating classes of interest, and interactive debuggers to help the programmer figure out what a module of code can really do.

Increasing Productivity

Extensibility and Maintainability

It is easier to modify and extend an object-oriented application. As shown in Figure 3.1, new types of objects can be added without changing the existing structure. Inheritance allows new objects to be built out of old objects. Methods are easy to change because they reside in a single location, rather than being scattered and potentially repeated throughout the program. Thus, with the object-oriented approach, it is no longer necessary to search and replace functions and variables throughout a large body of procedures.

The features of object orientation are extremely useful during maintenance. Modularity makes it easier to contain the effects of changes to a program. Polymorphism reduces the number of procedures and thus the size of the program that the maintainer must understand. Class inheritance permits a new version of a program to be built without affecting the old. The mechanism of inheritance documents program changes as subclasses representing the history of changes made to the superclass.

Creating a subclass, the object-oriented technique of defining a new class by describing only the differences between it and its parent class, makes it easier to determine how a program differs from its prior ver-

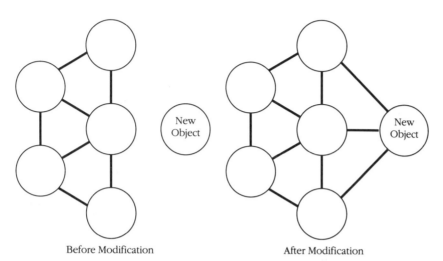

New Object

New Object

Before Modification

After Modification

Figure 3.1
Modifying an Object-Oriented Program Does Not Affect the Program's Structure (New Science Associates, 1989)

sion. A set of subclasses represents the history of changes made to a superclass. Inheritance mechanisms reduce the likelihood of human error because changes in one class are automatically propagated to all subordinate subclasses.

Object-oriented techniques are also being successfully combined with conventional systems. Hybrid systems, such as C + +, add object-oriented capabilities to established programming tools. This allows the developer to explore the new technology from familiar ground.

Programming by the User

Today's power user writes a remarkable number of programs. Typical programs are spreadsheet macros and Hypercard scripts, although users often consider macros and scripts not to be programs at all. In the future, users who perform object-oriented programming are equally likely not to recognize the tasks they are performing as programming *per se.* With object-oriented applications, programming tasks will become easier still, and many of today's nonprogrammers will become tomorrow's power users.

The ease of building object-oriented models and applications will attract people who would never identify themselves as programmers. And in fact they will not really understand exactly what they are doing. With the knowledge woven into models and class libraries, however, users will be able to build and extend applications. To the user, the real benefit of object orientation will be the delivery of content-rich class libraries that are intuitive in their representation of the real world process, as well as easy to modify and use.

Summary

Object-oriented programming improves not only the software development process but also the the flexibility and utility of the resulting software. The design process becomes more intuitive and inspectable as elements of the software correspond to elements in the application's real world domain. The programming process itself encourages teamwork, code reuse, and code polishing.

Reusability is the key to increasing productivity in the face of increasing complexity. Classes encapsulate modules of code so that complex tasks can be factored successfully. Supported by object-oriented concepts such as polymorphism and abstraction, programmers can extend class libraries or frameworks rather than writing code from scratch. The mechanism of inheritance automatically propagates methods from abstract classes down to the objects. Finally, development environments assist programmers in browsing a library to understand the use and availability of its prebuilt classes.

In addition to the increased productivity that results from reusability, using object-oriented technology can result in greater reliability because it reduces the risk of human error. Program structures remain intact, and change propagates naturally through the hierarchy of classes.

Flexibility is also a trademark of object orientation. Programmers are unleashed from the constraints of preestablished data types, allowing extensions of application functionality and bridging of heterogeneous applications.

Object orientation will affect all software users. First it will radically change the way that software engineers and programmers build applications. Later, applications will be enriched so that users will modify and enhance them.

Subsequent chapters of this book will provide additional depth and detail to explain further the benefits of object orientation.

Key Points

- The primary benefits of object orientation are improved management of complexity and increased programmer productivity.

- Abstract classes partition complex problems into simple modules and hide implementation detail. Conceptual clarity is present in the design, program, and ultimate application.

- Class libraries and frameworks provide a rich platform for object-oriented application development and code reuse.

- The structure and function of object-oriented software increases reliability.

- Applications that provide object-oriented facilities can enable users to extend and modify the software to their needs.

For Further Study

Johnson, R. E., and Foote, B. 1988. "Designing reusable classes." *Journal of Object-Oriented Programming,* Vol. 1, No. 2.

Johnson and Foote provide a deeper, more technical view of the benefits of object orientation. *The Journal of Object-Oriented Programming* takes a broad view of object orientations. Articles appear across the entire spectrum of object-oriented activities.

Jeffcoate, J., Hales, K., and Downes, V. 1989. *Object-Oriented Systems: The Commercial Benefits.* London: Ovum Ltd.

New Science Associates. 1989. *Object-Oriented Technology: Commercial Scopes and Limits.* Advanced Software Research Industry Report, Southport, Conn.: New Science Associates.

New Science Associates and Ovum Limited are market research organizations who have independently identified object orientation as an emerging technology of significant importance.

Part 2

The Object-Oriented Software Landscape

- **Languages**

- **Databases**

- **User Interfaces**

Chapter 4

Languages

In this chapter we shall examine the family of object-oriented computing languages. We shall compare procedural and object-oriented programming languages, briefly trace the history of the object-oriented languages, and then focus on their current and future functionality. We shall emphasize object extensions to procedural languages, such as C and Pascal. Pure object-oriented languages, such as Smalltalk, will be examined as well. The chapter concludes with a discussion of evolving technical issues related to object-oriented languages.

This chapter is the beginning point for programmers. Programmers will find Chapter 7, "Analysis and Design," and Chapter 8, "Programming and Maintenance" of additional value. Nonprogrammers are encouraged to review Chapter 2, "The Vernacular," before reading this chapter.

Read this chapter to understand the functional differences between traditional computer languages and object-oriented languages.

The object-oriented programming paradigm differs from the historical traditions of procedural programming. Procedural programming focuses on data and procedures with no constraints on which procedures may act on which data. Data are structured so that they can be acted upon (processed) by a separate and changing set of procedures. Both the structure of the data and the organization of the procedures are subject to change, each potentially invalidating the other. The languages, techniques, and tools of the procedural programmer are all built to support this procedural programming paradigm.

Several significant departures from the procedural approach drive the way object-oriented programs are constructed. First, programs are collections of only one basic entity, the object, which combines data with the procedures that act upon them (methods). Second, unlike traditional programs, which use procedures to accomplish actions on a separate set of passive data, objects receive requests and interact by passing messages to each other. These contrasts are illustrated in Figure 4.1. Finally, the hierarchical organization of objects into classes allows data and methods in one ancestor class to be inherited by its descendants.

The object-oriented programming paradigm can be exploited with conventional languages but requires the programmer to build the missing object-oriented extensions out of the traditional language. The more appropriate solution, as presented in this chapter, is an object-oriented language with the needed extensions built in. Object-oriented languages support the mechanisms of objects, classes, methods, messages, and inheritance. Traditional languages do not support inheritance, one of the

Traditional
Paradigm

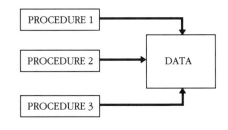

Figure 4.1
Comparison of Tra-
ditional and Object-
Oriented Paradigms

Object-Oriented
Paradigm

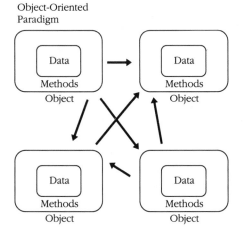

more powerful mechanisms of object-oriented languages. Inheritance
allows the object-oriented programmer to further abstract the definition
of similar objects into classes. Descendents of these abstraction are built

	Traditional	Object-Oriented
Accomplishing Actions	Procedures act on data	Messages sent to objects
Abstracting Data and Functions	Combinations of predefined data types and procedures acting on these data types	Methods and messages
Encapsulation	Library software components	Objects
Inheritance	(No analog exists)	Classes and subclasses

Table 4.1
Fundamental Differ-
ences between
Traditional and
Object-Oriented
Languages

through the mechanism of subclassing, allowing previously programmed methods to be inherited and differences only to be programmed. Table 4.1 illustrates the basic differences between procedural and object-oriented languages.

History of Object-Oriented Languages

The computing environments that evolved in the 1980s, and will become typical for the 1990s, are graphically rich. In this computing environment, intelligent workstations provide distributed end-user computing with access to multiple databases. The applications support multiple data types, including image, text, and video. Driven by this complexity, the emergence of object-oriented programming and languages to support the paradigm is no surprise.

A number of programming languages have contributed to the evolution of today's object-oriented languages, beginning with LISP in the 1950s. LISP, an acronym for list processing, is an artificial intelligence language that introduced the concept of dynamic binding and the benefit of an interactive development environment to the evolution of object-oriented languages. Simula, developed in the 1960s as a language for programming simulations, contributed the class concept and inheritance mechanisms. Data abstraction, in the form of abstract data types, was introduced in the 1970s, first in academic languages such as CLU, developed at the Massachusetts Institute of Technology (MIT), and later in more commercially popular languages such as Ada and Modula-2.

The main force behind the commercial development of object-oriented languages was the Smalltalk project at Xerox Palo Alto Research Center (PARC). Alan Kay described the original goals for Smalltalk in the early 1970s. These goals included the concept of classes, as used in Simula-67, and a graphical interface supporting direct manipulation by the user. Smalltalk was evolved through several releases by PARC, culminating in the release of Smalltalk-80 in 1981. More recently, Xerox encouraged the advancement of Smalltalk with the spinoff of ParcPlace Systems, a company aiming to achieve wider commercial acceptance of Smalltalk and derivative products.

Even with this early movement toward object-oriented languages, only small inroads were made in the general programming community. Progress away from the procedural languages was slow to occur as languages supporting the procedural programming paradigm were well entrenched by the time object-oriented languages arrived. Recently progress has accelerated, primarily due to the availability of object-oriented extensions to two popular languages, C and Pascal, and promised extensions to other commercially popular languages such as BASIC and COBOL.

Two major camps of object-oriented languages have emerged from the last decade of evolution of object-oriented language. One camp is the pure object-oriented language group, where almost everything is an object. This group includes Smalltalk, Actor from the Whitewater Group, and Eiffel from Interactive Software Engineering, Inc. The other camp is the hybrid group, whose object-oriented constructs are added to a procedural language. The members of this group include C++, Objective-C, the Common Lisp Object System (CLOS), and the various object-oriented Pascals.

In general the pure object-oriented languages emphasize exploration and rapid prototyping, while hybrid languages emphasize runtime speed and ease of incorporating object-oriented extensions for the procedural-oriented programmer. The more mature object-oriented languages, such as Smalltalk, also offer robust class libraries and rich sets of development tools. These capabilities are gradually being incorporated into the hybrid languages as well. Figure 4.2 illustrates the evolution of both object-oriented languages camps.

With the emergence in the 1980s of C as an extremely popular programming language across all platforms, the object-oriented extensions to C have been a primary reason for the increased attention to object-oriented programming itself and account for wider use of C++ in the programming community than Smalltalk. C++, Bjarne Stroustrup's object-oriented extension to C, has gained an early following in the workstation and minicomputer realm, and more recently in Microsoft's DOS and IBM's OS/2 implementations. Performance has been a key factor in the rise in popularity of C++. Code produced by C++ is nearly equal in performance to code produced by traditional C compilers, due to careful language design with an eye toward efficient code generation.

Object-oriented Pascal is another popular hybrid. Apple Computer incorporated the first object-oriented extensions to Pascal in 1985 for the Macintosh computer. Other object-oriented Pascals have been more recently released by Microsoft Corporation and Borland International, Inc., for use in DOS and OS/2 environments. Like C++, object-oriented Pascal has been developed with speed and efficiency as underlying requirements and imposes no significant performance overhead.

> The Smalltalk and C++ camps represent two distinct programming cultures. The "bitmap, window, and mouse" culture represented by Smalltalk is part of the user-interface revolution that began in the 1970's. On the other hand, the "single-character-prompt, save-memory-and-machine-cycles-if-it-kills-you" culture is represented by C++.
> *Rettig et al., 1989*

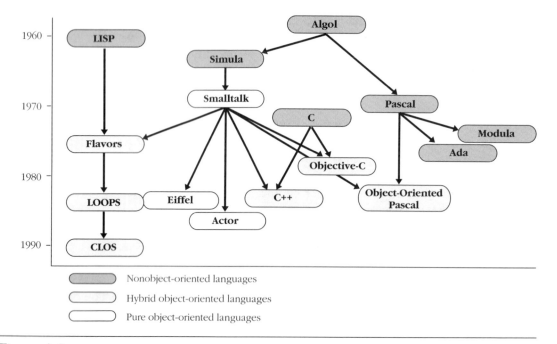

Figure 4.2
Evolution of Object-
Oriented Languages
(Modified after
Schmucker, 1986)

Backward compatibility is an extremely important benefit provided by C + + and object-oriented Pascal and not by the pure object-oriented languages. A large amount of the software industry's program code is already written in C and Pascal. Adding object-oriented techniques to an existing program in a familiar language is a great deal easier than rewriting an application in an entirely new language. Investment in programmer training and experience is retained, and learning time is diminished.

Object-oriented languages have also achieved wide usage outside the mainstream programming community. In the artificial intelligence (AI) community, LISP has evolved to incorporate object-oriented extensions. Object-oriented hybrids of LISP include LOOPS, developed by Xerox PARC; Flavors, developed by MIT; and the current standard, Common Lisp Object System (CLOS), developed by a consortium of AI researchers and practitioners.

In addition to object-oriented languages there are the objectlike languages. One major category, hyperware, includes such user-oriented products as Apple Computer's HyperCard. Although these languages serve to move programmers closer to the object-oriented paradigm, they are more like application frameworks for particular kinds of applications than general-purpose languages. In the case of HyperCard, for example, the metaphor consists of stacks of cards, each with button, text, and icon objects, and methods that can be associated with these objects. These objectlike languages do not provide the benefits of programming by subclassing with inheritance because inheritance is not supported. However, within their restricted metaphors, objectlike languages can provide considerable computational power with little programming effort.

Benefits of Object-Oriented Languages

A programming language that supports the object-oriented paradigm benefits the software developer by providing a natural way to model complex, real-world phonomena. Although the object-oriented paradigm of objects, methods, and messages is often difficult to grasp for programmers accustomed to the traditional metaphor of procedures and data, object orientation actually offers a more natural model of the real world. Programming no longer means just writing lines of code but instead means developing models using classes. With object-oriented programming, programs have fewer lines of code, fewer branching statements, and modules that are more understandable because the modules reflect a one-to-one relationship between the conceptual and object model.

Predefined class libraries, a component of the mature object-oriented languages, enhance the benefits of using object-oriented languages. Much of the programming done with Smalltalk, for example, can be done with objects and messages that already exist in the Smalltalk library. The programming task consists of finding the appropriate objects and messages in the Smalltalk library and combining them in the proper order. This use of a class library is similar to the use of function libraries, such as those used in C, but there is a significant difference. The C function library is relatively fixed. With the Smalltalk library and libraries that accompany other object-oriented languages, new members can easily be created through the use of inheritance.

The overall approach of reducing code via programming the differences with inheritance is one of the key tactics of object-oriented programming and is a unique capability of object-oriented languages. To illustrate this, consider the simple process of adding, changing, or deleting elements in an employee file. In traditional programming, as illus-

Figure 4.3
Traditional Approach to Modifying an Employee File

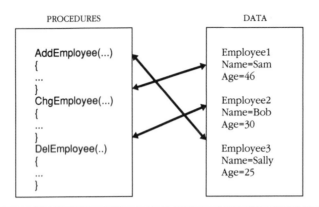

trated in Figure 4.3, a procedure such as AddEmployee() is called to perform its task and place data into a data structure or file.

In an object-oriented system, as illustrated in Figure 4.4, the message Add is sent to the class Employee to create a new Employee object. Changing the Add method does not affect other methods, nor does it affect the object's data structures in a way that would affect application code.

From a programming language standpoint, as shown in Example 4.1, the class of an object identifies both its data structures (e.g., an array of type char) and its methods (e.g., Add). In this example, the method Add works with two data structures, an array called name and an integer called age.

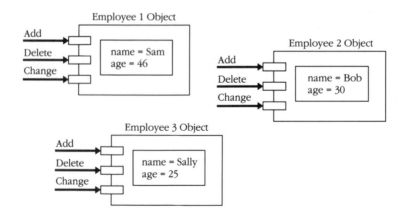

Figure 4.4
Object-Oriented Approach to Employee File

```
class Employee
    {
        char name [25], int age;
    public:
        virtual void Add(char *name, int age);
        virtual void Delete(char *name);
        void Change(char *name, int age);
    };
```

Example 4.1
Class Employee in
C+ +

Subclasses can duplicate, or inherit, the data structures and methods of existing classes. The subclass summarizes common elements from individual classes and allows applications to be factored into ever more refined modules. As shown in Example 4.2, the class Manager can be created as a subclass of the class Employee to describe further employees who are responsible for a group. Manager inherits all the data structures and methods from its parent class Employee without duplicating its code. Differences between Manager and Employee are expressed in the Manager's methods and data. New Manager data like Number__of__ employees are declared. Old employee methods like Add and Change are modified. Thus, a manager is like an employee, with some differences. As this example illustrates, a programmer is not required to build from scratch. Instead, object-oriented methodology supports programming the difference.

Object-oriented languages benefit the developer by supporting modular software development. Objects make it possible to keep related elements together and, in particular, to keep data and the methods that act on those data together. By keeping in one place all the important program parts that relate to a particular entity, program maintenance and upgrading are simplified. In contrast, with traditional languages,

```
class Manager: Employee
    {
        int Number_of_Employees;
    public:
        virtual void Add(char *name, int age, Num_of_Employees);

        virtual void Change (char *name, int age, int
            Num_of_Employees);
    };
```

Example 4.2
Class Manager in
C+ +

there is always the possibility that an update to a subroutine or data element will effect some routine physically far removed from the update. The object-oriented programmer need not scan through all of the source code to see if local changes will cause problems elsewhere in the system.

The benefits of object-oriented programming are substantial. At the same time, object-oriented programming and languages do have a few characteristics that are considered disadvantages by some. The most frequently cited disadvantage is that object-oriented programs run slower than programs written in procedural languages. Why this is so is explained later in this chapter, in the discussion of dynamic binding and polymorphism. Actual differences in execution speed between traditional languages and their object-oriented counterparts, however, do not prove to be very significant, except in the case of Smalltalk, which typically runs five times slower than C (Deutsch 1989).

Another potential problem with object-oriented languages is that a programmer must often learn an extensive class library before becoming proficient in an object-oriented language. As a result, object-oriented languages are more dependent on good documentation and development tools. On the other hand, the extra time spent becoming familiar with the offerings of a class library is more than made up for by the time saved in reusing the code in the class library instead of continually reinventing it.

Functionality of Object-Oriented Languages

Object-oriented programming approaches can be undertaken to some extent with existing languages. Object-oriented languages provide syntax to drive the paradigm and support the powerful mechanism of inheritance and dynamic binding that allows reuse of classes and class libraries. This section provides a review of the basic object-oriented functionality of object-oriented languages: objects with methods and messages, inheritance, dynamic binding, and polymorphism.

Object-oriented Pascal, in particular Borland International, Inc.'s Turbo Pascal 5.5, and C+ + will be used to illustrate the fundamentals of object orientation. These examples reveal differences in terminology and in function that exist between languages. For example, in C+ + a method is called a member or virtual function. In object-oriented Pascal a method is called a static or virtual method. Examples in this chapter will focus on features (syntax) of a programming language. Discussion of the tools and environments for program development occurs in Chapter 8, "Programming and Maintenance."

Object-oriented languages will be illustrated with an example that starts with a class called Location. Location contains internal *X, Y* coordinate data and has three methods:

1. initialization,

2. access to the value of the *X* coordinate, and

3. access to the value of the *Y* coordinate.

Subsequently Point and Circle will be created as subclasses of Location. Point and Circle will inherit the three methods and acquire new data and methods. Figure 4.5 illustrates the three classes. The example is adapted from Borland International (1989) programming guide for Turbo Pascal.

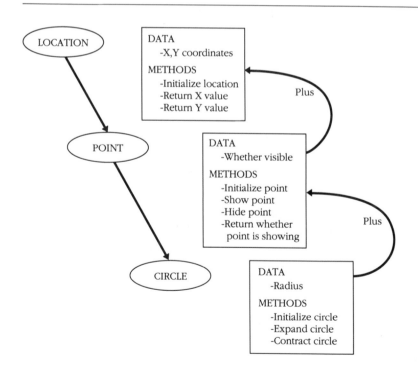

Figure 4.5
Location, Point, and Circle Classes

Objects and Classes

A class defines a set of run-time objects, or instances, each of which is characterized by the operations, called methods, and the value of its internal data, called instance variables. All objects of the same class have the same set of methods available to them. For example, all the objects of class Location share the three methods, Initialize location, Return X value, and Return Y value. Objects of the same class may differ in the values of their instance variables. That is, two instances of the class Location may have different X, Y coordinate data. Some object-oriented languages additionally support the concept of class variables. A class variable has a value that is shared by all objects of that class. The term *class data* is used to refer collectively to the class variables and instance variables.

Figure 4.6 shows an extension of class Location to include a class variable, count, the number of Location objects in existence. Three instances of class Location are shown. Each instance has its own values for its instance variables, X and Y, and all three share the common value of 3 for count. If a new instance of class Location is created, count would change to 4 in all instances of the class. Since class variables have shared values, they are usually implemented as pointers to a single copy.

The distinction between class variables and instance variables is an

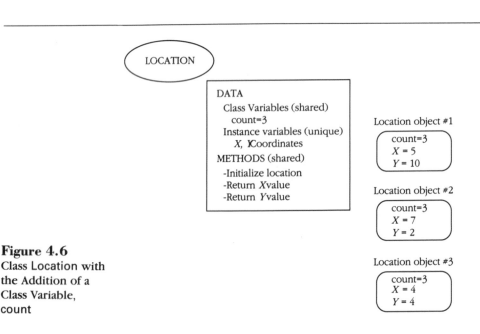

Figure 4.6
Class Location with
the Addition of a
Class Variable,
count

Object-Oriented Pascal	**C++**	**Example 4.3**
		Definition of Class
type	class Location	Location in Object-
Location = object	{	Oriented Pascal and
		C++ (Correspond-
	int X,Y;	ing Lines are Side
X,Y : Integer;	public:	by Side)
	virtual void Init(int InitX,	
procedure Init(InitX, InitY: Integer);	int InitY);	
	int GetX();	
function GetX: Integer;	int GetY();	
function GetY: Integer;	};	
end;		

important theoretical concept that clarifies the distinction between classes and objects. In most applications, however, class variables are much less useful than instance variables. In fact, many object-oriented languages do not permit their definition.

Methods and Messages

Objects, as previously defined, contain a set of shared procedures called methods. An object's methods are invoked only with a suitable message. The message may invoke a method to perform calculations, access and change the object's instance variables, or send messages to other objects as a part of its response. An object's instance variables can be manipulated only by its own methods. That is, messages telegraph a request for action to an object while the object's methods decide how to perform the action. Example 4.3 shows the definition of the class Location in object-oriented Pascal and C++. Class Location consists of data, coordinates X, Y, along with methods that initialize and return values for X and Y.

    A method definition is just like a procedure or function definition, with the addition of the class name prefixed to the method name. Ex-

Object-Oriented Pascal	**C++**	**Example 4.4**
		Method Definitions
function Location.Get X: Integer;	Int Location :: GetX()	in Object-Oriented
begin	{	Pascal and C++
		(Corresponding
GetX := X;	return X;	Lines are Side by
end;	}	Side)

Table 4.2
Invoking Methods
with Messages in
Object-Oriented
Pascal and C++

	Object-Oriented Pascal	C++
	X: Integer;	int X;
Defines ALocation	ALocation: Location;	Location ALocation;
Initializes ALocation	ALocation.Init(5,10)	ALocation.Init(5,10);
Returns the X value of ALocation	X: = ALocation.GetX;	X = ALocation.GetX();

ample 4.4 compares the definition of methods in C++ and object-oriented Pascal. In both object-oriented Pascal and C++, as Table 4.2 illustrates, methods are invoked by specifying the name of the instance followed by the name of the method.

Inheritance

Inheritance provides one of the unique advantages of object-oriented languages, the ability to extend and refine data types and functionality without duplicating or even having to access the original source code. Once the class Location is defined, descendant classes can then be defined. Class Point is defined through inheritance from class Location, with the addition of a Visible data item and methods for showing, hiding, and inquiring about the visibility of points. Example 4.5 shows the definition of class Point in both object-oriented Pascal and C++. Finally, as shown in Example 4.6, descendent class Circle is defined through inheritance from class Point, with the addition of an instance variable, radius, and methods for expanding and contracting circles.

Example 4.5
Definition of the
Class Point as a Sub-
class of Class
Location in Object-
Oriented Pascal and
C++ (Correspond-
ing Lines are Side
by Side)

Object-Oriented Pascal	**C++**
Point = object(Location)	class point: public Location
	{
Visible: Boolean;	boolean visible;
	public:
procedure Init(InitX, InitY: Integer);	virtual void Init (int initX, int initY);
procedure Show;	virtual void show ();
procedure Hide;	virtual void hide ();
function isVisible: Boolean;	boolean isvisible ();
end;	};

Object-Oriented Pascal	C++	**Example 4.6**

| | | Definition of the Class Circle as a subclass of class Point in Object-Oriented Pascal and C++ (Corresponding Lines are Side by Side) |

```
Circle = object(Point)       class circle: public point
                             {
   Radius: Integer;             int radius;
                                public:
   procedure Init(InitX, InitY,    virtual void init (int initX,
      InitRadius: Integer);           int initY, int initRadius);
   procedure Show;              virtual void show ();
   procedure Hide;              void hide ();
   procedure Expand             void expand (int expandby);
      (ExpandBy: Integer);
   procedure Contract           void contract (int contractby);
      (ContractBy: Integer);
end;                         };
```

A method in a descendant class can override a method in an ancestor class simply by defining a new method of that same name. The same method name, for example Show, can thus operate as appropriate for objects that are instances of different classes. By inheriting methods from ancestor classes that operate correctly for the descendent class, and by overriding those methods that must operate differently, the programmer truly extends an ancestor class without recreating it from scratch.

The most common form of class creation is specialization, in which a new class is created from an existing class, because the existing class is too general. For example, class Point is a specialization of class Location; a point is a location that also is able to show and hide itself. Another common form of class creation, which does not necessarily involve inheritance, is a combination in which a new class is created by combining objects from other classes as its instance variables. For example, a class could be defined as a collection of points and circles.

Inheritance is a fundamental characteristic of object-oriented languages. Without inheritance, the addition of a new type of object requires writing entirely new procedures for common operations, such as print. Without inheritance, there will be a great deal of similarity between different print methods, requiring continual maintenance of methods that differ slightly or not at all. Inheritance is the mechanism that largely relieves programmers of this burden.

Polymorphism

Object-oriented languages allow the creation of a hierarchy of objects with common method names for operations that are conceptually similar but that are implemented differently for each class in the hierarchy. As a result, the same message when received by different objects can cause completely different actions. This functionality is referred to as *polymorphism.* In the Location, Point, Circle example, instances of classes Point and Circle can each receive the message Show. In the former case, a point will be displayed; in the latter, a circle. The programmer need not write any special code to determine the object's type at run time.

In a traditional language without polymorphism, such as C, separate Show functions such as ShowCircle, ShowSquare, and ShowEllipse would be named for each type of object to be drawn. This results in a proliferation of code. Example 4.7 contrasts how two languages, one without polymorphism (C) and one with polymorphism (C++), solve the problem of writing one general routine to show both points and circles.

Example 4.7
The Advantages of
Polymorphism

Solution with no polymorphism

```
void show(obj)
    struct object *obj;
{
    switch (obj → objectType)
    {
    case POINT:
        showPoint (obj);
        break;
    case CIRCLE:
        showCircle (obj);
        break;
    default:
        printerror("incorrect object type");
    }
};
```

Solution with polymorphism

```
void show(obj)
struct object *obj;
{
    obj.show
};
```

Dynamic Binding

Binding is the process by which the caller of a routine is given the address of the routine. In a procedural language, binding associates the caller of a procedure with the procedure's address. In an object-oriented language, binding associates a message to an object with the method to carry out that message. This may happen when the program is compiled and linked, or when it is running. When binding occurs at compile-and-link time, the process is termed static binding, early binding, strong binding, or compile-time binding. When binding occurs at run time, the process is termed dynamic binding, late binding, weak binding, or run time binding. Traditional languages such as C and Pascal support static binding only. Dynamic binding is one of the major enhancements embodied in object-oriented languages.

In Example 4.7, the use of dynamic binding requires much less code, as it does not need to determine explicitly the object's type. Instead binding is performed dynamically at run time between the object and the Show method appropriate to it. More importantly, suppose that the program is modified to add a new kind of shape, such as a triangle. In both solutions, a new Show routine must be written. In the static binding solution, however, an additional call to this routine must be added to the Show procedure, as follows:

```
case TRIANGLE:
    showTriangle (obj);
    break;
```

In the dynamic binding solution, the Show routine remains the same. In other words, the addition of new kinds of data types does not require changes to existing code.

Multiple Inheritance

Two types of inheritance, single and multiple inheritance, are commonly used to relate objects. With single inheritance a subclass can inherit instance variables and methods from a single class. With multiple inheritance a subclass can inherit instance variables and methods from more than one class. Single inheritance provides a means to extend or refine classes. Multiple inheritance provides, in addition, the means to combine or unite different classes.

An example of multiple inheritance, taken from Meyer (1988) is a class describing windows in a windowing system, where windows can contain subwindows. This notion can be described by having class window inherit from three parent classes: screen_object, text, and tree, as shown in Figure 4.7.

Class screen_object provides the geometrical properties of windows, with methods to display and move the window on the screen.

Figure 4.7
With Multiple In-
heritance, Window
Inherits all Methods
from Its Three
Parent Classes.

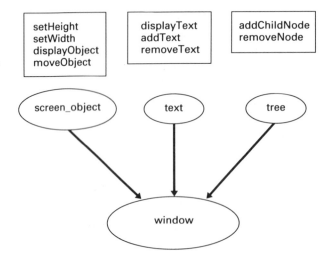

Class text provides the textual properties of windows, with methods to manipulate lines of text. Finally, class tree provides the hierarchical structure of windows, with methods to add and remove windows. Example 4.8 provides an example of how class window could be defined in C+ + as a subclass of screen—object, text, and tree.

Without multiple inheritance, the programmer could choose only one of the classes as the parent for window, as illustrated in Figure 4.8. The programmer would have to write specific routines to provide the features that are now unavailable from the other two unchosen classes. This requirement for support of multiple inheritance is controversial. Opponents state it is an unnecessary feature that is confusing and difficult to use correctly, that it has limited real value, and that it is wasteful of machine resources. Proponents state just the opposite when they argue that multiple inheritance is an essential language feature bringing great power, convenience, and generality to an object-oriented language.

Multiple inheritance certainly adds expressive power to a language, but at a cost in syntax complexity, as well as compilation and run-time overhead. Classes become more complex to design because there are more ways to inherit methods and data, with potential conflicts. For example, suppose a method in class text had the same name as a method in class tree. The programmer must then additionally specify which of these methods the instances of class window should inherit.

Multiple inheritance also complicates how messages are resolved. In a single-inheritance hierarchy, when a message is sent to an object and

```
class screen_object {
    // ...
public
    virtual void setHeight (int);
    virtual void setWidth (int);
    virtual void displayObject( );
    virtual void moveObject (int, int);
};

class text {
    // ...
public
    virtual void displayText ( );
    virtual void addText (char *);
    virtual void removeText( );
};

class tree {
    // ...
public
    virtual void addChildNode (node);
    virtual void removeNode (node);
};

class window:
public screen_object,
public text,
public tree {...};
```

Example 4.8
Multiple Inheritance
in C++

the object's class has no method for the message, the class's immediate ancestor is inspected, and so on up the class hierarchy until a matching method is found. With multiple inheritance, a more complicated search is required for the appropriate method. The search could, for example, proceed breadth first (i.e., search through all immediate ancestors before searching above them), or depth first (i.e., search all the ancestors of one immediate ancestor before searching the next ancestor). If the language implements only one search strategy, it runs the risk that it

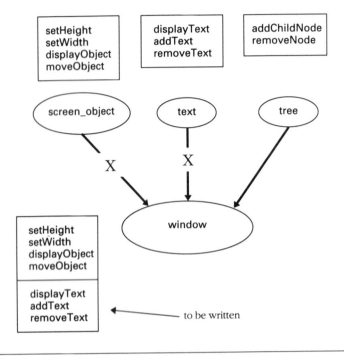

Figure 4.8
With Single Inheritance Window Inherits Methods from Only One Class

might be inefficient for certain kinds of problems. Some object-oriented languages solve this problem by permitting the programmer to specify the search strategy, but at the cost of increasing programming complexity.

Class Libraries

A class library is a collection of classes used for a particular programming task. The closer a class library matches an application, the less modification is needed. At one extreme is the class library of fundamental units of program construction, such as strings, stacks, and linked lists. These can be used by virtually any application, but only at the lowest level of granularity. Figure 4.9 shows a portion of such a class library available from Stepstone Corporation for its Objective-C language. The library includes collections as well as arrays, strings, and various graphical shapes.

At the other extreme are class libraries that provide a complete framework for a category of application, for example, a framework for building graphical user interfaces that includes classes for menus, cursors, and help screens. Here, the breadth of applications that can be

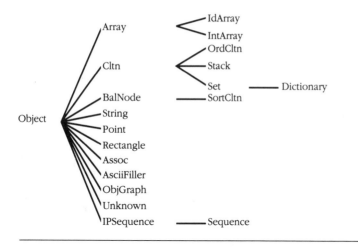

Figure 4.9
Portion of the Step-
stone Class Library
for Objective-C
(Stepstone, 1989)

programmed is more severely limited, but the support is at a much higher level of granularity. Figure 4.10 shows a portion of such a class library, also from Stepstone Corporation, for building graphical user interfaces.

Figure 4.10
Portion of the Step-
stone Class Library
for Graphical User
Interfaces (Step-
stone, 1989)

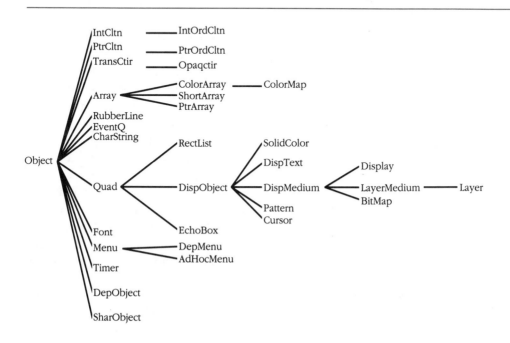

Good class libraries are difficult to produce. They require the somewhat unrelated skills of decomposing problems into their components, and abstracting and arranging their components into classes that are both general and useful.

Development Tools

The two most important tools for object-oriented languages are browsers and symbolic debuggers. A source-code browser is an interactive tool that provides views of both the application code and the class library. It is primarily a navigational aid, permitting the programmer to see the application's overall hierarchical structure, as well as to move from a class to its ancestor or descendant classes, from a method to the classes that implement the method, or from a message to the classes that use that message. In addition, browsers are tutorial aids because they make it easy to display and learn from existing class and method definitions and by providing templates for the creation of new classes and methods.

Symbolic debuggers for object-oriented languages provide the same capabilities of traditional debuggers, extended to the object paradigm. Object-oriented symbolic debuggers trace method calls, just as traditional debuggers trace function calls. Debuggers permit breakpoints to be set within methods, or at method invocation. In addition, debuggers can examine and alter the values of instance variables.

Much of the power of any debugger lies in its ability to view the program under test in different ways. An object-oriented debugger, in particular, should provide views into the individual objects during run time, views of the relationships among objects, and views of the classes from which the objects are derived. In fact, the functionality of object-oriented debuggers and source-code browsers often overlaps, so that it is often possible to set breakpoints from within the browser, or alternately to browse the class library from within the debugger.

Figure 4.11 illustrates the debugging environment for Borland International's Turbo Pascal. The Module window shows source code for class Location's methods. The Object Hierarchy window shows the hierarchy of classes the programmer has defined. The Object Type window shows the instance variables and methods for class Location. Finally, the Watches window displays the current values for programmer-specified variables, in this case an object from class Point called APoint.

For further discussion of the use of object-oriented programming tools, see Chapter 8, "Programming and Maintenance."

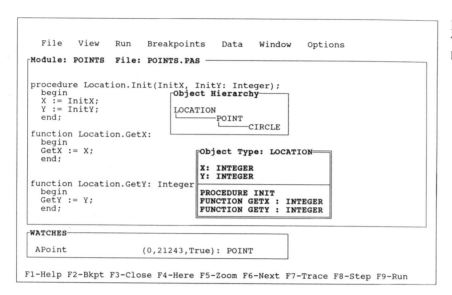

Figure 4.11
Turbo Pascal
Debugger

Survey of Object-Oriented Languages

This section surveys a representative sample of object-oriented languages. Four hybrids are explored, C++, Objective-C, object-oriented Pascal, and Common Lisp Object System (CLOS). Two pure languages are presented, Smalltalk and Eiffel. For each language, the survey includes a short history, information on commercial availability, a brief technical description of the language, including any unique features, and an assessment of the language's particular strengths and weaknesses. A table in each section indicates the language's specific use of the object-oriented vernacular.

C++

C++ is a superset of the C language. C++ was written by Bjarne Stroustrup at AT&T's Bell Laboratories in the early 1980s. Due in large measure to its C heritage, C++ has achieved the most commercial popularity of object-oriented languages used today.

AT&T has put the C++ language definition in the public domain. AT&T first licensed its C++ source-code translator to commercial language vendors in 1986. It is now available in source-code form from Bell Laboratories and in binary form from a number of other software vendors. Most commercially available products are derived from the AT&T

There is a gap between those languages which are highly practical and efficient but provide little for expressing higher level abstractions and those languages which are rich in abstraction facilities but are too inefficient to be practical. C++ bridges that gap, making all the benefits of higher level abstraction facilities available for use in production software development.
Hopkins, 1987

source, so there are few major language differences. Two notable exceptions are Zortech's C++ and Oregon Software Incorporated's Oregon C++, which are true compilers developed independently from the AT&T source code. Commercial products differ primarily in their development environments and their class libraries.

C++ is very nearly a proper superset of the X3J11 ANSI standard for C. Like C, C++ places a very strong emphasis on efficiency, both by avoiding language features that require more than minimal support at run time and by providing language features that permit low-level hardware and memory manipulation. For these reasons it is favored by many object-oriented developers and shunned by others. C++ was designed from the start to be implemented as a native code compiler rather than as an intermediate code interpreter. Due to this design goal of efficient code generation, code produced by C++ is identical in speed to code in C with the single exception of virtual function calls, which impose the small performance penalty of a call through a pointer to the function instead of a direct call to the function. C++ is efficient enough that AT&T and Sun Microsystems have chosen it to rewrite their UNIX operating system kernels.

C++ may be thought of as a multiparadigm language in which the programmer may choose the programming style and set of language features to suit the problem. In those situations where the focus is on operations instead of data, the programmer may choose to ignore the object-oriented features of C++ and concentrate instead on the development of functional algorithms. This approach would be appropriate for developing libraries of mathematical functions, for example, where the data types are few and unchanging, the individual building blocks are relatively small and easy to manage, and the emphasis is on efficiency and speed.

In those situations where the focus is on the design and manipulation of data types and structure, the programmer would instead choose to exploit C++'s object-oriented features. This use of C++ would be appropriate for developing classes for a windowing system, for example, where the data types are complex and changeable, the individual building blocks are relatively large, and the emphasis is on the organization and mastery of this complexity.

C++ supports the basic object-oriented concepts of object, class, method, message, subclass, and inheritance, including multiple inheritance, as previously illustrated in this section. Table 4.3 gives the C++ naming conventions for these concepts.

Concept	C++
Object	Object
Class	Class
Method	Member function
Instance variables	Member
Message	Function call
Subclass	Derived class
Inheritance	Derivation

Table 4.3
Naming Conventions for Object-Oriented Concepts in C++

The class construct in C++ provides the key mechanism for object-oriented programming. Each class construct contains definitions of the class data and methods. In addition, C++ class constructs provide flexible information-hiding options to the class developer. Each instance variable and method in a C++ class can be declared either private, protected, or public. Access to those declared private is restricted to methods within the class; access to those declared protected is restricted to methods within subclasses of the class; and access to those declared public is available to methods of any class. These restrictions can be overridden by declaring another method a friend of a given class, allowing it selective or total access to the class' private and protected data and methods. Messages in C++ are sent to objects using a mechanism similar to a function call.

Example 4.9 shows the definition of the class location, which has two private instance variables, X and Y, and three public methods, Init, GetX, and GetY. The default declaration of X and Y as private instance

```
class location
{
    int X, Y;
public:
    init(int InitX, int InitY);
    int GetX();
    int GetY();
};
```

Example 4.9
C++ Class with Private and Public Methods

variables means that no code can directly access X or Y except location's three methods. Assuming that a C++ program defines an object of class Location called ALocation, then

    XValue = ALocation.X;

is illegal. Instead, the public method, GetX, is used to retrieve the X value of ALocation as shown below:

    xValue = ALocation.GetX();

C++ classes can provide automatic initialization and deallocation methods called constructors and destructors, respectively. A class constructor is called whenever an object of that class is created. A class destructor is called whenever an object of that class is destroyed. These two methods assure the proper handling of an object at the beginning and end of its lifetime.

A C++ class can contain operator overloading constructs, enabling the new objects defined by the class to be used with the familiar operators, such as + and −, that C++'s built-in types can already be used with. For example, defining a class of complex numbers could include within the class definition a definition of how members of this class (i.e., complex numbers) will respond to the + and − operators. Once these definitions have been made, then

    z = x + y;

is legal when x, y and z are complex numbers. The + operator has been overloaded to be usable with complex numbers as well as ordinary numbers. C++ allows the programmer to define new data types that are just as easy to use as built-in types. This combination of the C++ class definition, constructors and destructors, and operator overloading permit the programmer to achieve this ideal.

C++ provides for inheritance through subclassing, which allows a class to inherit some or all of the methods of its parent(s), to redefine existing methods, and to define new methods. Example 4.10 shows an example of class point defined as a subclass of class location. C++ also supports multiple inheritance, as previously illustrated in Example 4.8.

C++ provides for dynamic binding methods called virtual functions within an inheritance hierarchy. By specifying a method in a parent class to be virtual and then redefining it in one or more subclasses, the compiler will specify that any messages to this method be dynamically

```
class point: location
{
    boolean visible;
public:
    virtual void show ( );
    virtual void hide ( );
    boolean isvisible ( );
};
```

Example 4.10
C++ Definition of
the Class point as a
Subclass of Class
location

bound at run time. The programmer is free to choose whether static or dynamic binding suits the various parts of the problem, thus allowing a certain measure of fine tuning. The strategy of redefining only methods in subclasses also guarantees that at run time at least one of the redefined methods will always be chosen. This is very different from Smalltalk, where any message can be sent to any object at run time, with no guarantee that the object will understand the message.

C++ is an attractive choice for the commercial software developer. As it is based on C, C++ has immediately garnered support, interest, and expertise from the enormous community of C developers. Because it is a superset of C, following the philosophy of "Add to, don't change," C++ guarantees upward compatibility with the existing base of C programs. Due to its philosophy of "Don't pay for features you don't use," it is relatively lean, requiring less memory to compile and run and preserving the speed and efficiency for which C has been famous. And finally, because C++ has attracted the most attention from software language vendors, it promises to have the largest array of compilers, tools, development environments, and class libraries of any object-oriented language.

One drawback often cited against C++ is that because it is a hybrid, rather than pure object-oriented language, it is not as good as a pure object-oriented language for teaching object-oriented concepts. The language does not require use of its object-oriented features. In this respect, C++ is probably not the best choice as a vehicle for learning how to program with an object-oriented language. Another near-term drawback with C++ is the lack of mature source-code debuggers, development environments, and class libraries. Fortunately, this lack is only temporary, as many software vendors are pushing hard to fill the gap.

Objective-C

Objective-C was developed by Brad Cox for Productivity Products International, now the Stepstone Corporation (Cox, 1987). Objective-C is another hybrid object-oriented language, formed by adding Smalltalk-inspired constructs to the C language. Objective-C was originally released in 1983. Though less well known and less widely used than C++, it has attracted attention as part of the initial development environment for the NeXT computer. Objective-C supports the basic object-oriented mechanisms of object, class, method and message, subclass, and inheritance. Objective-C supports multiple inheritance. Table 4.4 gives the Objective-C naming conventions for these concepts.

The Objective-C language is a strict superset of the C language. The object-oriented extensions are achieved by adding to the C language a new definition mechanism, the class definition; a new data type, the object type; and a new expression type, the message expression. In Objective-C, each class definition consists of two files, an interface file and an implementation file. The interface file defines what is available to users of the class: the class name, the name of its parent class, the declarations of the instance variables for objects of the class, and the declarations of the methods available to objects of the class. The implementation file contains the actual implementations of the class methods.

Sample interface and definition files for class Location are shown in Example 4.11. In the example, Location has the superclass Object. Each Location object has two instance variables, X and Y, and three methods: init, which creates a new Location object with X = InitX and Y = InitY; getX, which returns the X value of the object; and getY, which returns the Y value of the object. The + in front of init identifies it as a class

Table 4.4

Naming Conventions for Object-Oriented Constructs in Objective-C

Concept	Objective-C
Object	Object
Class	Factory
Method	Method
Instance variable	Instance variable
Message	Message expression
Subclass	Subclass
Inheritance	Inheritance

```
// interface file for class Location
@interface Location: Object
    { int X, Y; }
    + init; (int) InitX: (int) InitY
    − (int) getX;
    − (int) getY;
@end
```

Example 4.11
Class Location in
Objective-C

```
// implementation file for class Location
@implementation Location: Object
    { int X, Y; }
    + init: (int) InitX: (int) InitY
        {
        self = [super new];
        X = InitX;
        Y = InitY;
        return (self);
        }
    − (int) getX
        { return (X);}
    − (int) getY
        { return (Y);}
@end
```

method. Objective-C, like Smalltalk, blurs the distinction between classes and objects by permitting classes to receive messages and respond to them with their own class methods.

An example of an Objective-C object declaration is:

```
id aLocation; // declares aLocation to be an object identifier
```

A new Location object is created by sending the message init to the class Location (declared earlier) and assigning it to the id aLocation. For example, the message expression to create a new location at (5, 10) is as follows:

```
aLocation = [Location init: 5 : 10];
```

In Objective-C, message expressions are enclosed in square brackets with the receiver listed first, followed by the message. The receiver is always an object, and the message tells it what to do. For example, the X value of the Location object aLocation is obtained by sending aLocation the message getX:

```
xValue = [aLocation getX];
```

Objective-C, like C+ +, provides some flexibility in the amount of protection it affords the instance variables and methods of a class. Objective-C supports two categories of instance variables, private and public. By default, all the instance variables of a class are private; that is, they are accessible only through the class' methods. Instance variables can be declared public, in which case they are freely accessible.

The Objective-C compiler accepts Objective-C source code and outputs an equivalent C source code. The resulting C source code can then be compiled for execution on the target machine. This has resulted in substantial portability of the language and availability on a wide spectrum of computers.

One major advantage Objective-C has over C+ + is the maturity of its class libraries and development environment. The Objective-C class libraries, called ICpaks, implement basic data structures as well as graphical user interface classes. Brad Cox, the creator of Objective-C, coined the term "software-IC" to describe such a machine-independent class (Cox 1987), although the term is now used to describe any well-designed class.

In addition to its class libraries, Stepstone offers an interactive, interpretive development environment called VICI, which eliminates the compile-link process between code changes, offering immediate, interpreted execution of any C or Objective-C statement. With this development environment the developer can set breakpoints; trace statements, data, or methods; and single-step through source code. One interesting feature of VICI is its ability to mix interpreted and compiled classes. This can be advantageous when developing a large application with many classes, as only those classes under development need be interpreted. Previously developed classes run at compiled speed.

Object-Oriented Pascal

Object-oriented Pascal is available from a number of vendors. Like C+ +, object-oriented Pascal is a hybrid language, based on object extensions to the Pascal language. In the Apple environment, object-oriented Pascal is usually associated with MacApp, which provides a class library and Macintosh Object Pascal for developing Macintosh ap-

Concept	Object-Oriented Pascal
Object	Object
Class	Object type
Method	Method
Instance variable	Object variable
Message	Message
Subclass	Descendant type
Inheritance	Inheritance

Table 4.5
Naming Conventions for Object-Oriented Constructs in Pascal

plications. In the IBM personal computer environment, object-oriented Pascals are available from a number of vendors and include Borland International's Turbo Pascal and Microsoft's Quick Pascal.

The various versions of object-oriented Pascal support the fundamental object-oriented mechanisms of object, classes, methods, messages, and inheritance. Turbo Pascal includes capabilities derived from C++ such as objects, static and virtual methods, and constructors and destructors. The Borland compiler also uses a smart linker to strip away unused objects and methods during compilation. Examples in this section are written in Turbo Pascal 5.5. None of the object-oriented Pascals currently supports multiple inheritance, although this situation will undoubtedly change. Table 4.5 reviews the naming conventions in object-oriented Pascal.

In object-oriented Pascal a class is much like a record with the addition of the new reserved word object. The object syntax allows the creation of classes that can inherit. In Example 4.12, a Location class is defined with integer coordinates X and Y. In Example 4.13, a new class, Point, is created as a subclass of Location. With the use of the object(Location) syntax, Point inherits the X,Y coordinates and adds its own characteristics of a Boolean field Visible.

Inside the class definition a method is defined by the header of the function or procedure acting as a method. The definition of the method

```
type
    Location = object
    X,Y: Integer;
end;
```

Example 4.12
Definition of the Class Location

Example 4.13
Inheritance in
Object-Oriented
Pascal

```
Point = object(Location)
    Visible : Boolean;
end;
```

is qualified with the definition of the name of the type, as shown in Example 4.14.

Extensions to object-oriented Pascal, such as those from Borland, include the ability to store classes in separate files as units. These units can be separately compiled and accessed later through a uses statement. The units also provide a way for third-party vendors to develop and distribute class libraries without revealing their source code.

Like C++, object-oriented Pascal provides an important benefit that pure object-oriented languages lack: backward compatibility with most existing Pascal programs. These programs can have object-oriented constructs added to them in a controlled fashion, using the same programmers who wrote and understood the original Pascal programs. This provides a shorter learning curve to object expertise.

Smalltalk

Smalltalk's origins date back to the early 1970s when Alan Kay, then a graduate student at the University of Utah, realized that his work in graphics could be enhanced by some of the concepts contained in the Simula language. After joining Xerox PARC, Kay expanded these first

Example 4.14
Method Definition
in Pascal

```
type
    Location = object
    X,Y: Integer;
    procedure Init(NewX, NewY : Integer);
end;


procedure Location.Init (NewX, NewY : Integer);
begin
X : = NewX; { The X field of a Location
    object }
Y : = NewY; { The Y field of a Location
    object }
end;
```

ideas into the concept of a graphics-based, interactive personal workstation. Two other important contributors to the development of Smalltalk
were Adele Goldberg and Dan Ingalls.

Smalltalk went through a number of major revisions at Xerox PARC,
culminating in Smalltalk-80, which was released in April of 1983. In
1987, ParcPlace Systems of Mountain View was formed as a spinoff from
Xerox to commercialize the Smalltalk language. Smalltalk and its deriv-
atives are available from ParcPlace Systems and other vendors including
Digitalk, who offer Smalltalk/V.

Smalltalk originated much of the definitions of today's object-oriented
vernacular. In Smalltalk, the basic mechanisms are referred to as objects,
classes, methods, and messages. Inheritance is supported, although multiple inheritance is not. Smalltalk is the purest of "pure" object-oriented
languages. There is no form of data other than objects, and the only
operation that can be performed on an object is to send it a message.
Smalltalk even considers classes as objects, where each class is an instance of a higher-level metaclass, and messages can be sent to classes
in the same way as they are sent to instances of classes.

The naming conventions in Smalltalk are listed in Table 4.6. Because
Smalltalk established much of the terminology for object-oriented languages, the mechanisms and naming conventions are the same.

Smalltalk is distinguished from other object-oriented languages in
the richness and maturity of its programming environment, which includes a large library of several hundred classes covering basic abstractions such as collections and dictionaries, as well as graphical classes
covering useful interface components such as windows and scrollbars.
Thanks to the existence of this class library, the programmer need not
write original code for defining the class Location because its capabilities

Concept	Smalltalk
Object	Object
Class	Class
Method	Method
Instance variable	Instance variable
Message	Message
Subclass	Subclass
Inheritance	Inheritance

Table 4.6
Naming Conven-
tions for
Object-Oriented
Constructs in
Smalltalk

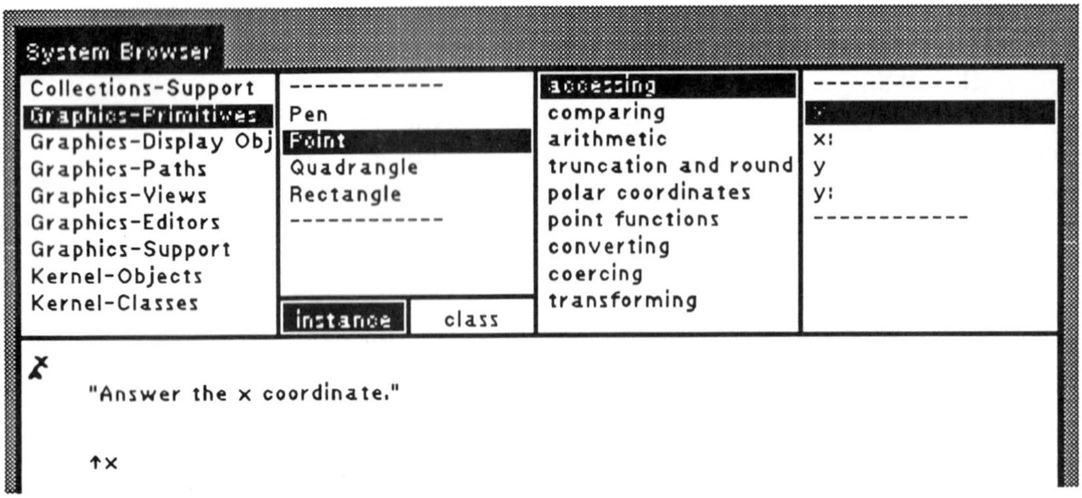

```
┌─────────────────────────────────────────────────────────────────────┐
│ System Browser                                                        │
├─────────────────────────────────────────────────────────────────────┤
│ Collections-Support │ ------------ │ accessing          │ ----------- │
│ Graphics-Primitives │ Pen          │ comparing          │ x           │
│ Graphics-Display Obj│ Point        │ arithmetic         │ x!          │
│ Graphics-Paths      │ Quadrangle   │ truncation and round│ y          │
│ Graphics-Views      │ Rectangle    │ polar coordinates  │ y!          │
│ Graphics-Editors    │ ------------ │ point functions    │ ----------- │
│ Graphics-Support    │              │ converting         │             │
│ Kernel-Objects      │              │ coercing           │             │
│ Kernel-Classes      │ ┌─────────┐  │ transforming       │             │
│                     │ │ instance│ class                               │
├─────────────────────────────────────────────────────────────────────┤
│ X                                                                     │
│                                                                       │
│      "Answer the x coordinate."                                       │
│                                                                       │
│      ↑x                                                               │
└─────────────────────────────────────────────────────────────────────┘
```

Figure 4.12
The Smalltalk Class
Point with
Method X

already exist in the Smalltalk class Point, a subclass of class Object. Class Point has two instance variables, X and Y, and many predefined methods, including X, which returns the receiver's *X*-coordinate, and Y, which returns the receiver's *Y*-coordinate. Figure 4.12 shows the actual code for class Point and its method, X.

Smalltalk's messages specify the object first, then the message to send to it, and finally any parameters required by the message. For example, X + Y in Smalltalk translates to "send to the object X the + message and parameter Y." Messages can have multiple parameters; for example, BusinessExpense spend: 50 on: 'lunch' sends a spend: on: message to the object BusinessExpense, with 50 and 'lunch' as parameters. The code shown in Example 4.15 creates an object of class Point and then calls the X method to get its *X*-coordinate. Variables are declared by placing their symbols between vertical bars.

Example 4.15
Creating an Object
and Calling a
Method with
Smalltalk

```
| aPoint xValue |
aPoint : = (5@10).
xValue : = aPoint X.
```

Smalltalk is a typeless language: There are no variable type declarations, and no type checking is performed. Smalltalk takes dynamic binding to an extreme by permitting you to send any message to any object; only at run time will Smalltalk be able to decide if the message is one that the object can understand and respond to. This is in contrast to typed languages such as C + +, where inappropriate messages to objects are caught at compile time.

Smalltalk is a language that is almost impossible to separate from its development environment. All Smalltalk language implementations come with a large class library of predefined classes that a programmer needs to write a program, such as compilers, debuggers, and editors. This is an integrated environment, in which there is no distinction made between applications, tools, and interfaces. All components are just objects in the Smalltalk class library. The environment gives Smalltalk a unity of concept that is especially helpful in learning the language and the object-oriented style of programming.

There is a common misconception that because any Smalltalk application can access and modify any class or object in the entire system, it becomes very difficult to extract the application from the surrounding system. However, tools exist to strip out the unused classes and to seal the image.

Despite its purity and the tight integration of the development environment, Smalltalk is considered to have some drawbacks. Since every aspect of the Smalltalk system is open to inspection and modifications, changes made by an application for its own purposes can affect the operation of the system. For example, an application can modify a class in such a manner that it unintentionally introduces errors into the compiler or the debugger. This can also cause problems for the distribution and continued support of applications. If users can change anything about their own systems, it becomes difficult to support an application that depends upon certain features of that system remaining stable. Similarly, user applications are vulnerable to the effects of system revisions by the system developer.

Compared to other object-oriented languages, Smalltalk's performance is slow. Because all Smalltalk messages are dynamically bound, including even the lowest-level constructs such as the + message in X = A + B, Smalltalk incurs a penalty every time a message is sent to an object. This run-time overhead is not incurred by statically bound languages, such as C + +. Smalltalk can also be bulky—Smalltalk-80 requires 2M bytes (Deutsch 1989).

Eiffel

Eiffel is a language developed by Bertrand Meyer and his colleagues at Interactive Software Engineering, Inc. Eiffel's notable capabilities include robust development tools, full typing, and multiple inheritance. Eiffel

Table 4.7	Concept	Eiffel
Naming Conventions for Object-Oriented Constructs in Eiffel	Object	Object
	Class	Class
	Method	Routine
	Instance variable	Attribute
	Message	Applying a routine
	Subclass	Descendant
	Inheritance	Inheritance

supports the basic object-oriented mechanisms of object, class, method and message, subclass, and inheritance. Eiffel also supports multiple inheritance. The naming conventions in Eiffel are outlined in Table 4.7.

In Eiffel, the class Location would be defined as shown in Example 4.16. In Eiffel the export clause lists the features available to users of the class: in this case the messages getX and getY. The feature clause lists the instance variables and methods of the class: in this case, instance vari-

Example 4.16
Eiffel Definition of
Class Location

```
class Location export
    getX, getY
feature
    X, Y : INTEGER;
    getX is
        do
            Result : = X
        end;
    getY is
        do
            Result : = Y
        end;
    Create (InitX, InitY: INTEGER) is
        do
            X : = InitX;
            Y : = InitY
        end;
```

ables X and Y, and methods getX and getY, which return values X and Y, respectively. In addition, class Location has a Create method, which is called whenever a new instance of the class is created. After the class Location is defined, the Eiffel code for creating an object or instance of Location and obtaining its X value is as shown in Example 4.17.

```
aLocation: Location;
xValue: INTEGER;
aLocation. Create(5, 10);
xValue : = aLocation.getX;
```

Example 4.17
Use of the Location
Object in Eiffel

Eiffel supports multiple inheritance with language features that re-solve name conflicts. When a class inherits from two parents that have instance variables with the same name, an Eiffel programmer can rename one of the instance variables with an inherit clause so that both instance variables can be used in the subclass without conflict. For example, as-sume that both class screen__object and text have methods named setHeight and setWidth, as shown in Figure 4.13. The Eiffel programmer can resolve this conflict by renaming text's setHeight and setWidth to setTextHeight and setTextWidth, respectively, as shown in Example 4.18.

In addition to resolving name clashes, renaming can be used in Eiffel

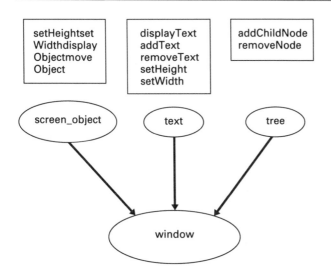

Figure 4.13
Multiple Inheritance
with Name
Conflicts

Example 4.18
Eiffel Code for Re-
solving Name Con-
flicts in Multiple
Inheritance

```
export
    setHeight,
    setWidth,
    displayObject,
    moveObject,
    setTextHeight,
    setTextWidth,
    display Text,
    addText,
    removeText,
    addChildNode,
    removeNode,
inherit
    screen_object;
    text rename
        setHeight as setTextHeight,
        setWidth as setTextWidth;
    tree
end
```

to provide a more appropriate and consistent set of names for the services a class offers. For example, the class window defined in Figure 4.13
could have renamed addChildNode as addChildWindow, removeNode as
removeWindow, so that all exported services refer uniformly to the window class from which they are derived.

Like C + +, Eiffel is a statically typed, dynamically bound language.
As previously discussed, static typing provides the benefits of compile-
time checking of types, guaranteeing that no message will ever be sent
at run time to an object that does not recognize it. Dynamic binding
guarantees that when a message is sent at run time to an object and
more than one version of the message's method is available through inheritance, the most appropriate version will be chosen.

The Eiffel language includes a rigorous exception-handling mechanism to increase its usefulness as a language for commercial software
development, especially in the areas of documentation, debugging, and
support for software fault tolerance. Assertions can be attached to a routine to check that preconditions are met before the routine is called and
postconditions are satisfied after the routine is completed. Assertions

called class invariants can also be specified for a class to check that all its instances obey the same constraints. Assertions are inherited in the same way that instance variables and methods are inherited, and can be turned on or off with appropriate compilation options.

Whenever an exception occurs during the execution of a routine, through the violation of its precondition or postcondition, for example, the routine's rescue clause is automatically called, which can clean up the environment, terminate, and report failure in an orderly fashion. Alternatively, the rescue clause can attempt to change the conditions that led to the exception and try the routine again with the retry instruction.

Eiffel also has built-in automatic garbage collection for the reclamation of the space occupied by objects no longer needed by the application. Eiffel's garbage collection scheme can be viewed as a competition between two coroutines: the application, which creates objects as it runs and destroys some of them; and the garbage collector, which collects all of the destroyed objects it can find and makes their space available again to the application. The garbage collection mechanism can be turned off and on dynamically to keep it from interfering with the application during time-critical phases.

The Eiffel development environment includes a class library and graphical class browser, an editor that knows Eiffel syntax, and configuration management tools. Eiffel's library provides a set of classes implementing basic data structures and associated operations. Eiffel's C package generation option produces self-contained programs, which can be moved to any machine with a C compiler and recompiled. Packages produced in his way are highly portable, meaning in particular that target systems need not be UNIX-based, the primary platform supported by Eiffel.

Eiffel's robustness as an object-oriented language is offset by its proprietary nature. Unlike C++ and Pascal, it is not a hybrid of an established language.

Common Lisp Object System

The Common Lisp Object System (CLOS) is a set of object-oriented extensions to the artificial intelligence language, Common Lisp. CLOS was defined in 1986 by groups from Xerox PARC, Symbolics, Inc., and Lucid, Inc. CLOS was then submitted to ANSI and formally adopted as a part of Common Lisp by the X3J13 ANSI committee, which is working on creating the ANSI Standard Common Lisp (Bobrow *et al.* 1988).

CLOS is a descendent of two other object-oriented extensions to

Table 4.8
Naming Conventions for Object-Oriented Concepts in CLOS

Concept	Common Lisp Object System
Object	Instance
Class	Class
Method	Method
Instance variables	Slots
Message	Generic function
Subclass	Subclass
Inheritance	Inheritance

Lisp, New Flavors and Common Loops. Although CLOS has achieved some popularity with AI programmers, it is not used in the mainstream computing community. CLOS provides support for the mechanisms of object, class, method, subclass, and inheritance. The major departure from the object-oriented concepts is the replacement of the message concept with generic function calls to allow programming of simultaneous events. CLOS also supports multiple inheritance. Table 4.8 overviews the CLOS naming conventions for object-oriented concepts.

The object-oriented extensions that CLOS adds to Common Lisp bear a superficial resemblance to the object-oriented extensions that C++ brings to C. Each CLOS object is an instance of a class. Instances of the same class have the same set of instance variables, called slots, and access to the same set of methods. CLOS objects send messages, called generic functions, to other objects, which act upon them by evoking appropriate methods. CLOS classes are arranged in a hierarchy, with subclasses inheriting both methods and instance variables from one or more superclasses. Example 4.19 shows the CLOS definition of the class

Example 4.19
CLOS Class with Two Instance Variables and Two Methods

```
(defclass location ( )
    (  ( X : reader : get-X )
       ( Y : reader : get-Y )))
```

location, which has two instance variables (X, Y), and two methods (get-X and get-Y). defclass is the CLOS macro for defining a new class. location is the name of the new class. Parentheses contain the list of direct superclasses, which is empty in this case. The two instance variables are coded as (X : reader : get-X) and (Y : reader : get-Y) with X and Y as the variables, each followed by the slot option, reader. get-X specifies the message for getting the value of X. The slot option : reader : get-Y specifies get-Y as the message for getting the value of Y.

With the class definition, a new location object is created by calling the function make-instance and providing it with the class name and initial values for its instance variables, as follows:

(make-instance 'location : X 5 : y 10)

The main difference between CLOS and other object-oriented languages is the flexibility it provides the programmer to customize virtually every aspect of the language, including the object-oriented paradigm itself. For example, CLOS directly supports three kinds of methods: The primary method is augmented with before-methods and after-methods that are used for setup and clean-up work. Furthermore, one class can provide the primary method, while other classes provide the corresponding before- and after-methods. The programmer can even define completely new method types or combinations. CLOS classes can also be dynamically redefined by the addition or deletion of instance variables, even after objects of the class have been created. When such redefinitions occur, CLOS automatically updates everything affected, including any existing objects. Finally, the programmer can override the class-inheritance hierarchy by redefining the precedence rules for selecting the appropriate method for a received message.

This power and flexibility is a two-edged sword. For certain specialized applications, such as language development and artificial intelligence research, CLOS can be a wonderful tool. For most standard uses, however, CLOS could overwhelm the programmer by its wide assortment of techniques and features.

Evolving Technical Issues

Throughout this chapter a number of issues have been described related to the future evolution of object-oriented languages. Many of these issues relate to the features of polymorphism, dynamic binding, and multiple inheritance.

Dynamic versus Static Binding

As described earlier in this chapter, dynamic binding is a mechanism required to support the object-oriented paradigm. Without dynamic binding, the flexibility and power promoted by the paradigm, in which operations are able to adapt automatically to the objects to which they apply, is not feasible. With dynamic binding, however, comes a performance penalty, as a run-time search is required to match a method to each message.

Dynamic binding leads to a large class of type-mismatch programming errors if sufficient program testing is not undertaken. Ordinarily caught at compile time by statically typed languages, these errors are not caught until run time by languages with dynamic binding. And then, the only help the program can give to the programmer trying to fix the problem is "an object was sent a message that it doesn't understand." Even with a sound testing methodology, some pieces of code may not be thoroughly tested because they are executed only in rare combinations of situations.

Some object-oriented languages, such as Smalltalk, which supports only dynamic binding, incur these penalties for every message sent. Other languages, such as C+ + and Eiffel, lessen the performance problem by using static typing to ensure that every message will be matched with an appropriate method during run time. A mixture of static typing and dynamic binding seems to offer an appropriate balance between programming flexibility and run-time efficiency.

Even with static typing, some applications are so time critical that they cannot tolerate this smaller run-time overhead. Reservation systems and real-time systems, for example, fall into this class. If an object-oriented language is to be useful in these application areas, it must permit the programmer to break out of the object-oriented paradigm completely, and program in static, non–object-oriented constructs that incur no runtime penalty. Hybrid languages, such as C+ + and object-oriented Pascal, provide this paradigm-mixing benefit; pure object-oriented languages such as Smalltalk do not, and therefore will always be at a competitive disadvantage in this area.

Software developers must weigh this minor limitation of slower execution speed inherent in object-oriented languages against the advantages of more rapid development time, smaller code size, and greater ease in modification and maintenance. As computing performance continues to improve, much of this execution speed disadvantage is mitigated.

Classes as Objects

The object-oriented paradigm makes a clear distinction between classes and objects. Classes are static templates that exist only in the body of a program's source code. Objects are dynamic entities that exist as areas of memory during the execution of the program. This fundamental distinction between objects and classes has been blurred in languages such as CLOS and Smalltalk, which, striving for generality, view classes as objects.

There are several arguments in favor of this generality of classes as objects. Having a single object concept instead of separate objects and classes provides greater conceptual consistency and simplicity for the paradigm. Because classes are treated as objects, they can be dynamically created, tracked, and debugged in run time, just as ordinary objects. Finally, considering a class as an object makes it an instance of a more general class (called a *metaclass* in Smalltalk), thus permitting the definition of class methods, which apply to the class rather than to its instances. In particular, object creation, which requires a special mechanism outside the object-message-method paradigm in languages that do not consider classes as objects, can be implemented in a class-as-objects language by providing each class with a method that responds to the create message by creating a new object as an instance of itself.

The opponents of this generality offer two arguments to support their case. First, they insist that the distinction between classes and objects is real: Classes are descriptions of things; objects are the things themselves. To treat classes and objects as one concept is simply wrong. Second, they point out that treating classes as objects does not simplify the paradigm but in fact makes it more difficult to understand, as evidenced by the difficulties learners of the Smalltalk system, for example, have in grappling with the concept of metaclass. Finally, they claim that the number of class methods required, such as create, is actually very few, and these have been implemented as reserved words in the languages that do not treat classes as objects.

To a certain extent, the choice depends on the programmer's application. For quick prototyping and experimentation, programmers choose the greater power and flexibility of a classes-as-objects language. For the development of more traditional applications, where such power and flexibility are not needed, less is better; and programmers choose languages that maintain the distinction between objects and classes.

Concurrency

The object-message-method paradigm is appealing because it accurately models most real-world objects and processes. Yet, because message passing is essentially a linear process, the paradigm starts to break down when it attempts to model concurrent processes. For example, in modeling the behavior of billiard balls on a pool table, each ball could be represented as an object with instance variables specifying its size, mass, elasticity, location, and velocity. A collision method would be needed, which calculates what happens to a ball's location and velocity when it collides with another ball. Collision messages must be serialized arbitrarily when modeling a collision between the two balls. A message must be sent first to one ball and then the other when in reality such messages should be passed simultaneously. Establishing such a linear order of events is, at best, arbitrary and can, at worst, significantly misrepresent the real-world process being modeled.

A commonly used technique for serializing such concurrent events uses semaphores. In Smalltalk, for example, a process waits for an event to occur by sending a wait message to a semaphore and signals that an event has occurred by sending a signal message to a semaphore. Smalltalk's process scheduler maintains a queue of ready but inactive processes, and it determines which process should next be activated by choosing the highest priority process in the queue. Generally, this kind of scheme will have a high process overhead and is best suited to modeling situations with only a few active processes.

A better solution toward modeling concurrent events is to not just simulate concurrency, but instead actually provide a means whereby objects can truly execute simultaneously. This requires hardware with parallel architectures and concurrent languages that can exploit it. Several research efforts are proceeding in this direction, including ABCL/R (Watanabe and Yonezawa 1988) and PROCOL (van den Bos and Laffra 1989). Alternatively, distributed languages have been developed which support concurrency by permitting objects on different machines to communicate concurrently via the sending and receiving of messages. Distributed Smalltalk, developed at the University of Washington (Bennett 1987) is an example of such a language. Although work on both concurrent languages and distributed languages continues, no commercial systems are yet available.

Standards

Although C++ has become a de facto standard for object-oriented languages, as of the publication of this book, no object-oriented language has been approved by ANSI. Such approval would stabilize the feature set and accelerate tool development. In addition, it is likely that ANSI could include basic class libraries to motivate increased development of additional libraries. ANSI approval also signifies stability to the more cautious and cost-conscious members of the programming community, corporate data processing and management information systems (DP/MIS).

Summary

Object-oriented programming represents a major shift from traditional procedural programming approaches. Although this new object-oriented paradigm can be supported to some extent by traditional languages, object-oriented languages provide the built in functionality of objects, classes, methods, messages, and inheritance to enable the creation of programs that are more exact and less complex. The function of inheritance, unique to object-oriented languages, also facilitates the creation of programs that are much easier to maintain.

Although object-oriented languages vary in their naming conventions, the fundamental functionality to support objects, classes, methods, messages, and inheritance is quite similar between languages. The support of polymorphism, dynamic binding, and multiple inheritance varies from language to language. Languages also vary in the robustness of their development environment and the completeness of their generic class libraries.

Acceptance of object-oriented languages has accelerated due to the availability of object-oriented extensions to popular languages such as C and Pascal. These hybrid languages not only offer familiarity but also facilitate using selected object-oriented techniques in applications not well suited for full object orientation. In addition, these languages combine static typing with dynamic binding to improve performance and run-time accuracy. Object-oriented extensions can be expected in most popular languages, such as COBOL and BASIC. Hybrid languages accelerate the transition to an object-oriented approach.

Key Points

■ Object-oriented programming represents a fundamental shift away from procedural programming.

■ The object-oriented programming approach provides a higher level of programming abstraction via the construction of objects.

- Object-oriented languages provide built-in support for fundamental object-oriented concepts: objects, classes, messages, methods, and inheritance.

- Object-oriented programming with traditional languages would require the programmer to manage intricate software with complex data structures, by building the missing object-oriented mechanisms out of the traditional languages.

- Object-oriented languages vary from pure object orientation, such as Smalltalk, to hybrids, such as C++.

- Smalltalk appeals to purists; the hybrids, primarily C++ and object-oriented Pascal, appeal to traditional programmers.

- Object-oriented languages simplify the programming model, make the solution more exact, and usually result in fewer lines of less complex code.

- No concensus has been reached in the definition of an object-oriented language.

- The robustness of development environments and the number of class libraries available are important elements in the utility of object-oriented languages.

For Further Study

Bobrow, D., DeMichiel, L., Gabriel, R., Kiczales, G., and Moon, D. 1988. *Common Lisp Object System Specifications.* X3J13 Document 88–002R, American National Standards Institute.
    This is a complete definition of CLOS as developed for the American National Standards Institute.

Borland International. 1989. *Turbo Pascal 5.5, Object-Oriented Programming Guide.* Scotts Valley, Calif.: Borland International.
    A part of Borland's documentation, this guide provides an in-depth review of Borland's object-extended Turbo Pascal.

Cox, B. J. 1987. *Object-Oriented Programming: An Evolutionary Approach.* Reading, Mass.: Addison-Wesley.
    This book provides a thorough overview of the Objective-C language.

Digitalk. 1989. *Smalltalk/V Mac, Tutorial and Programming Hand-book.* Los Angeles, Calif.: Digitalk, Inc.
   The Digitalk handbook is a programming manual accompanying Smalltalk/V. It is a good tutorial introduction to Smalltalk.

Goldberg, A., and Robson, D. 1983. *Smalltalk-80: The Language and Its Implementation.* Reading, Mass.: Addison-Wesley.
   This book provides a thorough overview of Smalltalk. It is referred to as the "Blue Book" by Smalltalk developers.

Keen, S. 1989. *Object-Oriented Programming in Common Lisp.* Reading, Mass.: Addison-Wesley.
   A programmer's guide to the CLOS concepts and techniques, with many code examples.

Meyer, B., 1988. *Object-Oriented Software Construction.* Englewood Cliffs, N. J.: Prentice Hall.
   An in-depth review of the Eiffel language by its creator.

Miller, W. M. 1989. "Multiple Inheritance in C++." *Computer Language,* August, pp. 63–71.
   This article provides an overview of recent enhancements to C++.

Miller, W. M. 1989. *What Is C++?* Sudbury, Mass.: Software Development Technologies. Videotape.
   A multimedia tutorial for novice C++ programmers.

Schmucker, K. J. 1986. *Object-Oriented Programming for the Macintosh.* Hasbrouck Heights, N.J.: Hayden Books.
   This book reviews in detail Apple's Object Pascal, as well as the MacApp development environment. Other object-oriented languages available on the Macintosh are also reviewed.

Stroustrup, B. 1986. *The C++ Programming Languages.* Reading, Mass.: Addison-Wesley.
   Written by the creator of C++, this book reviews the C++ language in depth. It contains a reference manual for C++ that serves as a default definition of the language.

References

Deutsch, L. P. 1989. "The past, present and future of Smalltalk." *ECOOP '89, Proceedings of the 1989 Europe Conference.* The British Computer Society Workshop Series, Cambridge: Cambridge University Press, pp. 73–87.

Rettig, M., Morgan, T., Jacobs, J., and Wimberly, D. 1989. "Object-oriented programming in AI: New choices." *AI Expert,* January, pp. 53–69.

Stepstone Corporation. 1989. *Objective-C Language: Version 4.0.* Sandy Hook, Conn.: The Stepstone Corporation.

van den Bos, J., and Laffra, C. 1989. "*PROCOL: A parallel object language with protocols." *Proceedings of Object-Oriented Programming: Systems, Languages, and Applications 1989* (OOPSLA '89). *SIGPLAN Notices,* Vol. 24, Number 10, October, pp. 95–102.

Watanabe, T., and Yonezawka, A. 1988. "Reflections in an object-oriented concurrent language." *Proceedings of Object-Oriented Programming: Systems, Languages, and Applications 1989* (OOPSLA '89). *SIGPLAN Notices,* Vol. 23, Number 11, pp. 306–315.

Chapter 5

Databases

In this chapter we shall provide an overview of object-oriented databases. We shall describe the functionality of object-oriented databases and identify their strengths and weaknesses, particularly with respect to relational databases. The chapter will conclude with an overview of evolving technical issues.

Read this chapter to learn what object-oriented databases are, how they have evolved, and what additional functionality they offer beyond current database technology.

Object-oriented databases provide central storage for data, mechanisms for sharing these data among users, and ways to ensure the integrity and security of the data. Recently, database technology has struggled to find ways to continue to provide these benefits, while at the same time storing increasingly diverse and complex data.

Following closely on the heels of object extensions to programming languages, object-oriented databases promise to bring the same benefits to the world of data management that object-oriented languages bring to the world of programming. As in object-oriented programming, object-oriented databases attempt to reduce complexity by increasing the capability of the software building blocks.

Object-oriented databases and object-oriented extensions to existing database technologies offer not only ways to store and retrieve data but also mechanisms to define and manage the complex relationships among data. Object-oriented databases do not store data in isolation but rather follow the object-oriented paradigm of binding data together with associated behavior into objects. Functional capabilities of object-oriented databases include support of rich data-modeling constructs, direct support for inference, and the ability to store novel data types such as images, voice, and video. Object-oriented databases go beyond the simple representation of data as passive numbers and text, and instead more exactly model the world with its richness and texture. For a review, see Stein (1988).

History of Object-Oriented Databases

Databases were initially built to support applications that process large volumes of uniformly structured data items with little or no internal structure. With the advent in the 1970s of hierarchical databases, applications and data were separated. Successful data models developed for the applications of the 1970s were similarly uniform and simple in structure. The models often were record-oriented, with a single atomic piece of data in each field. This simple model, referred to as the hierarchical model, allowed for development of such features as ad-hoc query languages, query optimization, constraint checking, and control over underlying storage management.

Relational databases appeared in the late 1970s and offered several advantages over the hierarchical model. The relational form, the table, is simple and understandable. Methods for manipulating data in tables are well known and reasonably efficient. Relational algebra provides a formal mathematical foundation capable of supporting data-analysis methodologies. Finally, with the ability to join data into virtual tables dynamically at run time, relational databases facilitated the development of applications with a higher level of data independence than their predecessors.

The relational model, however, suffers at least one major disadvantage. It is difficult to express the semantics of complex objects with only a table model for data storage. Although relational databases are adequate for accounting or other typical transaction-processing applications where the data types are simple and few in number, the relational model offers limited help when data types become numerous and complex.

Just as the step from hierarchical to relational was taken to reduce the attention to structure, so is the step from relational to object-oriented. New applications for the 1990s require support for complex and extensible data structures, complex data access, and high performance. Traditional database concepts are gradually being extended with object-oriented capabilities to meet these needs. The evolution of database technology over the last 20 years, as illustrated in Figure 5.1, represents this shift to more complex data management.

This need to support object-oriented functionality in a database is also driven by particular application needs. Object-oriented databases are favored for applications where the relationships among elements in the database carry the key information. Relational databases are favored when the values of the database elements carry the key information. That is, object-oriented models capture the structure of the data; relational models organize the data itself. If a record can be understood

> Relational database management systems are really for records data. But most of the real world is not made up of records.
> *Eugene Bonte (Whiting 1989)*

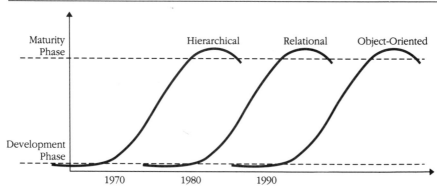

Figure 5.1
Evolution of Database Technology

in isolation, then the relational database is probably suitable. If a record makes sense only in the context of other records, then an object-oriented database is more appropriate.

Engineering and technical applications were the first applications to require databases that handle complex data types and capture the structure of the data. Applications such as mechanical and electrical computer-aided design (MCAD and ECAD) have always used nontraditional forms of data, representing such phenomena as three-dimensional images and VLSI circuit designs. Currently these application programs store their data in application-specific file structures. The data-intensiveness of these applications is not only in the large amount of data that need to be programmed into the database, but in the complexity of the data itself. In these design-based applications, relationships among elements in the database carry key information for the user. Functional requirements for complex cross references, structural dependencies, and version management all require a richer representation than what is provided by hierarchical or relational databases. Figure 5.2 compares the increasing complexity of modeling and managing data with the different database models.

While the transition to object-oriented databases is beginning with the many types of design applications, such as MCAD and ECAD, it is gradually extending to many other applications that manage complex data. Examples of these applications include computer-aided software engineering (CASE), computer-aided publishing (CAP), and materials requirements planning (MRP). These applications, like design applications, are data intensive in programming and in respect to type of data

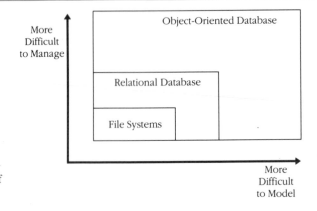

Figure 5.2
Volume, Complexity and Varieties of Database

stored. They need storage techniques that recognize subtype relationships such as design versions in CAD or parts implosions in MRP. They also require consolidation of near replicates of data, such as the variations of program design stored in a CASE repository.

Many other applications also share the requirement for a multimedia database. This growing set of applications requires that relational data must be processed along with text or graphic information in an integrated fashion. These future applications include advanced office systems and other document management systems.

Artificial intelligence (AI) applications, such as expert systems, also drive the need for the development of object-oriented databases. Expert systems are characterized by the need to handle many instances of different, often complex, data types. Object-oriented databases, as opposed to relational databases, are able to handle these requirements without suffering degradation as the number of data types increases. Figure 5.3 shows the fit of applications to the hierarchical, relational, and object-oriented database systems.

Driven by these diverse application needs, a few commercial and many research-based object-oriented databases began to appear in the late 1980s. Most of these initial object-oriented databases were used in design-based applications in the scientific and engineering area. Examples of these early commercial object-oriented databases include Gra-

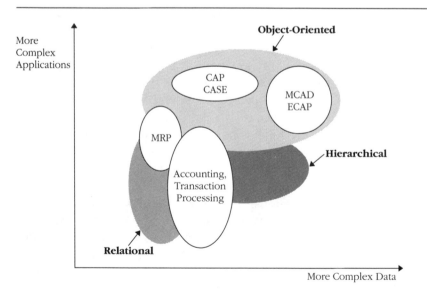

Figure 5.3
Data and Application Complexity (Modified after Ontologic, Inc., 1989)

phael's G-Base, Ontologic's Vbase, and Servio Logic's GemStone. G-Base, introduced in 1987, was Lisp-based, with a tightly coupled expert system application development language, G-Logis. Ontologic's Vbase included a proprietary schema generation language called Type Definition Language (TDL) and a procedures language, C Object Processor (COP). Gemstone is a multiuser object-oriented database management system, which is controlled by a proprietary data definition and manipulation language, OPAL. Gemstone provided development flexibility by permitting its users to perform data manipulation in C or Smalltalk, as well as in OPAL.

These early object-oriented databases had several characteristics that limited their use in the general commercial area. First, the orientation toward design assumed that the user would execute a limited number of extended transactions, as compared to the frequent, high-volume transactions of many business applications. Second, engineering users, much like programmers, accessed the objects through browsing, whereas commercial users require easy-to-use query facilities such as those provided by Structured Query Language (SQL).

In addition, attempts by proprietary object-oriented database vendors to provide new database definition and manipulation languages in the commercial sector were also unsuccessful, as SQL has become the standard in the relational area. Ontologic's early failure with COP is one such example. Lastly, these early implementations suffered from low performance, making them unsuitable for large-scale, high-volume applications. Clearly, the focus on design applications yielded a disparity between user functionality, performance, and optimization needs of the commercial database.

Newer products and improvements to earlier versions of existing object-oriented databases, such as Ontologic's Ontos, have attempted to correct many of these limitations. Ontos, for example, is written in C++ and is designed to be open to compilers and development tools of other vendors. Performance is also improved in newer versions via a variety of approaches including compilers that analyze workflows to optimize the positioning of objects in the system's memory, cache, or storage.

Another recent advancement in object-oriented databases has been the extension or hybridization of existing relational databases to accommodate much of the functionality of a pure object-oriented database. Object extensions to the relational model focus on optimization for commercial applications in performance, physical representation of the objects to deal with a heterogeneous and distributed environment, and extending the SQL model to include the object-oriented paradigm. Such efforts are evident in the current work of established relational database vendors. These vendors include INGRES Corporation with the INGRES Object Management Intelligent Database, IBM Corporation with their DB2-based repository, Hewlett-Packard with IRIS, and Oracle with its Oracle database.

These extensions of the relational database model to support objects have taken one of two primary approaches. One approach is to allow the objects themselves to act as relational tables. In this approach a shell is created which allows objects to act as tables. The shell decomposes object structures and flattens them so that they could be stored in relational tables, as illustrated in Figure 5.4. The objects then act as virtual tables and are called as needed, using a standard query language, such as SQL. These shells store information about the data as objects, but the data themselves remains in relational tables. The shell stores and retrieves only entire objects. This is adequate when objects can be indexed by regular data fields. This object-extended approach also suffers from a performance tradeoff. The relational search-and-match process is slower than search in a full object-oriented database where queries have direct references to data. When objects must be located through relationships with other objects, a full object-oriented database is preferred.

A second approach to extend the relational model is to allow the relational table to contain pointers to the objects. With this approach objects are another data type in the table. Data-manipulation operators

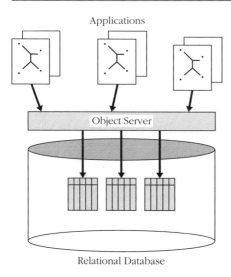

Applications

Object Server

Relational Database

Figure 5.4
Relational Database with Objects Flattened into Tables

function at the table level, and objects are called into an environment external to the database where they can then be acted upon by messages. This method avoids the overhead of flattening objects for storage in tables but limits the kinds of queries that can be made to them. This approach is illustrated in Figure 5.5.

Object-oriented extensions are widely accepted as the direction that relational database companies will adopt in the coming years. Already second-generation relational databases have been introduced by companies such as Sybase, whose product provides for rules stored along with data in the form of triggers and stored procedures. Another example of a relational model that has been extended to support non-conventional data types is INGRES Corporation's Object Management Intelligent Database. Both databases, although much richer, are still relational, with the structure primarily determined by joining tables.

Eventually, fully object-oriented databases will be commercially available. These object-oriented databases will store and retrieve complex and interrelated data structures. The databases will act as repositories for interrelated sets of objects, which themselves consist of both data and methods. In addition to supporting the richness of applications that cannot be supported by today's relational model, object-oriented databases will also support systems developed with object-oriented languages.

Debate already focuses on the hybrid (database with objects) versus pure object-oriented database models, an issue that separates object-

> I think by 1995–1997 relational database implementations will have reached their peak. The next evolutionary step will be object-oriented databases and knowledge-based information processing based on the semantic model. Databases have to represent real life, which is fuzzy.
>
> *Shaku Atre, cited in Chapnick (1989)*

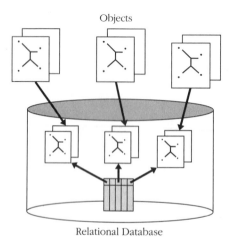

Objects

Relational Database

Figure 5.5
Relational Database with Tables Pointing to Objects

oriented languages as well. If relational databases are extended to support more complex applications, it is likely that object-oriented databases will not replace relational systems in the short term. It is also likely that SQL will be extended to support user defined functions, types, and objects in such a way that the relational model is incorporated in an object-oriented model rather than existing alongside it. Objects with user-defined types will then be permitted to cross the interfaces between the database, the application, and the user. Full object-oriented databases will probably be used primarily for specialized applications that are currently built upon proprietary databases and for new classes of applications. Likely candidates for applications will include CAD, CASE, and CAP. A secondary use for object-oriented databases will be to add persistence to applications developed in object-oriented languages.

Benefits of Object-Oriented Databases

Systems developed with object-oriented languages have many benefits, as previously discussed in Chapter 4. Yet, as also described, these systems have particular attributes that can be complemented with object-oriented databases. These attributes include lack of persistence, inability to share objects among multiple users, limited version control, and lack of access to other data, for example, data in other databases.

In systems designed with object-oriented languages, objects are created during the running of a program and are destroyed when the program ends. Providing a database that can store the objects between runs of a program offers both increased flexibility and increased security. The ability to store the objects also allows the objects to be shared in a distributed environment. An object-oriented database can allow only the actively used objects to be loaded into memory, and thus minimizes or preempts the need for virtual memory paging. This is especially useful in large-scale systems. Persistent objects also allow objects to be stored for each version. This version control is useful not only for testing applications, but also for many object-oriented design applications where version control is a functional requirement of the application itself. Access to other data sources can also be facilitated with object-oriented databases, especially those built as hybrid relational systems, which can access relational tables as well as other object types.

Object-oriented databases also offer many of the benefits that were formerly found only in expert systems. With an object-oriented database, the relationships between objects and the constraints on objects are maintained by the database management system, that is, the objects themselves. The rules associated with the expert system are essentially replaced by the object schema and the methods. As many expert systems currently do not have adequate database support, object-oriented databases afford the possibility of offering expert system functionality with much better performance.

Object-oriented databases offer benefits over current hierarchical and relational database models. They enable support of complex applications not supported well by the other models. They enhance programmability and performance, improve navigational access, and simplify concurrency control. They lower the risks associated with referential integrity, and they provide a better user metaphor than the relational model.

Object-oriented databases by definition allow the inclusion of more of the code (i.e., the object's methods) in the database itself. This incremental knowledge about the application has a number of potential benefits for the database system itself, including the ability to optimize query processing and to control the concurrent execution of transactions.

Performance, always a significant issue in system implementation, may be significantly improved by using an object-oriented model instead of a relational model. The greatest improvement can be expected in applications with high data complexity and large numbers of interrelationships. Clustering, or locating the related objects in close proximity, can be accomplished through the class hierarchy or by other interrelationships. Caching, or the retention of certain objects in memory or storage, can be optimized by anticipating that the user or application may retrieve a particular instance of the class. When there is high data complexity, clustering and caching techniques in object databases gain tremendous performance benefits that relational databases, because of their fundamental architecture, will never be able to approach. Figure 5.6 illustrates likely performance trends.

Object-oriented databases can store not only complex application components but also larger data structures. Although relational systems can support a large number of tuples (i.e., rows in a table), individual tuples are limited in size. Object-oriented databases with large objects do not suffer a performance degradation because the objects do not need to be broken apart and reassembled by applications, regardless of the complexity of the properties of the application objects.

Since objects contain direct references to other objects, complex data sets can be efficiently assembled using these direct references. The ability to search by direct references significantly improves navigational

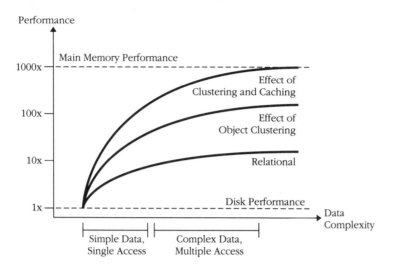

Figure 5.6
Relational versus
Object-Oriented
Database Perfor-
mance (Modified
from Ontologic
1989)

access. In contrast, complex data sets in relational databases must be assembled by the application program using the slow process of joining tables.

For the programmer, one of the challenges in building a database is the data manipulation language (DML) of the database. DMLs for relational databases usually differ from the programming language used to construct the rest of the application. This contrast is due to differences in the programming paradigms and mismatches of type systems. The programmer must learn two languages, two tool sets, and two paradigms because neither alone has the functionality to build an entire application. Certain types of programming tools, such as application generators and fourth-generation languages (4GLs) have emerged to produce code for the entire application, thereby bridging the mismatch between the programming language and the DML, but most of these tools compromise the application programming process.

With object-oriented databases much of this problem is eliminated. The DML can be extended so that more of the application can be written in the DML. Or an object-oriented application language, for example C++, can be extended to be the DML. More of the application can be built into the database itself. Movement across the programming interface between the database and the application then occurs in a single paradigm with a common set of tools. Class libraries can also assist the programmer in speeding the creation of databases. Class libraries encourage reuse of existing code and help to minimize the cost of later modifications. Programming is easier because the data structures model the problem more closely. Having the data and procedures encapsulated in a single object makes it less likely that a change to one object will affect the integrity of other objects in the database. Concurrency control is also simplified with an object-oriented database. In a relational database, the application needs to lock each record in each table explicitly because related data are represented across a number of tables. Integrity, a key requirement for databases, can be better supported with an object-oriented database, because the application can lock all the relevant data in one operation. Referential integrity is not guaranteed with a relational database, where deleting a record from one table may leave a pointer to it in another record dangling unless the application specifically checks for this situation. Referential integrity is better supported in an object-oriented database because the pointers are maintained and updated by the database itself. Finally, object-oriented databases offer a better user metaphor than relational databases. The tuple or table, although enabling a well-defined implementation strategy, is not an intuitive modeling framework, especially outside the domain of numbers. Objects offer a more natural and encompassing modeling metaphor.

Functionality of Object-Oriented Databases

Object-oriented databases offer some of the same functionality as object-oriented languages. They permit encapsulation within objects of data and the methods that act upon them. They activate methods by messages to the objects. They permit declaration of hierarchical relationships among objects through the use of inheritance. In addition, object-oriented databases offer traditional database functionality that object-oriented languages lack, such as persistence and sharing.

Overview

Programming languages have historically focused on processing, rather than on data. The goal has been to improve the tools available to programmers who build complex systems involving large amounts of code and relatively small amounts of data (as compared with databases). For some time, languages have offered support for more complex structuring of data, including graphical structures and complex interrelationships. The emphasis, however, has clearly been on local data. Language facilities for handling large amounts of data on secondary storage have been minimal and usually limited to file-level access, leaving the programmer with the responsibility of managing the organization of these complex data objects in the files. Sharing of data among programmers has, in general, been accomplished through the sharing of these files, with none of the support provided by databases.

Object-oriented languages are ordinarily memory based and geared toward supporting a single-user application. Objects created when an application is run are either not saved between executions or are saved in a primitive manner that does not lend itself to concurrency or sharing. Database technology depends on several important features beyond those offered by object-oriented languages. These features include:

persistence: creating objects that survive the process that created them,

integrity: guaranteeing that changes to the database do not destroy its consistency,

sharing: allowing multiple processes to coordinate simultaneous access to the objects in the database, and

querying: using logical expressions to define a subset of the database for access.

Table 5.1 summarizes the basic functionality of object-oriented databases.

Over the years there has been a consistent movement within database technology to incorporate more semantics into the data model. If data more closely reflect the design of an application, then the data are more easily available to the end user, and the need to understand how the data are stored is diminished. Object-oriented databases extend data semantics even further. By permitting the definition of arbitrarily complex data types and providing a means to associate behavior with data,

Object-Oriented Features	Database Features	
Objects	Persistence	**Table 5.1**
Methods	Integrity	Object-Oriented and Traditional
Inheritance	Sharing	Database Features of Object-Oriented
	Querying	Databases

the semantics of object-oriented databases are closer to their programming language counterparts.

Object orientation shifts a programmer's attention to focus more closely on the concerns of database designers by emphasizing the organization of software around the data rather than the flow of control. Object-oriented languages and object-oriented databases are natural complements of one another. Languages emphasize processing, complex structuring, and local data. Databases focus on a more declarative approach, shared data outside the domain of applications, and support for large amounts of data. One of the goals for both object-oriented languages and object-oriented databases is to create a clean fusion between them yet still retain their individual strengths.

Object-oriented databases differ significantly in functionality from relational databases. Relational databases are based on deriving a virtual structure at run time based on values from sets of data stored in tables. Object-oriented databases contain predefined objects that do not need to be derived at run time. In a relational database, views are constructed by selecting data from multiple tables and loading them into a single table. In an object-oriented database a view is obtained by transversing pointers from object to object.

An object-oriented database plays a very active role, whereas a relational database is passive. While the relational database primarily offers the ability to add or delete records, the object-oriented database offers the ability to incorporate methods within objects, thus allowing the database to incorporate many of the operations that must be left to the application with a relational database. The following section reviews the fundamental functions of an object-oriented database.

Objects

Objects are the elements that an object-oriented database stores, modifies, and retrieves at the behest of the application program. These objects may be as simple as numbers and strings or as complex as the complete specifications for an electronic circuit. Multiple data types, including graphics, sound, and video, are also accommodated. One major advantage that object-oriented databases have over traditional databases is their ability to represent almost any real-world entity as an object. The alternative, as discussed before, is to squeeze data into disconnected tables. Figures 5.7 and 5.8 illustrate the fundamental differences between database objects and tables, using the example of a student's scholastic data stored in a relational database and an object-

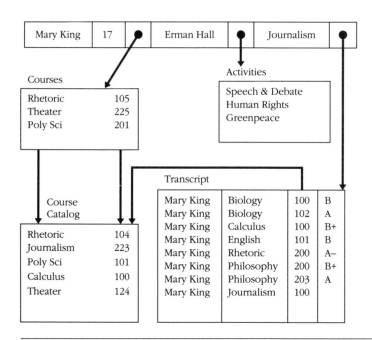

Figure 5.7
Scholastic Data
Stored in Relational
Tables

oriented database. Notice how an object can contain other objects to any level of nesting, thus providing tremendous flexibility in defining new object types. As illustrated in the example, objects make writing applications easier, because all of the data for a particular entity are located in one place. The programmer need not search through multiple files via pointers to determine where the student's transcript is stored, for example. In addition to the data, objects can store relationships, rep-

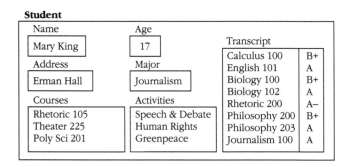

Figure 5.8
Scholastic Data
Stored as a Set of
Related Objects

resented internally as links to other objects, and they can store behavior, represented internally as methods.

Objects can also make applications run faster. Since the data for an entity are logically related, the object-oriented database has the means to optimize their physical location. Applications are able to read fewer files in order to retrieve all relevant data. Traditional CAD systems, for example, often store each component of a design in a separate file and use a database to hold the names of the files. To access the full design, the CAD application must open and close all of the files in the file list. In an object-oriented database, the entire design with all of its components can be stored in one object, greatly reducing the number of file operations needed to access the design.

Storing objects as data elements changes the implementation of other features that all databases must provide. Because objects can be efficiently transferred in a single operation, it is easier to develop disk caching algorithms for transferring logical groups of objects. Concurrent multiuser access, transaction processing, version control, security, and recovery schemes are easier to implement because a single lock can be put on all relevant data at the object level, rather than requiring the application program to try to set multiple locks through the related but scattered data in a relational database.

Unlike relational databases, which only allow sets of data of the same type, object-oriented databases allow arbitrary collections of objects. These collections can be manipulated by the user or the application, locked for transaction management, or clustered for optimization of performance and ease of access.

Methods

Each object in an object-oriented database can have encapsulated within it a number of methods for acting on its data. These methods are activated when the application program sends messages to the object.

To continue the example shown in Figure 5.8, a student object might contain a method for determining the student's grade point average. The method calculates the grade point average by sending the message get-grade to each of the student's course objects, averages the responses, and returns the result. Any application program that needs the GPA of a student need only send the message gpa to the student object, rather than going through the calculation on its own. The encapsulation of methods and data removes much of the programming burden from the programmer, shifting the responsibility for database retrieval and update to the database itself.

Although the application software can perform data integrity checking, it is easier and less error-prone to let the database take care of it. For example, specific courses may have prerequisites, limited enrollment, or other constraints. If the application software is responsible for checking these constraints, then every application that adds students to courses must contain code to check those constraints. And each time the constraints change, then all the application programs must be updated. In contrast, an object-oriented database can encapsulate methods that check constraints with the course objects themselves. This guarantees that the course constraints will be satisfied every time an application program accesses the courses. In addition, an object-oriented approach localizes the constraint code so that it is easy to update the database to reflect changes in constraints.

Inheritance

Inheritance provides a means for reducing the effort required to develop and maintain a database. But its ability to allow a database to age gracefully is far more important. When used properly, inheritance allows new features and data types to be added to a database while requiring only very localized changes.

A relational database has only a limited set of built-in data types (e.g., integer, string, date), and a limited set of built-in operations on these data types (e.g., get a field's value, set a field's value). A relational database designer can create more complex data structures by combining basic types linearly, as fields in records, for example:

Employee = | Name | Age | Address |

Unfortunately, because there is no way to add new operations for these new types, the operations on them are restricted to those defined for the basic types. An object-oriented database provides an equivalent set of built-in types and operations. More importantly, each object in an object-oriented database is a member of a class, which determines the object's structure and defines what operations can be performed on it. New classes are created from existing classes through the technique of subclassing and overriding of inherited methods. This results in arbitrarily complex data types and operations, which may then be treated as if they are the built-in types.

Not only does inheritance assist in this process of defining the type and relationship of data to be stored in a database, but also it reduces the effort required to accommodate the inevitable changes to the database structure. Adding a new data type is easily accomplished through subclassing, with the guarantee that existing data types and methods are unaffected by the change. Changing the internal representation of an existing data type or method can be localized to the one class in the class hierarchy where that data type or method is defined. Finally, because changes to the database hierarchical structure continue to associate data that are logically related, the inheritance mechanism supports database functions such as locking, authorization, and query.

Class Libraries

Predefined class libraries are supplied by object-oriented database vendors. Class libraries allow programmers to reuse rather than reinvent commonly needed data structures such as arrays, dictionaries, tables, and dates. Class libraries include methods as well, such as linear traversal or hashing. Analogous to programming with object-oriented languages, database programmers fine tune class libraries and hierarchies by adding new methods, overriding old ones, and adding new instance variables to suit the application's needs. Finally, class libraries provide great tutorial value to the programmer, who can learn from browsing through their carefully constructed class definitions and method implementations.

Class libraries for object-oriented databases differ from class libraries for object-oriented languages primarily in the kinds of classes they define. Both typically include classes for basic types such as integers, reals, and strings, as well as aggregate types such as lists, sets, and arrays.

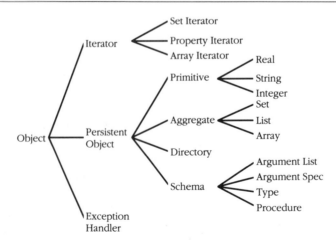

Figure 5.9
Typical Class Library for an Object-Oriented Database

Class libraries for object-oriented databases also include classes for persistent objects, exceptions, directories, locks, schemas, and other database-specific functionality. Figure 5.9 shows part of a typical class library for an object-oriented database. It is instructive to compare this class library with the libraries for an object-oriented language illustrated in Chapter 4, Figures 4.9 and 4.10.

Persistence

An object is said to have persistence if it continues to exist after the application program has finished. Typically, the objects that exist during the execution of an object-oriented program come into existence in one of three ways:

1. The object is created statically or dynamically by the program.

2. The object is retrieved from a file or a relational database and translated into the form of an object.

3. The object is retrieved from an object-oriented database and is ready to use.

Persistent objects contain data that remain in existence beyond the duration of the application program. Unlike applications built from object-oriented languages, where the objects are created at run time and end with the application session, the objects in a database survive multiple sessions. And unlike data from files or relational databases, persistent object data do not change their forms, although they may move between applications and the database in which they permanently reside.

Object persistence is closely tied to the concept of object identity, which requires that every object have something about it that is unique and unvarying, no matter how the object changes. Object identity permits efficient handling of complex relationships. If objects refer to each other by their unique object identifiers, then their relationships will continue even as the objects change their state or location. Object identity contrasts with value-based databases, such as relational databases, where entities are identified by their attributes and hence can change over time. In other words, object identity is especially useful in maintaining persistence of object relationships. This persistence of objects and their relationships requires a different mechanism for object deletion than is used in a relational database. If an object in an object-oriented relational database is simply deleted, other objects may be left with references to the deleted object that are now incorrect. Instead, many object-oriented databases do not delete objects immediately. Rather, the database deletes references to a deleted object. The deleted object is removed when all references to it have been removed, and then space is reclaimed.

Query

One major difference between relational and object-oriented database systems is in the amount of information that moves between the application and the database management system. Applications send queries to the relational database, which then returns a number of values. These values are typically stored as a part of the application's data structures, manipulated, and then shipped back to the database for storage. In contrast, when applications send messages to object-oriented databases, the database manipulates data with methods, retrieves or computes a value, and returns the value to the application.

There is much more traffic between an application and a relational database that stores objects. In such a relational database, complex objects are broken up and stored as fields in separate tables, so that a number of queries must be applied to retrieve and reassemble a single object. These queries are applied sequentially, with one query depending on the result of the previous query. The database does not know about the global request; it knows only about the individual queries and therefore cannot reorder the queries to optimize them. In a fully object-oriented database, a single message takes the place of many relational database queries. A message can request computations and cause messages to be sent to other objects before returning a result. This alleviates the problem of needing sequential queries.

As SQL has become a de facto standard in relational database query, object-oriented databases have been forced to incorporate it. This is despite the fact that the relational structure and SQL are not consistent with object-oriented database structures. The relational predicate queries are directed against unknown structures, but the object-oriented query navigates through pointers that define a known structure. To resolve these differences, object-oriented databases take two major approaches. One approach is to extend the types recognized by the SQL syntax to allow objects as well as tables to be queried. Another approach is to issue SQL and object queries in tandem and subsequently bring the two queries together in the application. The main concern with object-oriented extensions to SQL has been performance; the relational search and match process is inherently slow when contrasted to a pure object-oriented database where queries directly reference objects.

Integrity

Each program that accesses a database is a potential threat to the database's integrity. Database management systems guard against these threats by providing integrity constraints, or conditions that data items must always obey. One example of an integrity constraint is a restriction on the values of data items, that is, requiring that an employee's age must be between 0 and 100. Another example is a restriction on the number of data items requiring that there be only one employee for each employee identification number. A third example is the requirement that data items referred to by other items actually exist, for instance, requiring that if a student record shows enrollment in Art 101, then that course must be in the curriculum database. These integrity constraints apply equally to traditional and object-oriented databases.

There is, however, an additional type of integrity constraint, called an instance-level constraint, that is derived from the object-oriented paradigm. An instance-level constraint can be applied to a subset or subclass of the data, unlike most integrity constraints, which apply to all data items of the same type. For example, suppose a particularly valuable employee is to be awarded a salary in excess of the constraint that all other employee salaries must obey. It is convenient to attach an instance-level constraint to this employee's salary through the subclassing mechanism without altering the salary constraint for other employees. Traditional database management systems do not provide this capability.

One means used by object-oriented databases of blocking constraint violations is an exception mechanism, such as that used in Persist (Juniper 1989). When an exceptional situation is encountered in a Persist database, the program raises an exception by creating an exception object and transferring control to the appropriate exception handler. The exception object can then be interrogated by the exception handler to communicate information about the exceptional situation. Because an exception is an object, it has a type, thus permitting the grouping of similar kinds of exceptions by types, such as DivideByZero and OverFlow, both subtypes of ArithmeticError, with an exception handler appropriate to each type.

Another means of providing constraint integrity is through triggers. Triggers are mechanisms attached to specific data items within a database which are activated whenever an attempt is made to access or change data items. Triggers check that nothing illegal or incorrect is being done to the data items. Triggers can also perform updates to make the database consistent. For example, consider a database with manager and employee records. Whenever an employee's manager is updated, a trigger can automatically adjust the list of direct reports for the old and new manager. Object-oriented databases provide a unique method for implementing triggers by monitoring method invocations. Since data can be accessed only through methods, the database can identify attempted changes to data by monitoring those methods that have access to the data and by invoking an appropriate trigger whenever a method is invoked. In large databases it is often inefficient to check all triggers and other integrity constraints before an update is made. In an object-oriented database in particular, where any operation can be user-defined, the system cannot easily determine ahead of time what other operations might be affected. The problem is to locate those critical points where integrity constraints must be activated. This is a general problem that has yet to be solved.

Evolving Technical Issues

As object-oriented databases move from research projects to commercial products, developers face an evolving set of technical issues. With an object-oriented database significant challenges are posed in providing good performance, concurrency, integrity, reliability, and flexibility. Some challenges are peculiar to object-oriented databases; others are a continuation of current technical challenges faced by relational database developers. This section discusses both kinds of technical issues. General database issues include query optimization and database distribution.

Query Optimization

When dealing with large amounts of data, it is imperative to be able to search the database as efficiently as possible. Relational database performance depends heavily upon automatic query optimization for this. Such optimization is needed for object-oriented databases to be successful. In relational databases, query optimization exploits the algebraic properties of relational operations and physical structure of relations. For example, it is known that join and select commute. Heuristics can be applied because of the uniform structure across all data. One heuristic, for example, might be: "Select first on fields for which indexes exist." This will narrow the set over which a join must be performed.

In an object-oriented system, there can be no standard set of operations across all data, since operations or methods are defined on a per-type basis. Furthermore, there is no way to determine in general whether any two operations commute. Hence, the standard query optimization techniques are not useful. One suggested technique, called revelation, would overcome these difficulties (Dawson 1989). The revelation technique permits the optimizer to check inside class definitions and inquire about their otherwise hidden implementation details. While this strategy violates the object-oriented paradigm's principle of privacy of a class's implementation, it is difficult to imagine how the query optimizer can otherwise achieve its goals.

On the other hand, in the object-oriented model there will be cases in which links between two kinds of objects exist. These objects can be retrieved directly, whereas in the relational model, a join would have been necessary. More sophisticated structures are possible in object-oriented databases and might make some optimizations unnecessary. For example, queries such as, "Select all the parts that make up component XYZ," are readily handled in an object-oriented database, since each component object is stored along with all its part information.

Distributed Database

Distribution independence is the latest in a series of steps toward independence that began in the late 1960s with device independence and continued through the late 1970s and early 1980s with data independence. Most technical issues related to the implementation of distributed relational databases also apply to distributed object-oriented databases. Distributed database systems are commonly discussed in the context of a client/server model.

A database is said to satisfy the client/server model if most of the data and related processing logic reside on one or more servers, while each client locally processes only enough data and querying logic to allow it to send queries and receive data subsets from the server(s). Figure 5.10 illustrates the client/server model. Note that the client/server model does not imply a distributed database; a client/server model is distributed only if it has more than one server.

There are several advantages of the client/server architecture. One advantage is greater ease in imposing data integrity, locking, and secu-

Figure 5.10
Database Server
with Clients on a
Local Area Network

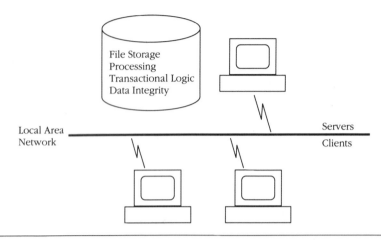

rity, because data are checked in and out of only one place. Another advantage is greater ease in expanding to larger systems by adding servers and clients. In addition, it can be less expensive because less processing power and storage capacity are required for each client. Lastly, there is reduced network traffic because the server returns to the client only the subset of data requested.

A number of problems for the distributed approach remain unsolved. For one, it is not yet clear how best to identify objects and broadcast the identifiers among machines to make identity valid network-wide. A strategy is needed to make objects transparent in a distributed scheme. The strategy must allow a single object to behave correctly with multiple interfaces or even multiple file systems. Keeping track of the locations and movements of objects presents another problem. Sub-databases, such as a location broker database, can facilitate these functional requirements.

One suggested extension to the current client/server model is called the *client and broker* model. In this model, clients are consumers of various services such as accessing files and printers. Objects residing in the network contain either simple uninterpreted information or actual procedures, for example, procedures for placement of a document into a printing queue. The broker creates a function that names and locates objects and users in the system, authenticates clients of objects, locates idle computing resources in the network, and so on.

Other methods of distributing include remote procedure calls (RPCs) between local object managers and object databases on servers.

RPCs as a form of interaction between objects provide the benefit of being both network independent and application independent. Although the object database on each server functions as a location broker, object-oriented databases on different servers will communicate using the same RPC mechanism used for client/server interaction.

Concurrency

Traditional implementations to guarantee database integrity during concurrent operations are generally based on the rule that each data item to be read or written during a transaction should be made unavailable to other transactions. For example, before a transaction to update an employee record can begin, the database must gain exclusive access to that record. In simple transactions, this type of transaction management at the read and write level is not a problem. However, for more complex applications such as those found in a cooperative CAD environment, a single transaction might involve access to a large number of interrelated data records. If the transaction must gain exclusive access to all of these records, then it may seriously degrade the performance of other concurrent transactions. For cooperative applications, this traditional transaction mechanism to guarantee integrity is overkill. It is based on the assumption that transactions should not interact during their executions. Cooperative applications, however, are based on the opposite premise that work units must interact so that their results are sharable. Object-oriented technology is being applied to this demand for better and more efficient concurrency control among cooperative transactions. Practical solutions have yet to appear.

The complexity of transaction management also extends to the locking mechanism. The relational model allows locking of sets of data (tables and rows), but the decision as to what extent an object and its related entities are locked must be derived by the database designer. Concurrency control is generally provided at the object level or under the definition of the data definition and modeling language. However, locking decisions can take on the complexity of deciding whether locking occurs at the object attribute level, the composite object level, or across other defined relationships of objects.

The tradeoff between optimistic concurrency, which allows anyone to act on an object and notifies all active users of changes made, and pessimistic concurrency, which does not allow access by other users until a particular user's transaction is complete, must also be considered. Change conflict and version management become issues if optimistic concurrency is allowed. At the same time some of the complexity of the locking decision in an object-oriented database can be offset by the database's inherent embedded knowledge, which allows database procedures to execute particular transaction controls when events occur.

Performance

Because data are stored in many places in an object-oriented database, the efficient clustering of objects is a key factor in performance. Such clustering can be by class hierarchy or by other relationships of the objects. Clever caching schemes are also needed to enhance the performance of any object-oriented database. The goal is to keep objects as close as possible to their point of use.

The performance of an object-oriented database can be potentially improved, particularly in a distributed environment, by taking advantage of the fact that the application programs that access the database can also be considered as objects, and hence they can be moved around the database just like data objects. In performing a query, the database has the option of moving data to the program, or the program moving the data. In a typical situation where a small program object is accessing a large data object, it is often more efficient to move the program to the machine where the data are, rather than the converse.

Late binding of messages and methods can potentially cause performance problems. When an application sends a message to a data object, the object might require several database accesses as it searches the class hierarchy for the appropriate method. Requiring overridden methods to reside physically close to each other can help mitigate this problem.

Schema Modification

Schema modification or the restructuring of a database will become an issue as upgrades or new versions of object-oriented databases are required. This has always been a problem in the relational model when large amounts of data must be converted to a new format. With a pure object-oriented database, the problem could be minimized by subclassing. In a hybrid relational database with objects in tables or pointers to objects in tables, the schema modification issues cannot be totally mitigated by adding subclasses.

Language Support

With the advent of C+ + as the *de facto* standard of object-oriented languages, object-oriented database vendors have been forced to abandon support of proprietary languages such as Ontologic's TDL or Servio Logic's COP. The use of C+ +, however, as a data definition and manipulation language presents some issues to the object-oriented database developer. The selection of C+ + as the primary language interface requires that extensions be built into the language or that an underlying proprietary language is simply hidden from view and invoked with a C+ + function call. Essentially, the issues are whether to continue to support a proprietary language, extend C+ +, or support the needed extensions in methods embedded in the class hierarchy of the database.

The extensions of C+ +, as supported by the language vendors, could allow objects to be defined as persistent and registered with a database. Such an approach is already supported in Interactive Software Engineering's Eiffel language. Another example is Object Design, Inc.'s use of the C+ + new command to create persistent types independent of any particular classes in its ObjectStore database. Extensions facilitated through the C+ + language could insure that the resulting structure would be acknowledged by the compiler potentially resulting in more optimized performance, as well as debugging efficiency than keeping the schema and object definition separate as subroutine calls or as methods in the object.

Standards

One argument in favor of the hybrid relational model for object-oriented databases, in which object-oriented constructs are grafted onto an existing relational database, is that object-oriented standards could be more easily defined as extensions to the already established and accepted relational standard.

Relational database management systems have benefited greatly from a standard model for data definition and retrieval, as described in the 1986 ANSI SQL standard. In contrast, no standard data model for object-oriented databases has emerged, nor have any guidelines for designing object-oriented databases. This is to be expected, because there are only recently established de facto standards for object-oriented languages (that is, rules for encapsulation or inheritance). When developers of object-oriented languages cannot decide what an object is, it is not surprising that object-oriented database developers, who must integrate their databases with these languages, cannot decide how to query the object. The problem is aggravated by the natural resistance of developers to setting standards. Developers want flexibility so that they can meet the needs of changing markets. And they want to differentiate their products to maintain an edge over their competitors. For widespread acceptance, a common data model is needed so that applications written in different languages can easily share database objects.

The lack of standards has also contributed to the dearth of tools for object-oriented databases. The popularity of relational databases has been accompanied by a rich set of tools for both the user and the developer. As in object-oriented languages, the availability of tools for browsing the structure and hierarchy of objects is a requirement. Query, reporting, schema design, and optimization tools will also be required.

Applications

The semantic content of the database increases when methods are encapsulated with data. More information resides in common repository, rather than being scattered among applications. With the trend to move more and more code from the applications to the database, a problem arises: What code should be transferred? For example, what happens when the applications that perform sensitive or confidential functions are moved into a company's corporate database? How can the company guard against unauthorized access to these without inhibiting the usefulness of the database? This is just one aspect of a general problem where the sharing and flexibility of complex objects is inhibited by binding with them application-specific knowledge of the data. Should object-oriented databases provide a complete picture of executing applications, or should the database provide a simple repository for persistent objects? In particular, should active objects execute within the database, or to take a more traditional view, should an application's procedures remain explicitly outside the database?

Summary

Object-oriented databases are evolving as a result of the current limitations of the relational model in its inability to support numerous and complex data types. Object-oriented extensions to existing relational databases are likely to set the direction for database companies. Full object-oriented databases will likely be implemented for specialized engineering- and design-based application areas such as CAD and CASE.

Not only do object-oriented databases complement object-oriented languages; they also offer benefits over the current relational model by supporting complex applications, enhancing programmability and performance, improving navigation access, simplifying concurrency control, and lowering referential integrity risks.

Many of the same issues related to the relational model also apply to both hybrid and pure object-oriented databases, including distribution, concurrency, and schema modification. Query optimization, language support, and standards are also important issues for the object-oriented database.

Key Points

- Object extensions to relational databases focus on optimization of commercial applications.

- Object extensions to relational databases are usually implemented as objects flattened into tables or with tables containing pointers to the objects.

- Pure object-oriented databases will be targeted on specialized applications such as CAD and CASE.

- Object-oriented databases compliment object-oriented languages in the areas of persistence, version control, concurrency, and code sharing.

- Object-oriented databases allow a database to incorporate many of the operations previously left to the application.

- Object-oriented features are being added to databases to increase their support for complex data types and complex data access.

- Object-oriented models capture the structure of data; the relational model organizes the data themselves.

- Applications best suited to object-oriented databases include those that handle complex data types and stat structures such as CAD, CASE, MRP, and CAP.

- Early implementations of object-oriented database had many limitations including poor performance and query facilities, proprietary database definition, and manipulation languages. Newer object-oriented databases overcome many of the early weaknesses.

■ Remaining technical challenges include query optimization, distribution mechanisms, concurrency, and schema modification.

For Further Study

Bochenski, B. 1989. "Object-oriented cells bring new life to DBMS". *Software Magazine,* June.
This article provides a good introduction to object orientation, with excellent figures and many testimonials from actual users. It includes an overview of contemporary OODBMS companies.

Dawson, J. 1989. "A family of models." *Byte,* September.
This article reviews the fundamental issues related to object-oriented database implementation.

Dyson, E. 1989. "Object-oriented database roundup." *Release 1.0,* September 22. New York: EDventure Holdings Inc.
This report provides an overview of commercial object-oriented databases current at the time.

Juniper Software Corporation. 1989. *An Introduction to the Persist Object Model.* Chelmsford, Mass.: Juniper Software Corporation.
This publication provides a clear overview of a pure OODB, with good explanations of exception handling, object types, and object creation and deletion. It includes a useful glossary of terms and suggestions for further reading. The publication is available from
Juniper Software Corporation
23 Longmeadow Road
Chelmsford, MA 01824

Zdonik, S., and Maier, D., eds. 1990. *Readings in Object-Oriented Databases.* Palo Alto, Calif.: Morgan Kaufmann Publishers.
This book provides an updated collection of papers from leading researchers and developers in object-oriented databases.

References

Chapwick, P. 1989. "Interview: Shaku Atre." *Database Programming and Design,* August.

Ontologic Inc. 1989a. *Vbase.* Billerica, Mass.: Ontologic, Inc.

Ontologic Inc. 1989b. *Product Description.* Billerica, Mass.: Ontologic, Inc., March.

Parsaye, K., Chignell, M., Khoshafian, S., and Wong, H. 1989. *Intelligent Databases: Object-Oriented, Deductive, and Hypermedia Technologies.* New York: John Wiley & Sons.

Stein, J. 1988. "Object-oriented programming and databases." *Dr. Dobb's Journal,* March.

Whiting, R. 1989. "The quest for a better way to develop software." *Electronic Business,* July 10, pp. 16–17.

Chapter 6

User Interfaces

- **History of Object-Oriented User Interfaces**

- **Benefits of Object-Oriented User Interfaces**

- **Functionality of Object-Oriented User Interfaces**
    Windows and Presentation Manager
    X Window
    NeXTStep's Interface Builder
    Apple Macintosh

- **Development Tools for Object-Oriented User Interfaces**
    Smalltalk
    NewWave
    Caseworks
    CommonView
    NeWS
    Metaphor

- **Summary**

This chapter provides an overview of the object-oriented functionality of both the user and developer environments associated with graphical user interfaces. We shall review current and evolving object orientation of graphical user interfaces. We shall explore object-oriented toolkits for construction of graphical user interfaces.

Read this chapter to see how object-oriented graphical user interfaces affect both the end user's experience and the developer's working environment.

History of Object-Oriented User Interfaces

With the introduction of the Macintosh in 1984, Apple Computer popularized the user interface as it is known today. Apple's user interface evolved from work done in the 1970s at Xerox's Palo Alto Research Center (PARC) and is now commonly referred to as a graphical user interface, or GUI. The GUI has become associated with a common feature set (Hayes and Baran 1989) available in a number of product offerings. Common features include:

- Secondary user-input devices, usually a pointing device and typically a mouse.

- Point-and-shoot functionality with on-screen menus that appear or disappear under pointing-device control.

- Windows that graphically display what the computer is doing.

- Icons that represent files, directories, and other application and system entities.

- Dialog boxes, buttons, sliders, check boxes, and many other graphical metaphors that let the programmer and user tell the computer what to do and how to do it.

Figure 6.1 shows the basic functionality of the GUI as seen by the user. Today's GUIs have expanded this basic functionality to support not only graphics but also dimension, color, light, video, and highly dynamic interaction. Modern user interfaces can simulate a very realistic view of a real, three-dimensional world.

Both the user environment and the development environment for GUIs are object-oriented to some extent. The external object orientation of the GUI, in particular, is quite vivid. From the user perspective, the screen contains various visual objects such as windows, buttons, scroll bars, and icons. The user can interact with these objects via the keyboard or, in most cases, with a mouse. Objects that closely resemble the real world environment contain data and procedures to allow some amount of direct manipulation without continually invoking an application program.

From the developer's prospective, some object-oriented features exist in the windowing subsystems of most GUIs, as will be described later in this chapter. Full object orientation of the GUI development environment can be limited. NeXTStep's Interface Builder from NeXT is an example of an object-oriented GUI development environment.

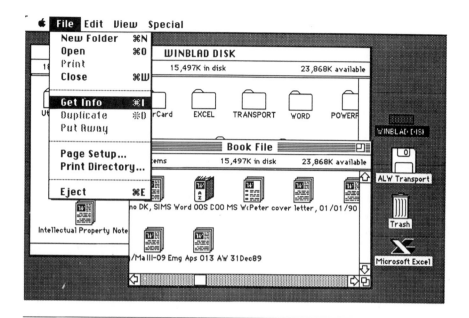

Figure 6.1
The Apple Macintosh Graphical User Interface

NeXTStep provides a set of predefined objects in an application kit. When an application draws to the screen or deals with a user event, the objects in the application kit are used. These objects provide the core functions for constructing an application. Programmers are also allowed to modify the instance variables of the predefined objects. An object called the Application object provides the fundamental support structure for the application's execution. This object establishes the application's connection to the windowing system, NeXT's Window Server. The Application object's function is analogous to the event loop skeletons used by Macintosh or IBM personal computer programmers. Events received from the NeXT Window Server are translated into event messages and then passed to the appropriate object. The complex event loop that manages the user interface is encapsulated in the Application object. Interface Builder's techniques of visually creating the message routes in an application makes the programmer's job of designing the connection between the GUI's windowing system and the application program interface (API) straightforward.

Object-oriented improvements, such as NeXTStep, which address the programming complexity of the GUI are becoming more important. In building user-interactive applications and in increasingly treating an application as a simulation, much of the user application is the interface itself.

Benefits of Object-Oriented User Interfaces

Although users and developers experience the same benefits from modern GUIs, their perspectives are different. For the user, the interesting thing is the visual and interactive experience, or look and feel, which is very similar across all currently available computer platforms. Objects on the screen can be manipulated to control the behavior of the computer. Just as the techniques of object-oriented programming encapsulate data and procedures into a single object, so too do the icons that the user sees and manipulates. For the developer, however, the GUI is more than the look and feel; it is the control panel that manages interaction between the operating system environment, the underlying application, and the user.

The user's experience with GUIs has been generally positive. GUIs are easier to use than impoverished character-based interfaces, and there is a good deal of consistency from one application to the next. The novice enjoys immediate ease of use, and the experienced user moves more quickly to an application's advanced features. Specialized knowledge of their computer is no longer a prerequisite. Users of contemporary GUIS are able to draw upon common sense, experience, and everyday spatial reasoning skills.

Object-oriented GUIs cause applications to look much more like real world functions and much less like programming processes. This, in turn, allows users to manipulate familiar images. The ultimate benefit lies in helping users to navigate in an environment that is more like a simulation of the real world and less like a computer program. This allows the user to focus on the task rather than being distracted by the tools. In other words, the user spends less time navigating in and out of programs and more time performing an immediate task. For example, to create a newsletter, the user could open a newsletter object and the object could load all the necessary desktop publishing tools.

Today's GUIs hide some program navigation from the user in several ways, not all of which are object-oriented. In today's graphic environments, the icons are graphic representations of either data or programs. Interaction between these objects is usually supported by some form of rapid context switching. The Apple Macintosh supports rapid program loading and switching with the MultiFinder operating system, which provides for transfer of data between programs with a cut and paste function. Within Microsoft's Windows, program switching is performed by DDE, which provides a dynamic link between data and applications. In both of these cases, however, the user is still bound to one particular application at a time.

In an object-oriented GUI application binding is overcome by providing the user with objects that combine functionalities that were previously spread across applications. Rather than cutting and pasting passive parts from one application to another, object-oriented systems link objects among applications. Cut-and-paste operations come alive when changes to an object, such as a graph or a table, in one document are reflected automatically in other documents. Links are bidirectional; that is, modifying data elements will cause the graph or table to be updated, and modifying the graph or table will cause the underlying data to be updated. Apple refers to this future direction as *live copy and paste* (Poole 1989).

To describe this future linking, Apple uses the metaphor of publisher and subscriber. As shown in Figure 6.2, elements of documents can be copied (formerly cut) with the publish command and inserted into other documents with the subscribe command. The elements selected with publish are saved as separate documents with their own publication icons. Publishers and subscribers are sections of documents themselves. Subscribers are notified (not automatically updated) when a change occurs in a publication. A published element can appear in one or more subscribers.

Fully object-oriented GUIs would allow the icons to tie programs and data together. A complete object-oriented operating environment would also make use of the icons as dynamic links to other programs and data, allowing users to access data instantly and seamlessly from a multitude of sources. In some cases, such as with NewWave, these en-

> The whole thrust behind an object-oriented system is that, when you go for a task, the tool appears to let you do the task. In theory it's like picking up a nail and having a hammer suddenly appear in your hand.
> *Millikin 1989*

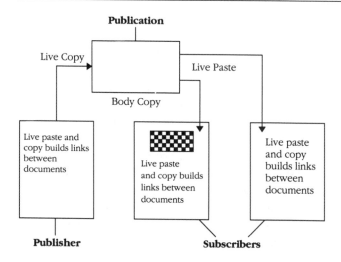

Publication

Live Copy

Live Paste

Body Copy

Live paste and copy builds links between documents

Live paste and copy builds links between documents

Live paste and copy builds links between documents

Publisher

Subscribers

Figure 6.2
Dynamic Linking with Live Cut and Paste as Facilitated in Apple Macintosh System 7.00

vironments can also allow bridging standard character-based products with the object-oriented world. GUIs developed within this environment could offer both improved ease of use and increased breadth of access across various operating environments.

The benefits to developers of object orientation in GUIs are also substantial. Object-oriented programming, as a process of modeling objects from the real world, is a natural fit for programming the window environment. In a user interface, the things on the screen are programmed as objects with direct correspondence between display and code objects; and overlapping and nested windows, with their need to refresh themselves whenever the display changes, map cleanly into objects.

The object-oriented approach to user interface construction allows the developer to abandon the disconnected statements of traditional languages and instead to use objects representing the key elements of the interface, such as as buttons or dialogue boxes. Programmers can enjoy all the benefits of the object-oriented programming paradigm including modularity, reusability, and extensibility. Object-oriented user interface development tools can also make it easier to enhance the user interface domain with extremely high resolution images, full motion video, and new ways of interacting with the data, such as gesture and eye tracking.

The development environments for GUIs contain varying levels of object orientation. In fact, object-oriented programming has been introduced to many system developers as primarily a method to design and code application interfaces in a fraction of the time required to code in a procedural-style language. For example, Glockenspiel's object-oriented GUI toolkit, CommonView, can reduce the amount of code needed to be written for a Microsoft Windows application by 75% (Imagesoft 1989).

Much of the developer's domain of most GUIs is already objectlike and closely resembles or actually supports the basic object-oriented mechanisms of methods, messages, classes, and inheritance. For example, most GUIs are event-driven. This event process is typically supported by a message-based architecture, one of the fundamental mechanisms of object-oriented systems. Because of polymorphism the same message sent to different GUI objects produces different results. When an event occurs, the system environment determines what the event is and causes the appropriate function to be executed.

Most GUI windowing subsystems provide some predefined classes and support some mechanism for inheritance. For example, PM creates windows from predefined window classes. These include classes for frame windows, border windows, button windows, scrolling bar windows, and text entry field windows. Programmers can also define their own window classes. The class definition includes not only the allocation of data that are unique to each window, based on the class, but also a window procedure that is responsible for processing messages, including messages for user input to the window and for displaying output on the screen.

The benefits of having object-oriented mechanisms and of using an object-oriented programming approach to creating the GUI can be illustrated with an example from programs that use a mouse to select a push button on the screen. In the traditional method of programming, the program is constructed to draw a button on the screen and display text. If the program detects a mouse click, it determines whether the mouse was positioned on the button and, if so, carries out the command for the button. The traditional process of building this function involves extensive coding, without access to the inheritance or encapsulation features of object-oriented environments.

Using PM under IBM's Operating System/2 (OS/2), for example, the object-oriented programming approach entails creating a window based on the preexisting button class. The window procedure for the button window class, which processes all messages that are sent to the push button, is in one of PM's dynamic link libraries. This preexisting class is already programmed to specify the size, text, and position of the button. The programmer need not write new code to draw the push button, because the push button can draw itself, using the internal methods of the preexisting button class. The PM routes mouse input to the window underneath the mouse at the time of the mouse input event. When the user positions the mouse over the push button and clicks, the mouse messages are sent to the button window procedure, not to the program's client window. The program does not need to check if the mouse click occurred over its window. The PM button window is a true object with the definition of the data type and a set of procedures that act on the data. Just as the user perceives the screen as containing various objects, so does the program.

Using inheritance, a capability not available in procedural programming or function libraries, the programmer can create subclass windows that already have the functionality of standard, predefined window classes and program only the differences. For example, in the hierarchy of classes illustrated in Figure 6.3, the programmer creates PublishWindowClass and then requests that it Enter Text. Since PublishWindowClass does not have a method of its own to perform this task, it relies on the EnterText method previously programmed in the preexisting class TextWindowClass.

Figure 6.3

Using Inheritance
Mechanisms in PM

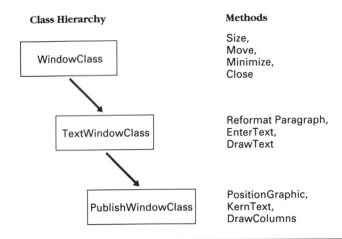

Class Hierarchy

Methods

WindowClass — Size, Move, Minimize, Close

TextWindowClass — Reformat Paragraph, EnterText, DrawText

PublishWindowClass — PositionGraphic, KernText, DrawColumns

PublishWindowClass routes the EnterText message through the system object manager to its parent, TextWindowClass, where the method exists to perform the requested task.

Even with basic object-oriented capabilities of the windowing system, GUI development environments present many complexities to programmers. These are in addition to the challenging human factor issues associated with ease of use and complex design issues related to the visual representation of information. For example, Microsoft's Windows environment contains approximately 450 C programming functions, and PM has over 500 operating system function calls. Although preexisting class libraries can significantly improve the programming process, these classes also contain hundreds of methods that require at least some familiarity by the programmer.

The event-driven paradigm of most GUIs can also present enormous complexity to the developer. This structure provides the flexibility for a graphical user interface to respond to events (keystrokes and mouse clicks), but many GUIs require programming of a complicated "event" code loop that manages this process. The programmer in essence becomes a slave to the GUI, writing an event handler to deal with the interaction of the user interface and system environment layers and responding to Windows or PM messages.

Until recently, user interfaces of most currently available interactive software systems were built in an ad hoc manner on top of the windowing subsystems of the GUI system environment. Even with the object-oriented capability of the windowing subsystem this was a costly and time-consuming approach. Experienced Macintosh or IBM personal computer programmers eased their programming burden by keeping skeleton files or frameworks to handle the complexities of the event loop and assist in the programming. Today, generalized object-oriented frameworks consisting of abstract classes for each major component of the user interface are available. These frameworks, HP's NewWave or Apple's MacApp, for example, decrease the complexity of user interface programming. However, most of the frameworks do not eliminate all of the programming complexity because, in exchange, they require intimate knowledge of yet another underlying structure and implementation.

Functionality of Object-Oriented User Interfaces

The development environment for most GUIs consists of four major components:

- A windowing system

- An imaging model

- An application program interface

- A set of tools and frameworks for creating interfaces and developing integrated applications

Windowing systems allow programs to display multiple applications at the same time. Windowing systems include programming tools for building movable and resizable windows, menus, dialog boxes, and other items on the display. Some GUIs contain proprietary windowing systems, such as Apple's Macintosh. Others use common windowing systems such, as X Window from the Massachusetts Institute of Technology. X Window, often called simply X, is the windowing system for the Open Software Foundation's MOTIF and Digital Equipment's DEC-Windows.

An imaging model defines how fonts and graphics are created on the screen. Imaging models handle, for example, typeface and size in a word processor or curves and lines in a drawing program. This component of the system environment has taken on increasing sophistication as applications incorporate complex curves, color, shading, and dimension. Two examples of imaging models are Apple's QuickDraw for the Macintosh and Microsoft's Graphic Programming Interface (GPI) for PM. Some GUIs support more than one imaging model.

The API is a set of programming language functions that allow the programmer to specify how the actual application will control the menus, scroll bars, and icons that appear on the screen. Like windowing models, APIs align with particular GUIs. Examples of APIs are Sun Microsystems' OpenLook and Digital Equipment's X-User Interface (XUI).

Finally, GUI development environments can include toolkits and frameworks. Most of these toolkits are object-oriented. Examples include Hewlett-Packard's (HP's) NewWave, MIT's X, Window's Xt, and components of NeXT's NeXTStep, as well as Microsoft's forthcoming Application Factory.

Although the structure of the basic development environment for most GUIs is similar, there are major differences in how the GUI is integrated with the operating system. Some, like the Macintosh and NeXT GUIs, are closely integrated with the operating system. Others, like X Window or Microsoft's Windows, can be set up as options to be selected by the user when the computer boots up.

Programming of software for GUIs across these components is fairly complex and challenging. Commercial developers who want to support multiple environments find their task further complicated by the absence of standards across heterogeneous computing platforms. The higher-level toolkit component is intended to mitigate much of this difficulty.

The GUI components that are most affected by object-oriented techniques are windowing systems and high-level toolkits. Together these two components control all interaction between the user and the application, as well as the interaction between the GUI developer and the system environment.

Although the graphical user interface has become a standard component of most systems, no standards in windowing systems, imaging models, APIs, or high-level toolkits have emerged. However, three major camps of GUIs dominate. The first camp is IBM's System Application Architecture (SAA), which includes primarily Microsoft's Windows and PM. The second camp is UNIX systems, usually build around X Window. NeXT, although included in this UNIX camp, is one major exception, as it does not use X. The third camp is the Macintosh. This section will describe the object-oriented functionality of representative GUIs in these camps, including Windows, PM, X (upon which most of the UNIX camp is based), NeXT, and Macintosh.

Windows and Presentation Manager

The PC-level GUIs that implement SAA are Windows from Microsoft and PM from IBM and Microsoft. These GUIs reflect IBM's SAA Common User Access (CUA) standards. Several GUIs based on X also have an SAA/

Windows/PM look and feel. This SAA class of GUIs includes several distinctive look and feel features, including optional use of the mouse, the menu or action bar, and the style of windows used; particularly the stretching of borders to enlarge the windows and the ability to minimize a window. DOS-based Windows and OS/2's PM share the same look and feel dictated by IBM's CUA guidelines. As Figure 6.4 shows, each has its own API, imaging system, and windowing system.

Microsoft Windows, announced in late 1983 and first released in 1985, is an operating environment that runs under MS-DOS version 2.0 or later on IBM personal computers and compatibles. PM, released in late 1988 as part of OS/2 version 1.2, is an integral part of the OS/2 environment, also for IBM personal computers and compatibles. PM is basically a collection of dynamic link libraries (.DLL files) that extend the functionality of OS/2 to include window management and graphics.

Development of Windows and PM was strongly influenced by existing object-oriented environments, such as Xerox's Smalltalk and the Macintosh interface; and, like these environments, Windows and PM use a message-based architecture that conveys data to predefined objects used by the environment. Different external events cause an object to execute different operations or the same operations in different ways. Windows and PM also support a class structure for the windowing system.

The primary object in Windows and PM is called window. To the user, this object is the rectangular area that divides the screen into separate programs. To the programmer, window is an object that receives and processes messages informing itself of all events that affect the win-

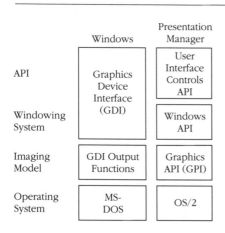

Figure 6.4
SAA GUI
Components

dow such as input of keystrokes or mouse clicks. The response of the window to the message is determined by the window's methods, called *window functions.* The window is a true object. It paints itself on the screen using internal methods, and it uses its internal methods to determine how to respond to user input (messages).

To create windows on the screen the programmer must initially set up a window class structure. In both Windows and PM windows have a parent-child relationship. When a parent window is created in a program, almost any other window in the same program is a descendent. Descendents inherit the parent window's controls, including title bar, sizing, and system menu. The child windows inherit some methods that cannot be changed by the programmer; for example, a child window must always display within a parent. All windows are descendants of the desktop windowClass. Because windowClass defines general characteristics of a window, the programmer creates most windows by subclassing from windowClass and adding more detailed information to the instances of the subclasses. A window class is registered only for the first instance of the program, but a separate window is created for each instance, all based on the same window class. Figure 6.5 illustrates the usual components of a typical parent window.

The windows used in these environments fit to some degree our description of objects, with one exception. The programmer is responsible for writing the window procedure, which becomes part of the window object. As in other object-oriented environments, objects are distinguished by the handles used to reference them. A handle is a

Figure 6.5
Presentation Manager Window as Defined by IBM's CUA

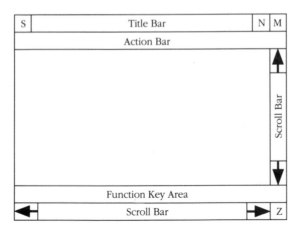

system-defined 32-bit value in PM and 16-bit value in Windows that identifies the object. The programmer supplies the variable name for the handle; PM or Windows supplies the arbitrary system value. One common handle is the window handle. When a window is created, the handle is returned to the calling program. This handle refers to the window in subsequent function calls that act on the window. When the window is eventually destroyed, the window's handle becomes invalid.

The consequence of making a handle the first parameter of every function is that every PM function either acts on an object or causes an object to act on itself. This syntax of PM functions is objectlike. Essentially handle is the object, fn name (function name) is the message, and params is the parameters of the message. Standard objects are available with a defined datatype and variable name used to reference the handle.

The programmer at the higher toolkit level is rarely privy to these internal workings of an object. In this environment, a message is similar to a standard function call. Messages, however, have some unique characteristics not found in functions. For example, the message always carries a selection mechanism or the parameter that distinguishes it from other messages and consequently tells the object what operation to perform. As previously described, the message is the fn name, and the first parameter is often, but not always, the handle to the object. A function always references a definite address in memory where the code for the function resides; a message does not reference memory, but tells the current instance of the object what memory address to reference. A function not only specifies an operation but also carries the information on how to perform the operation. The encapsulated window procedures (methods) specify how to perform the operation. Messages simply specify the operation.

Windows has one system message queue, and each program currently running under Windows has its own message queue that stores all messages for all windows in that program. Every message goes first to the system message queue and then is routed to the appropriate application. Figure 6.6 diagrams the typical message routes in a Windows application.

Windows and PM are responsible for generating many messages. In PM there are more than 100 general-purpose messages. In addition, there are more than 150 special-purpose messages that service such controls as dialog box windows and scroll bars. In all, there are four categories of messages:

Input messages: generated in response to keyboard and mouse input.

Figure 6.6
Sending Messages to
Various Window
Functions

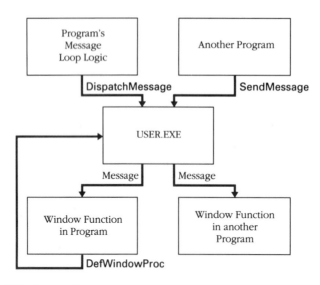

System messages: generated in response to a programmed event or a system interrupt.

Control messages: provided for two-way communication with a child window, including menus, scroll bars, title bars, list boxes, entry fields, pushbuttons, and display objects.

User messages: defined by the programmer and used within an application to convey data after a predefined event occurs.

Each category of general-purpose message is handled differently by PM. Ultimately, messages from each category are processed through the application message queue (called the window message queue when more than one queue is in effect). The programmer must anticipate which messages will emerge from the application message queue. The routines the programmer codes are based on this process of anticipation. In the end, however, many messages are processed in a default way by PM itself.

Before keyboard and mouse messages enter the application message queue, PM converts raw input into message form. Upon doing this, it places an input message into the system message queue. An input message proceeds to the input router, which selects the application to receive the message. Its selection is based on the current state of the input focus. PM establishes the input focus as a result of user actions such as

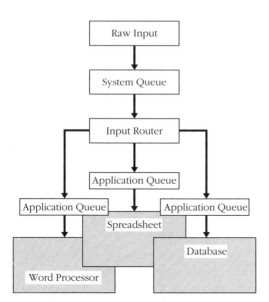

Figure 6.7
The Flow of an Input Message in PM

a mouse click in a window. It can also set input focus as the result of a programmed event such as a function call. Figure 6.7 shows the flow of a logical input message.

System messages are more complex than input messages because some system messages require processing through PM's system message queue, while others do not. One category of system message is all DDE messages. Other system messages go directly to the application message queue, including messages that create and destroy windows, clipboard messages, and more.

The third category of messages acts as the interface to PM's special control objects: dialog boxes, list boxes, pushbuttons, and a host of others. Some of these messages may never be required by the programmer; for example, it is entirely possible to write an application that does not include a list box. On the other hand, some control messages are used quite frequently. Typically, a control message carries information back to a control object from a window procedure, such as a request to a menu to deemphasize a previously selected menu item.

The fourth category of messages is user messages. The programmer creates these messages by defining them either at the top of the program or in a separate header file. In general, these messages never leave the application; instead, they are posted to the application message queue from one part of the program so that they are processed by another part.

User messages are often employed to process menu selections. A user message is associated with a menu item and then processed after emerging from the application queue.

In summary, Windows and PM are event-driven interfaces and share object-oriented characters of predefined classes for inheritance-based programming.

X Window

X Window was developed at Massachusetts Institute of Technology (MIT), in cooperation with Digital Equipment Corporation (DEC). MIT issued the X.11 version of X in September of 1987 and introduced X.11.2 in March 1988 to the current X Consortium. The name X, as well as part of the initial design, was derived from an earlier window system called W developed at Stanford University. Currently the X Window system is supported by an X Consortium of primarily UNIX-based hardware and software vendors as a standard base for user interfaces across most UNIX product lines. Figure 6.8 illustrates the components of UNIX GUIs based on X Window.

The X Window System does not define any particular style of interface but rather provides a mechanism for supporting many styles. X is also network-based. In contrast with PM, the X architecture is based on the premise that an application can run on one computer, while the graphical presentation of the application's output and responses from the user can occur on another computer. As such, X provides a flexible set of primitive window operations but carefully avoids dictating the look and feel of any particular application. X's device-independent functionality allows it to serve as a base for a variety of interface styles. X does not provide user interface components such as buttons, menus, or dialog boxes.

All interfaces supporting X can theoretically use any X Window display. The application program sends calls to the X Window Library, which packages the display requests as X packets and sends them along to the X Window server. The server decodes the X packets and displays them on the screen. Exactly how the packets will be displayed (i.e., will look) on a workstation depends on the set of predesigned window elements called *widgets* that are unique to the particular workstation in the system environment. The ultimate look on one workstation may differ substantially from that on another, but the response to a user's action on these different-looking interfaces will be the same. Several hybrids of X exist, such as Open Windows from Sun Microsystems, which runs on

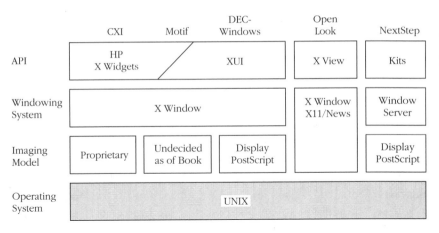

Figure 6.8
Components of Major UNIX-Based GUIs

Sun's NeWS in parallel with X Window. Open Windows sends some display functions through X Window and others through NeWS. This hybrid and others usually include more complete sets of widgets, standards for using them, and more comprehensive (and incompatible) APIs.

This hybridization has created many "look" variants of X Window GUIs. Examples include HP's API, called HP X Widgets, DEC's XUI, and HP's and Microsoft's Common X Interface (CXI). CXI has the look and feel of PM implemented within an X environment. Some standardization of X variations is likely with the emergence of Motif from the Open Software Foundation. Motif attempts to consolidate the hybridization. It is based on X Windows, looks like PM, but it uses components of the DEC and HP APIs.

The application programming model for X, like PM and Windows, is event-driven, and the categories of events are similar. Like PM, X programs rest in wait loops until the underlying window-management system generates an event. Window hierarchy management is also common to the architecture of both systems. Like PM's windows, windows in X are organized as parents and children, so attributes can be inherited and effects of the events applied to related members.

Since X does not support any particular interface style, most programmers build applications with libraries that provide an interface to the base window system. One standard programming interface to X is the C language library known as X Library or Xlib. This library defines functions for access and control over the display, windows, and input devices. Although commonly used, the library can be difficult and tedious to work with and often results in hundreds of lines of code for a

GUI. A better solution is a higher-level toolkit, such as the X Toolkit (Xt), upon which many other X Window toolkits are based.

Each high-level toolkit supports a specific and different widget set. At the time of this book's publication, the X Consortium had not recognized any widget set as standard. Three sets are generally available as contributed software to the Consortium and include X Widget from HP, Xsw from Sony, and the Athena widget set from MIT's Project Athena. Other commercially available widget sets include HP's and Microsoft's three-dimensional Common X Interface (CXI), DEC's proprietary DecWindows widget set, AT&T's OpenLook-based widget set, the Open Software's Motif widget set, and the X Consortium's CoreComponents widget set. In addition to the Xt toolset, there are other high-level X Window toolkits. These include InterViews built at Stanford University, Andrew from Carnegie Mellon University, Clue from Texas Instruments, and Xray from HP. Each widget set has a different appearance or style of interaction.

X Toolkit is the foundation upon which most of the commercial toolkits are based and is a good example for describing object-oriented functionality. The X Toolkit consists of two parts: a layer known as Xt Intrinsics and a set of widgets. Xt Intrinsics supports many of the available widget sets. The widget set, as previously described, implements user interface components including scroll bars, menus, and buttons. Xt Intrinsics provides a framework that allows the programmer to combine the components. Both parts are integrated with Xlib, allowing programmers access to higher-level libraries. A typical X programming environment is illustrated in Figure 6.9.

The common distinction in object-oriented programming between an application programmer (consumer) and a class library programmer (producer) fits well to the X environment. The X application programmer is likely to use a combination of a higher-level toolkit (e.g., the X Toolkit's Xt Intrinsic), Xlib, and a widget set. The class library programmer, whose job is to create new widgets, is likely to use the capabilities from within one of the higher-level toolkits.

Depending on the toolkit, the widget programmer may be able to take advantage of object-oriented capabilities. Xt Intrinsic, for example, uses an object-oriented approach and organizes widgets into classes. Xt Intrinsic defines the basic architecture of a widget. This allows widgets to work together smoothly when built by different programmers or potentially when selected from different widget sets.

A typical widget consists of two basic parts: a class record and an instance record. Each of these components is implemented as a C struc-

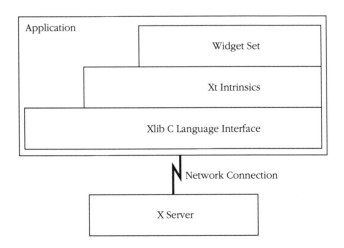

Figure 6.9
Typical X Window
Development
Environment

ture containing data and pointers to methods. Intrinsics defines the organization of each structure. All widgets belonging to a class share a copy of common data and methods for that class. Each individual widget has its own copy of instance-specific data. A widget's class record is usually allocated and initialized statically at compile time; a unique copy of the instance record is created at run time for each individual widget.

Since all widgets belonging to the same class share the same class record, the class record must contain only static data that do not relate directly to the state of an individual widget. For example, every widget's class record includes a field containing the widget's class name. The class record also contains methods that define the appearance and behavior of all widgets in the class. Although most of these methods operate on the data in the widget's instance records, the methods themselves are shared by all widgets in a class.

Many object-oriented languages provide inheritance as a language construct. The Xt Intrinsics is written in the C language, which does not directly support object-oriented programming. Xt itself supports inheritance with a subclassing mechanism. To use Xt's subclassing capabilities, the programmer first finds an existing widget with similar functions (a common step in object-oriented design), writes a subclass that can inherit existing data and methods, and then adds new data and methods as needed.

If a similar widget cannot be found, then a foundation class called Core is subclassed. All widget classes are subclasses of the Core widget class. Like the class Window in PM, Core contains the basic methods for initializing, displaying, and destroying widgets, and reacting to external resizing. Core also stores basic properties (e.g., the geometry) of widgets and the data for handling events.

New widget classes inherit the methods (called *resources*) defined by their superclass by specifically including the definition of the super-class structure in the definition of the new class. Xt Intrinsics provides two mechanisms for inheriting the methods defined by a superclass. The first mechanism is referred to as *chaining*. When a method is chained, Xt Intrinsics invokes the method defined by a widget's superclass first and then invokes the widget's method. This allows a widget to inherit part of a method from its superclass.

Xt Intrinsics also provides a mechanism for inheriting methods that are not chained. This is done by using special symbols to specify the methods in the widget's class record. Each symbol is defined by the superclass that added the method to the widget's class record. These symbols can be used by any subclass of the widget class Core and do not have to be redefined by each widget class. Only classes that contribute new methods to the class record need to define new symbols. When a widget class specifies one of these symbols in the class record, Intrinsics copies the corresponding method used by the widget's superclass into the widget's class structure at class initialization time. Figure 6.10 illustrates this architecture and shows the relationship between the class record and instance records of several widgets belonging to widget class Core.

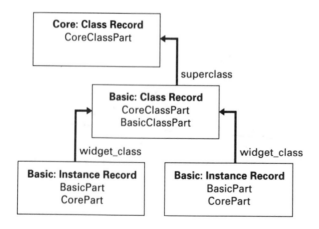

Figure 6.10
Inheriting from
Widget Class Core

The Xt Intrinsics uses a data-abstraction technique to hide the implementation of a widget from applications that use the widget. Applications that use a widget see only the incomplete definition of the widget and therefore cannot directly access fields in the widget structure. Applications declare all widgets as type Widget, which is known as an opaque type. This means the application has a pointer to the widget structure but does not have access to the real definition of the data that it represents. The application cannot access the contents of the data structure.

Another object-oriented technique promoted in X Window is to extract some general functionality from two or more new widget classes and create a metaclass. A *metaclass* is an abstract class that is not intended to be instantiated directly but serves as a superclass for other similar widgets. When creating a complete new widget set, it is frequently useful to create a hierarchy of metaclasses. With this approach, the top metaclass in the hierarchy defines elements that all widget classes in the set have in common, and each subclass becomes more and more specialized. Such an organization allows the widget programmer to create new widget classes with the least amount of effort, although there is some extra initial effort required to design and create metaclasses. For example, this approach is used by the X Widget set from HP, where most basic widgets inherit from the Primitive metaclass and most composite widgets inherit from the Manager widget class.

NeXTStep's Interface Builder

NeXTStep is a large component of the NeXT Computer's operating system. Unlike other UNIX-based platforms, NeXT does not support X. Instead, NeXTStep provides a complete object-oriented programming environment that consists of four components:

Window server: handles drawing to the screen, hardware events generated by the keyboard, and events related to managing the display; and includes embedded Display Postscript from Adobe Systems.

Workspace manager: manages files and applications on the system and launches applications from their icons.

Application kit: is a class library of 38 objects; provides some visible objects: window, button, view; and provides some invisible objects: application, speaker, archiver.

Interface builder: supports prototyping of user interfaces with existing objects or by creating custom objects; provides a visual interface so that prototyping is done with mouse clicks and keystrokes; and creates a description file for objects and their instance variables.

NeXT applications are constructed in three steps:

1. Designing and testing the user interface, using Interface Builder.

2. Identifying the underlying objects that satisfy the application's design requirements.

3. Implementing the objects.

When unique code is needed to implement application-specific functions, the Objective-C language preprocessor is used. Objective-C, originally developed by Stepstone Technologies, and an ANSI C compiler are bundled with the NeXT computer.

The Application Kit provides objects that can be used when an application draws to the screen or handles a user event. The Application Kit does not provide source code for these objects, but the Interface Builder can be used to modify the behavior of these objects without resorting to editing and recompiling their original source code.

The central object that provides the fundamental support structure for an application's execution is called Application. Each application must have one, and only one, Application object. Application connects an application to the Window Server, reads the Interface Builder description file, and instantiates the application's objects and their instance variables based on this file's contents. Application also manages a list of all the windows used by the program.

The function of Application is analogous to the event-loop skeletons used by Macintosh and OS/2 programmers. Application receives events from the Window Server, translates events into messages, and then sends these messages to the appropriate objects for processing. For example, when a mouse is clicked in a window, Application receives the event from the Window Server and translates it into an event message. This message is passed to the Window object associated with that particular event. Window may then pass this message to objects visible in the window. Visible objects in windows (or Panels, special types of objects used to present dialog boxes and menus) are called Views. Many objects in the Application Kit are descendant classes of View. A View object supplies the framework for drawing in a window and the methods for acting upon event messages dispatched to a window. View defines the location, size, and orientation of the PostScript coordinate system. View also handles any image clipping. A drawSelf method, containing Objective-C code and PostScript commands, draws the View's image. All Views in the window are ultimately owned by a single View, called a Content View. The hierarchy between Views and their subviews determines the order in which Views are drawn and receive event messages. This View hierarchy is used for managing images in a window.

Communication between control objects and application objects is through a target/action paradigm. For example, an event associated with a control object such as a Button sends an action message (save file) to a target object. The target object responds by executing the action method that saves data to a file on the disk drive. The target/action paradigm encourages designers to be precise in routing messages between the user interface and the methods that perform the work. It also helps the programmer use Interface Builder to change these routes to different objects at a later date. The programmer's task of designing the connections between the user interface and the application code becomes straightforward with the Interface Builder because it provides a simple, powerful way of visually establishing the message routes in an application.

Apple Macintosh

The Macintosh User Interface Standard, introduced in 1984, is an Apple-proprietary GUI. Figure 6.11 illustrates the components of the Apple GUI. Apple Computer has an object-oriented application framework, MacApp, designed specifically for creating interfaces and developing integrated applications for the Macintosh. MacApp builds code for the Macintosh GUI and has over 40 classes to handle standard features including menus, undo, exception handling, multipage print, desk accessories, MultiFinder, scrolling, zooming, and opening and closing of windows. MacApp is written in Object Pascal, and developers can expand an application either by using the predefined class set or by using an object-oriented language such as Object Pascal or C + + directly. The environment forces strict adherence to Apple compatibility guidelines.

Before MacApp, most Macintosh software was application-specific, with each program having its own code for managing all of the various interactive events that could occur while the application was running. Although applications could take advantage of Apple's ROM Toolbox to help develop interfaces that conform to the Macintosh User Interface

Figure 6.11
Macintosh GUI
Components

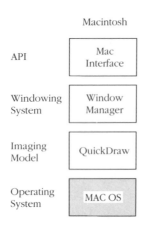

Macintosh

API   Mac Interface

Windowing System   Window Manager

Imaging Model   QuickDraw

Operating System   MAC OS

Standard, they still had a significant amount of development inefficiency. Most of the code required by the Macintosh User Interface Standard had to be reengineered by each developer.

MacApp is a framework only for building applications; it is not an appropriate tool for building other types of Apple programs such as device drivers, desk accessories, or HyperCard external commands (XCMDs). MacApp enforces the Apple standards; the programmer customizes or builds the application by supplying code to fill the windows with contents and putting working items in the pull-down menus. Code is then implemented as a set of classes with methods to respond to standard MacApp messages. MacApp also provides a browsing function referred to as the *view architecture* to view the class hierarchies, as well as to view and edit class structures.

MacApp has six primary classes for constructing user interfaces. These classes are defined as follows:

TApplication: manages interactions between the application and the Finder, manages the event queue, creates TDocument objects, and tells TDocument when to perform certain actions.

TDocument: manages the documents owned by an application, creates TView, TWindow, and TFrame objects, and tells view and window objects when to perform certain actions.

TWindow: manages the windows, and tells the frame objects comprising a window when to perform certain actions, such as scrolling.

TFrame: manages how windows are scrolled and resized and how coordinates are transformed, and tells the view object that displays it when to perform certain actions.

TView: manages rendering the images in a window or frame, including drawing, and creates TCommand objects

TCommand: manages everything to do with the user interface that affects the data in the document, specifically, mouse and keyboard input, undo, and redo; and interacts with the Clipboard and tells TDocument when to perform certain functions.

A simple example—a user interface with a single type of window and only one type of view—illustrates the use of the MacApp classes. To construct this interface, the programmer defines three new classes:

- a subclass of TDocument that defines a document to hold information needed by the application,

- a subclass of TView that defines a view capable of drawing whatever the application wants to show on the screen to represent the data in the document, and

- a subclass of TApplication that builds an application to invoke the view and use the document.

The subclassing method is similar to that of PM. Creating these three subclasses merely creates the items on the screen. Interaction in application-specific ways is not yet programmed, only the application-independent interaction, such as scrolling in both directions, using the menus, activating desk accessories, opening multiple windows, moving any of these windows, and printing the view.

The Macintosh GUI is also based on the event paradigm. On the Macintosh, the lower-level system software manages an event queue into which events are posted for later processing. Events of various types are placed in the event queue, packaged with all their appropriate information, such as the location of the mouse when it was clicked or the time when a key was pressed. The main event loop processes and dispatches these events in the order of their occurrence. Three kinds of events are stored in the queue:

- mouse events, including the press of the mouse button (a mouse-down event) or the release of that button (a mouse-up event),

- keyboard events, and

- window events, including the activation or deactivation of a window.

MacApp preprocesses many of these events and prompts the application with a higher-level event. For example, a Macintosh application must respond when a mouse-down event occurs in the menu bar by displaying the appropriate menu. MacApp performs this function and presents the application with a menu event when the user chooses a menu command. The application need handle only the higher-order event, the actual choice of a menu command; it does not have to be concerned with menu display and interaction. MacApp handles other events such as Switcher events, AppleTalk events, or events occurring on the serial communications lines.

MacApp provides a number of support tools, including window and dialog-box design tools: ViewEdit and MABuild. ViewEdit provides a WYSIWYG editing environment to create resource views that describe windows and dialog boxes, the boxes used for entering values into each view resource field. ViewEdit also allows drawing, resizing, and moving of views using the standard Macintosh interface, and it allows rearranging of view hierarchies. MABuild is a Macintosh Programmer Workbench (MPW) tool that controls the building of an application from its source file.

Also included in MacApp are debugging and inspecting tools. The integrated object-oriented debugger provides support for breakpoints, stack crawl, trace, and single stepping. The Object Inspector allows one or more Object Inspector windows to open and display the current values of the fields of any object. Multiple objects in multiple windows can be open simultaneously. The Object Inspector can display the contents of toolbox data structures as well as MacApp objects.

Like other high-level toolkits, MacApp imposes some limitations on the applications it builds. Performance is acceptable, but applications will not necessarily run as fast as those carefully coded in Object Pascal or C + +. To build a complete interface or an application, the developer must learn MacApp for the windowing system and use either Object Pascal or C + + to program the API.

Development Tools for Object-Oriented User Interfaces

There are two main difficulties in developing GUIs. The first is the problem of working with current low-level windowing systems, such as those provided with Windows and PM, a problem evidenced by the "API shock" most programmers suffer when they encounter the hundreds of function calls provided with the GUI toolkits. The second is the issue of application portability across operating environments and hardware.

Several object-oriented higher-level tools already exist to ease the programming burden of the GUI. Some, such as Xt, Interface Builder, and MacApp, have been discussed in the previous section because they are closely coupled with particular GUIs. Many tools were initially developed to address the GUI only, but some have expanded to address full application development. Such tools will be discussed further in Chapter 8, "Programming and Maintenance."

The role of a high-level toolkit or application framework is to provide higher-level abstractions that simplify development, potentially mitigate some of the complexity of the intricate event loop, and provide transparency across systems environments. One such toolkit is Xt, previously described in this chapter. The familiar program to display "Hello World" takes approximately 40 executable call statements to write in X Library, but in Xt it requires only about 4 statements (Asente 1989). NeXT's NeXTStep includes functionality to automate the event loop, and Glockenspiel's CommonView uses a common library for Windows, PM, NeWS, and X Window.

Most high-level toolkits exploit many features of object-oriented programming. For example, to write a main routine that forms the heart of the expandable application, programmers utilize dynamic binding, a feature present in object-oriented languages. To add new functionality to a portion of the main routine, the programmer overrides a method in one class with a new method in one of its descendant classes.

Smalltalk

As discussed in Chapter 5, Smalltalk is not only a language but also a window server and a collection of other tools. Smalltalk, originally produced by Xerox PARC, is the common ancestor of most window systems. With its uniform, comprehensive structure, Smalltalk is the simplest architecture for GUI construction.

Interactive interfaces in the Smalltalk environment are constructed using Smalltalk's class mechanism and Model/View/Controller (MVC) methodology. MVC is the underlying methodology used by most other high-level toolkits. The methodology is based on three classes—Model, View, and Controller—that work together as components of an interactive system. The division of labor among the various components in the Model-View-Controller design is shown in Figure 6.12.

Figure 6.12
Model-View-Con-
troller Relationships
(Dodani *et al.*
1989)

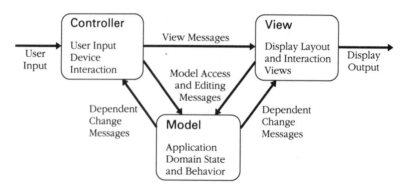

Model is the basic application. Its goal is to capture the features of some real-world situation. One model can have many views, for example, a graphical view and a list view. View renders the information contained in the model into an image that can be seen by the user. A number of operations can be performed on a view, including adding subviews and positioning them within the view, deleting subviews, transforming the view, and displaying the view.

Controller coordinates the user's input with the view and its model, relaying key presses or mouse activity to the model and the view and sending them messages to modify or update themselves based on this input.

The MVC methodology is implemented in Smalltalk as follows. Each of the three MVC classes is a direct subclass of class Object, Smalltalk's most general class. Class Model has only one feature that distinguishes it from the class Object; class Model describes objects that have other objects that are affected by the model's current state. In the MVC paradigm, any view and controller related to a model must be informed of when something happens that changes the state of the model so that the new information can be displayed on the screen and be made available to the user. To implement this, class Model has a variable called dependents that refers to the views and controllers that depend on it for information and enables it to broadcast messages to its dependents when something in its state has changed.

Because a view must be able to both send messages to its model requesting information about the model's state and to receive messages from its controller when a mouse or keyboard event has taken place, instances of class View inherit data and methods that enable it to reference a particular model, a particular controller, and various features of the display. Similarly, a controller object has instance variables establishing a relationship to a particular model, a particular view, and various forms of user input, enabling it (the controller) to coordinate the three.

The Smalltalk class library contains a variety of types of view and controller classes that can be further refined to meet the needs of a particular application. Thus, it can be used as a prototyping environment for exploring alternative user interfaces.

NewWave

In November, 1987, Hewlett-Packard introduced NewWave, a software framework for object-oriented programming. NewWave is task oriented rather than application oriented. Users create and define objects that can be linked or embedded with other objects regardless of the application in which the objects were created.

Originally released in early 1988 as an extension to Microsoft's Windows, the product is now available across many GUIs. NewWave features an Object Management Facility (OMF) that lets software pieces be incorporated from a number of applications into NewWave documents. A task master called the Agent acts as a macro processor to automate repetitive tasks. NewWave, as such, is partially a GUI and partially an application framework. The NewWave architecture consists of two primary extensions to the GUI: the Object Management Facility (OMF) and the NewWave API. OMF is a collection of system routines that allows objects to exist and then manages static and dynamic relationships between the objects and among tasks. OMF also provides a database of objects, managing the relationship between objects and binding objects to the appropriate executables. Finally, OMF provides an application interface that helps the application programmer maintain consistency in the NewWave environment.

NewWave compensates for the absence of an object-oriented file system in MS-DOS or OS/2 by offering object management on top of these operating systems to incorporate existing non-object-oriented applications. This is similar to another product, Metaphor, from Metaphor, Inc., which provides an environment within which users can access a full object-oriented environment. Metaphor, however, remains closed to existing applications.

NewWave is designed to help users move between applications, create multimedia documents, and update related files from different applications automatically. NewWave treats each object (i.e., a single word, a spreadsheet, or an individual bar in a bar chart) as a separate entity that can be incorporated into other applications and merged with like or unlike data.

NewWave's macro-like *agents* are programmable by users to accomplish frequently performed tasks, for example, the preparation of a sales report. Agent tasks are either performed at the user's command or automatically triggered by a predetermined event. For example, the agent can be taught to check sales totals from a database at certain times of the day and send an electronic message summarizing the data to the sales manager. However, to exploit fully the agent capabilities within an application, a developer must program for NewWave API. Agents can also record and replay keystroke macros for non-NewWave applications.

The *hot connect* facility of NewWave automatically updates files created in different applications. Hot connect can be used, for example, to keep a spreadsheet in the accounting department in alignment with a database in the order-processing department. Like Windows' DDE, NewWave links allow one application to update a linked application automatically without any intermediate program invocation by the user. NewWave's hot links are more advanced than DDE's because they are persistent. When two programs linked by DDE are shut down, the link is lost.

NewWave uses a database to record a list of the links created among applications. This database causes the application to perform object-oriented-like behavior. For example, when a spreadsheet object is changed and the spreadsheet is linked to a report object, the changes made in the spreadsheet are also reflected in the report. This is similar to Apple's live cut and paste, previously described. The database can accommodate standard character-based programs and data through its encapsulation facility, which essentially repackages character-based graphics elements that can be recognized by NewWave. This allows a smooth development path for systems developers. A developer can write a browser for an encapsulated word processing system, for example. The browser provides a graphics-based screen that reflects absolutely the data represented in the underlying application. These encapsulated objects can then be used as elements (objects) within a NewWave compound document.

Copying and sharing of data is also allowed within OMF. Sharing allows an object to be displayed in several places concurrently without replicating the physical data. Manipulating any one of the shared data images causes a concurrent change to all other images of the object, as well as the original object. Sharing provides three types of links: simple,

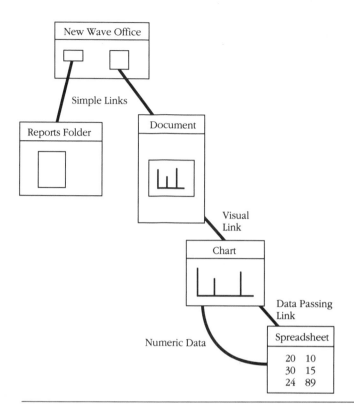

Figure 6.13
Three Types of
Linking Objects
under OMF

visual, and data processing (or numeric). All shared and linked objects are persistent.

Simple links refer to containment (such as a file within a folder). Visual links allow objects to appear as parts of other objects, for example, when a graphic appears in a document. The host object has no knowledge of the guest object; OMF maintains the link. Thus, adding a new data type (e.g., voice or video) is simply a matter of writing to the OMF API. No changes to other objects in the system are needed. Data processing links provide direct connection to a data source. For example, a document may contain a visually linked chart, while the chart has a data processing link to a data table. Figure 6.13 illustrates OFM's three types of linking.

The distributed version of NewWave, for IBM's OS/2 operating system, also supports the concept of distributed objects. This means that an object can reside on a workstation while the application that created it resides on a server. Users can update an object on one workstation and expect that the update will appear instantly in other files containing that object across the network. In the near future, the Agent facilities will likely be expanded to allow users to create and save tasks spanning several applications across a network of workstations and servers.

Caseworks

CASE:W and CASE:PM from Caseworks, Inc., are examples of code generation tools to build GUIs for Windows and PM that use expert system technology. Caseworks products are based on a proprietary Software Engineering Language (SEL), which is part of an expert system (or inference engine) that automates code generation for graphical features such as dialog boxes and pull-down menus.

CASE:W is a Windows application development system that provides a convenient programmer interface to the Windows Software Development Kit, as well as the compilers and linkers required to develop Windows applications. A high-level prototyper allows construction of the Windows interface and automatically generates the C language program modules and associated files needed to make the program. Entry points, or *hooks*, are provided for linking user-generated program codes. CASE:W and user-generated code is automatically regenerated each time the Window components are redesigned.

CASE:PM is a PM application development system that generates the standard OS/2 PM interface routines (i.e., Main, Winpro, and Dialog Processing) and provides a framework for application-specific code. CASE:PM also generates an application's header (.H file), resource scripts (.RC files), module definition (.DEF files), and its make file. The program provides configuration management and a make facility.

The embedded expert systems of both CASE:PM and CASE:W contain a knowledge base of code sets and production rules for effective PM and Windows development. The expert system evaluates the prototype the developer builds as a preprocess to code generation. Used in combination with Hewlett-Packard's NewWave, Caseworks products provide a development environment similar to NeXT's NeXTStep. Used in isolation, Caseworks tools generate only an application skeleton of the GUI for complex environments such as Windows and PM.

CommonView

CommonView is a C++ library designed by Glockenspiel Limited for windowing applications using C++. Targeted for a number of windowing systems including Windows, PM, X Window, and NeWS, CommonView

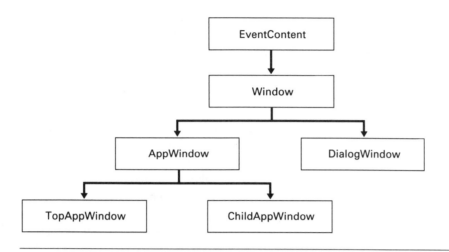

Figure 6.14
Window Hierarchy
in CommonView

encapsulates the large set of function calls used in these environments. For example, the entire Windows interface, representing over 400 function calls, is encapsulated into 30 classes. Because CommmonView is written in C++, it includes all the object-oriented features of the C++ language (cf. Chapter 4). Within CommonView there are several class hierarchies. The Window hierarchy, as illustrated in Figure 6.14, contains the classes concerned with the generation, reception, and handling of events.

CommonView event handlers are provided with each window and determine the effects a particular user action will have on the window. Actions cause the dispatcher or event handler to invoke the correct handler on the window. Event handlers are implemented as virtual functions within the window class and as such can be overloaded by the programmer. Default and programmer-overloaded event handlers control the interactions of the windowing system and user or applications program.

Three sets of functions determine the on-screen characteristics of the window. These function sets include size and appearance, painting and drawing, and selection (e.g., cursor, bitmap). AppWindow class contains subclasses TopAppWindow (the parent) and ChildAppWindow (the child). ChildAppWindow may have only one parent. DialogWindows are input/output objects representing legal controls available to the user. EventContent class abstracts the commonality of the CommonView event receiver classes and contains the CommonView event-dispatching mechanism. The Dispatcher is a default event handler implemented as a protected virtual function (i.e., method). The Window class, which is derived from EventContext, contains the actual Dispatcher for all CommonView applications. When a message is received from the underlying windowing system for which there is no CommonView event then Default is evoked. It is also evoked if a message is received for which the Default is not overridden.

Other classes provided with Common View include the Standard-Components classes (e.g., cursor, brush, icon), the Controls classes (e.g., the scroll bars and buttons), and the Container class library (e.g., heap, stack, ring, and table). CommonView, like other high-level toolkits, provides a higher level of abstraction via the class library; this results in less complexity in development and less code. In addition, the C++ language upon which CommonView is based provides the full features of an object-oriented language, as well as the familiarity of the C and C++ language.

NeWS

Sun Microsystems' Network/Extensible Window System (NeWS), announced in late 1986, is a "synthesis of the window server and page-description technologies" (Gosling et al. 1989). NeWS is based on both X Window and Carnegie-Mellon University's Andrew.

NeWS runs on a variety of Sun platforms with one or more bit mapped displays. NeWS acts as a window server that manages input and output on its host machine. Application programs (called clients) send messages from anywhere on a network causing NeWS to render images on the display. Figure 6.15 shows the basic NeWS architecture.

NeWS does not enforce a particular user interface. In fact, several different window styles are implemented by packages dynamically downloaded into NeWS when requested by individual users on a distributed network. These packages are typically programmed with high-level toolkits such as Xt. As a default the user interface can be programmed directly to NeWS using the Adobe PostScript program.

Figure 6.15
NeWS Protocol over a Network Connection (after Gosling et al. 1989)

NeWS provides mechanisms to support an object-oriented style of programming as implemented in PostScript code on the server. Predefined classes, represented as dictionaries, can be used on new subclasses created. Unlike most object-oriented languages, NeWS allows new methods to be added to a class at any time by sending code for the method to the object. Lite is a NeWS user interface kit which provides a basic Object class and Window, Menu, and Stem subclasses. The user interface can be constructed by writing subclasses for these predefined classes. Window is a drawing surface with methods such as resizing and repositioning. Menus associate keys with actions. Items are graphic interactive objects, such as a slider or scrollbar.

Metaphor

Metaphor is a user interface for database access. Metaphor is not a database engine itself; actual information from a database is obtained by generating SQL searches. Any task or series of operations defined for the system can be saved in a procedure, which Metaphor calls a capsule. Capsules can also call other capsules and can be either private or public.

Metaphor is not object oriented in the full sense, but has objectlike functionality. Capsules, like objects, can contain both data and procedures, and one capsule can invoke another capsule. However this invocation is more like a function call than message passing. Inheritance is also not provided, although users can modify the contents of established capsules.

Summary

While graphical user interfaces have greatly improved applications' ease of use, they have equally increased the difficulty and complexity of the programming task. Standards in look and feel of the GUI, led by the Apple Macintosh and IBM CUA definitions, have allowed the evolution of predefined class libraries to mitigate some of this inherent programming complexity. Most development environments for GUIs focus primarily on the windowing system and employ predefined classes and subclasses with inheritance. Few classes provide tools to program automatically the intricacies of the message-based event loops controlling the user and application interfaces.

High-level toolkits are available for many of the GUIs. These toolkits provide more robust class libraries and further abstract the voluminous function libraries present in GUIs, such as Windows and PM. Some, like NeXTStep, also automate much of the complex event loop and message queue.

Key Points

■ GUIs consist of four components: windowing system, imaging system, API, and tools.

■ GUIs employ object-oriented functions, primarily in the windowing components and toolkits. Such functions include support of predefined classes, subclassing via inheritance, and message-based event control.

■ The user capability for direct manipulation of screen-based objects is directly related to the level of object-orientation supported in the GUI development environment.

■ Complete interoperability between applications from different vendors is usually not supported by most GUI development environments.

■ Three categories of GUIs exist: IBM, SAA (PM and Windows), UNIX (X and NeXT), and Apple Macintosh. Each has numerous high-level toolkits that provide more robust class libraries and expanded object-oriented functionality.

■ The object-oriented functionality of the high-level toolkits is gradually being integrated into the basic development environment delivered with GUIs.

For Further Study

Apple Developer University Register, 20525 Mariani Avenue, Cupertino, Ca. 95014. (408)974-6215.
  Contact Apple Developer University Register for information about courses on MacApp and object-oriented programming.

MacApp Developer's Association, P.O. Box 23, Everett, Wa. 98206. (206)252-6946.
  The MacApp Developer's Association offers a number of useful products and a monthly newsletter.

The following books are guides to using various GUI toolkits:

Gosling, J., Rosenthal, D., Arden, M. 1989. *The NeWS book: Introduction to Network/Extensible Window System,* New York: Springer-Verlag.

Hewlett-Packard. 1988. *HP NewWave Environment: General Information Manual for Software Developers.* Palo Alto, Calif.: Hewlett-Packard.

Neuwirth, C.M., and Ogura, A. 1988. *The Andrew System Programmer's Guide to the Andrew Toolkit, Volume 1: Theory and Examples.* Pittsburgh, Pa.: Carnegie-Mellon University.

Petzold,C. 1989. *Programming the OS/2 Presentation Manager.* Redmond, Wa.: Microsoft Press.

Robertson, J., Mauro, T., and Helbrig, K. A. 1988. *Guide to Andrew (X Version 11, Release 3)* Pittsburgh, Pa: Information Technology Center, Carnegie-Mellon University.

Schmucker, K. J. 1986. *Object-Oriented Programming for the Macintosh.* Hasbrouck Heights, N.J.: Hayden Books.

Southerton, A. 1989. *Programmer's Guide to Presentation Manager.* Reading, Mass.: Addison-Wesley.

Young, D. A. 1989. *X Window Systems Programming Applications with Xt.* Englewood Cliffs, N.J.: Prentice Hall.

References

Asente, P. 1988. "Simplicity and productivity," *UNIX Review,* September.

Dodani, M. H., Hughes, C. E., and Moshell, M. J. 1989. "Separation of powers." *Byte,* March.

Hayes, F., and Baran, N. 1989. "A Guide to GUIs." *Byte,* July.

Machtrone, B. 1989. "Object-oriented: Old wine, new bottles?" *PC Magazine,* May 16.

Millikin, M. 1988. Remark made at Patricia Seybold's Technology Forum on Object Orientation. Boston, Mass., April 5.

Neuwirth, C.M., and Ogura A. 1988. *The Andrew System Programmer's Guide to the Andrew Toolkit, Volume 2: Reference.* Pittsburgh, Pa.: Carnegie-Mellon University.

O'Reilly, T. 1989. "The toolkits (and politics) of X Windows." *UNIX World,* February.

Petzold, C. 1989. "The truth about Presentation Manager." *PC Magazine,* April 11.

Poole, L. 1989. "System 7.0." *MacWorld,* August.

Thompson, T. 1989. "The NeXTStep." *Byte,* March.

Young, D. A. 1989. *X Windows Systems Programming and Applications with Xt.* Englewood Cliffs, N.J.: Prentice Hall.

Part 3

Developing Object-Oriented Applications

- **Analysis and Design**

- **Programming and Maintenance**

- **Emerging Applications**

Chapter 7

Analysis and Design

- ■ **History of Object-Oriented Analysis and Design**
    Structured System Analysis
    Object-Oriented Analysis

- ■ **Benefits of Object-Oriented Analysis and Design**

- ■ **Process of Object-Oriented Analysis and Design**
    Identifying and Defining the Objects
    Defining and Organizing Classes

- ■ **Emerging Methodologies**

- ■ **Summary**

This chapter provides an overview of the basic issues and approaches associated with the analysis and design of object-oriented systems. In this chapter we shall compare conventional structured analysis techniques with object-oriented techniques. We shall identify and define the key issues of object-oriented design. We shall also examine the alternative approaches to automated and paper-based analysis and design methodologies.

Read this chapter to examine the process of designing object-oriented systems.

Automated structured analysis and design tools, promoted with front-end Computer-Assisted Software Engineering (CASE) products, achieved considerable popularity in the 1980s. These tools have had particular appeal to management information system (MIS) managers who anticipated developing much better controlled software assembly lines. Although such software automation aids won many converts among programmers in the data-processing and management information systems (DP/MIS) organizations, they were not accepted by the programming community at large nor by commercial software developers in particular.

The introduction of object-oriented programming has been much different. The movement to accept this new paradigm has been a grass-roots one. The traditional spokesmen of structured systems (e.g., De Marco and Constantine) have not encouraged the object-oriented paradigm; rather, it has been ushered in by major software companies such as Microsoft Corporation, Borland International, and Software Publishing Corporation, whose programmers are already using object-oriented techniques. Such acceptance is soon likely to be mirrored in the DP/MIS community. This acceptance will force extension or replacement of current structured analysis and design methodologies.

History

Given the importance of understanding and communicating a system's requirements before it is programmed, system designers have continued to search for improved approaches for this early phase of the development process. Early approaches relied heavily on paper-based textual descriptions. These approaches led not only to ambiguity but also to difficulty in supporting change and an inability in supporting design of very large systems. Structured analysis, based primarily on decomposing functional components of a system was developed in the 1960s and introduced a more manageable and definitive approach to systems analysis. Object-oriented systems analysis is a new approach that emphasizes defining the characteristics and behavior within a system of objects.

Structured System Analysis

Traditional programmers are familiar with the processes of structured system analysis. The formalization of structured analysis was driven by the realization that subprograms could serve as an abstraction mechanism for building large and complex systems. The oldest and most familiar of structured analysis processes is functional decomposition. As the name indicates, functional decomposition views a system as a set of functional areas that can be divided into processes. These processes are then decomposed into steps or procedures understandable by those who are involved in the system design, including end users and developers. As shown in Figure 7.1, the decomposition of a distribution function yields process and subprocesses that ultimately result in procedural parts. The resulting notation, a structure chart, shows specific function

Functional Areas   **Processes**   **Parts of a Procedure**

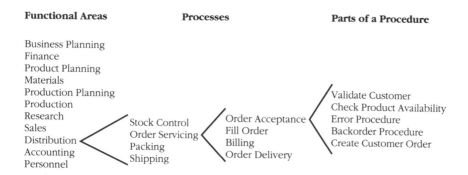

Figure 7.1
Functional Decomposition: The Top-Down Approach of Structured Analysis (Martin and McClure 1988)

modules and their activation by other modules. The final program specifications fit well with the sequence, selection, and repetitive control structures provided by procedural languages.

Functional decomposition has achieved great popularity since its introduction in the late 1970s. Popular methods and notations for functional decomposition are identified by the names of their authors: Yourdon, Constantine, DeMarco, and Gane. For real-time systems, functional decomposition methods were extended by Hatley and Pirbhai.

Because standards exist for its notation and software is available to support the design process, the functional decomposition approach has a strong following. However, functional decomposition has disadvantages. The structural design approach is straightforward, but it forces programmers to focus on operations with little regard for the structure of the data. The designs often result in more code and less data, because the organization of data is a derivative of the processes and their need to interact. Also, the design approach is not well bounded; different analysts working on the same design are likely to arrive at different results.

A second type of structured analysis is referred to as event response. This form was introduced in 1984 by Stephen McMenamin and John Palmer and was later adapted for real-time systems by Stephen Mellor and Paul Ward. Unlike functional decomposition, event-response analysis focuses on external events to derive the system's processes. The system is viewed as a black box that responds to events occurring outside of it, with each event resulting in the definition of a system process. As in functional decomposition, the final stage of the design is to link the processes together with data. Like functional decomposition, the models are easy to understand and often result in excessive code.

Object-Oriented Analysis

Information modeling, popularized by Peter Chen in the 1980s, is the closest precursor to object-oriented analysis and design. The end result of information-modeling analysis is an entity relationship diagram, developed by listing attributes, sorting them into entity categories, and then adding the relationships between them. The initial model is subsequently refined with a hierarchy of subtypes and associative objects. Although this approach is closely related to object-oriented analysis, there is no encapsulation of data; that is, the processing requirements for each object and its attributes are not treated as a combined entity. Neither are inheritance and message-passing supported in the information-modeling approach.

The first published material on object-oriented analysis was from Sally Shlaer and Stephen Mellor (1988). Their approach, as will be detailed later in this chapter, starts by defining objects and attributes. Life cycles of the objects are then defined in state models to capture the events acting on the objects. The last step is process definition, based on the objects and their life cycles. Unlike the functional decomposition and event-response methods, the object-oriented approach results in minimal data-driven code that remains stable even when requirements are changing.

The three components of a system—process (what is being done), data (what the process is being performed on), and control (when it is being done)—are given different priority and emphasis in the functional decomposition, event-response, and object-oriented approaches. Table 7.1 summarizes the components of these three approaches to analysis and shows the sequence in which they are considered.

In an object-oriented system the emphasis is not on transformations of input to output, but on the content of entities, the objects. The criterion for grouping functions together is not process; rather, methods are grouped together if they operate on the same data abstraction. Neighboring methods in a sequence may well reside in different objects.

	Functional Decomposition	Event Response	Object Oriented
Table 7.1 Three Approaches to Systems Analysis	1. Process 2. Control 3. Data	1. Control 2. Process 3. Data	1. Data 2. Control 3. Process

Structured Analysis and Design	Object-Oriented Analysis and Design	**Table 7.2** Structured Analysis Compared to Object-Oriented Analysis
Top-down: Functional decomposition based on subprocess of higher level process	Bottom-up: Class composition based on data abstraction	

It is message passing among objects that determines the sequence of operations. Table 7.2 summarizes the divergence of the top-down approach of structured analysis from the bottom-up approach in an object-oriented system.

Benefits

Few of the current structured analysis and design tools address the mechanisms of object-oriented programming. Some methodologies embedded in automated tools are promoted as object-oriented. In most cases the objects referred to are processes, modules, or just binary large objects (blobs), usually diagrams. To support object-oriented programming, the analysis and design tools must focus on:

- the identification of objects and definition of classes,

- the hierarchical organization of classes,

- the reuse of classes, and

- the construction of application frameworks from class libraries.

Not only do structured methods not apply to design of object-oriented software, but, in fact, there is no widely accepted object-oriented design method. Perhaps one reason for this is that the object-oriented programming paradigm itself contains important design techniques. The emphasis on reuse, modularity, and encapsulation, as well as the strong linkage between design and code are integral parts of object-oriented systems. Because object-oriented systems contain a great deal of the design information, the implementation and design processes merge closer together. Object-oriented programming lets the design of a program shine through the code. A good initial design can be expressed as an early version of the code or the code an early version of the design.

Regardless of the close linkage between design and programming, good analysis and design is still important and yields better systems.

Poorly designed object-oriented applications have the potential for inherent complexity beyond the capabilities of individual programmers. An object-oriented design begins with a set of class definitions. Each class has a set of methods that it defines and a list of objects to which its instances pass messages. A design is complete when each class, method, and message is defined. This design process is often incremental, and designers rarely begin from scratch; instead, they often start from and reuse existing class libraries and tailor generic classes to the system requirements. Therefore, a methodology for this approach needs to provide rules for identifying, defining, and organizing classes and their accompanying methods and messages. It also needs to provide strategies for organizing class libraries and guidelines for building applications from existing frameworks or class libraries.

Object-oriented analysis and design offers significant benefits. For one, good design approaches can insure that the maximum benefit of an object-oriented programming language will be realized, especially where preexisting, robust class libraries are lacking. In fact, even when the design is not implemented using an object-oriented language, an object-oriented design can bring some of the benefits of object-oriented systems to languages that do not fully support the concepts. An object-oriented design also usually results in less, more reusable, code than the process-intensive procedural decomposition approach produces.

In addition, the object-oriented design approach tends to result in systems that are resilient to change. It focuses on the elements of the system that are most stable—the objects. This stability and resiliency is present in the design itself. When change is necessary, the unique property of inheritance allows reuse and extension of the existing model.

The modularity of the object-oriented approach benefits the development team as well. Because the data and processes are localized within objects, it's easy to have several teams working independently on different parts of the design. Finally, the object-oriented design approach is more intuitive, not only to the analyst but also to the end user, because its approach to organizing and understanding the problem space is natural; it is based on the way humans think.

Process

The result of an object-oriented design is a hierarchy of classes. Each class is a self-contained module with both control and data structures. The problem domain can be viewed more naturally and realistically as a collection of objects and associated methods. The initial elements of an object-oriented design are the objects. Later, as commonalties are identified, objects are clustered into classes which are in turn subclassed into more abstract classes. The highest level of abstraction is commonly referred to as a framework. A framework is a set of classes that express a design for a family of related applications. Structured approaches and accompanying structure charts define an application as a sequential set of interdependent modules with shared data. Object approaches define a set of self-contained communicating modules with limited visibility to one another.

In essence, object-oriented design consists of four fundamental steps:

1. Identifying and defining objects and classes.

2. Organizing relationships among the classes.

3. Cultivating frameworks in a hierarchy of classes.

4. Building reusable class libraries and application frameworks.

Like the prototyping approach applied to traditional systems, object-oriented design is cyclical. Programmers start with a set of classes, extend them, modify them and assemble them as a prototype of an application. Interaction with end users usually causes the prototype to be revised and then the analysts or programmers take over again. Throughout this cycle, classes are refined and reorganized, and whenever it is noticed that a class is generic enough to be reused in subsequent applications, it is added to the standard class libraries. Framework designers subsequently spot similarities among applications and develop class-bound frameworks that are useful as programming solutions to similar future problems.

Identifying and Defining the Objects

The design of an object-oriented system begins with objects. Finding these objects is perhaps the central challenge of object-oriented analysis and design. Several approaches have been used for object identification, including grammatical inspection of documents and derivation from data flow and entity relationship diagrams.

Grady Booch (1983) originated the grammatical approach and suggests that the designer start with a prose description of the desired system and look to the nouns as potential identifiers of the classes of objects. Verbs, on the other hand, identify methods. The resulting list of classes (nouns) and methods (verbs) is then used to start the design process.

What follows is an example of Booch's lexical approach to object-oriented systems design. Booch's methodology, although tied to Ada, is useful for procedurally-oriented programmers who want to gain an object-oriented perspective. Booch's methodology begins with a definition of the problem and a description of the solution, as shown in the following example.

- *Statement of the problem:* Develop a very simple word processing program.

- *Description of the solution:* The word processing system allows users to create documents. Created documents are saved on a user's directory. Users can print or display documents. Documents can be changed. Documents can be deleted from a user's directory.

The next step is identifying potential objects by underlining the nouns (and noun phrases), as shown below:

The word processing system allows creation of documents. Created documents are saved on a user's directory. Users can print or display documents. Documents can be changed. Documents can be deleted from a user's directory.

Document and directory appear to be key concepts, and hence, objects. It should be noted that not all nouns that appear in an initial description of the system ultimately become objects. Although the grammatical method is a good way to develop an initial list of possible classes, it will generate a number of concepts that are outside the system being modeled and don't need to be incorporated into the software. Our description contains a classic example of this in the noun *user*.

After the objects are identified, Booch suggests associating attributes with each object. In the word-processing example, the objects and their attributes are as follows:

Object	Attributes
Document	can be created
	can be deleted
	can be saved (on disk)
	can be printed
	can be displayed
	can be changed

Object	Attributes
Directory	contains one or more documents
	documents may be saved on the directory, deleted from the directory

The next step in the Booch process is to identify potential methods by underlining the verbs, as follows:

The word processing system <u>allows</u> users <u>to create</u> documents. Created documents <u>are saved</u> on a user's directory. Users <u>can print</u> or <u>display</u> documents. Documents <u>can be changed</u>. A document <u>can be deleted</u> from a user's directory.

These methods are then collected with their respective objects, as follows:

Object	Method	
Document	create	save
	print	display
	change	delete
Directory	save	delete

Defining the interfaces among objects is the final step in the Booch process. Again a written description is created. From the example this description would be as follows:

The system is implemented as two classes, document and directory.

The class document contains an instance variable called documentid (its own name) and the following methods: create, save, print, display, change, and delete. The class directory contains directoryid and methods for save and delete.

Booch provides a simple strategy for identifying objects and methods by analyzing a text description and mapping nouns to objects and verbs to classes or methods. This noun and verb approach is a reasonable start, but it hides some of the complexity in class definition. Often classes are needed for operations in the verb part of the problem domain. For example, descriptions of compilers consist primarily of verbs describing how the compiler operates on a source program. But, because compilation is so complex, it is wise to identify separate compiler objects, for example, a parser and a code generator. Subdividing compilation into classes illustrates that a procedure can be implemented as a method in a class or as a separate class.

Even with the straightforward Booch approach for finding classes, achieving a high-quality result is difficult. In particular, it is difficult to come up with useful abstractions from the problem definition. A useful abstraction results from a clever factoring of the problem description into independent and intuitively correct elements. Useful abstractions are usually created by programmers who have both an obsession for simplicity and the patience to rework the design several times until the classes are easy to understand and easy to specialize. Even more rare are programmers who can go a step further to make application-specific solutions into elements of a generic library. Preexisting class libraries mitigate some of these design challenges.

Beyond the Booch approach, methodologies to support object-oriented analysis and design are in their initial stages of development, and few automated tools are available. Most early users of object-oriented languages and tools have relied on combinations of paper-based methodologies and published experience of practitioners.

No strict rules exist for identifying classes, but experienced practitioners have offered various rules of thumb. There is general agreement that the following guidelines help to identify and define classes and methods.

- Model with classes the entities that naturally occur in the problem domain.

- Design methods with a single purpose.

- Design a new method when faced with a choice of extending an existing one.

- Avoid lengthy methods.

- Store as instance variables the data that are needed by more than one method, or by a subclass.

- Design for the class library, not for yourself alone or your current application.

Practitioners have also identified mistakes that novices commonly make in this initial phase of designing object-oriented systems. Common mistakes include creating unneeded classes and declaring classes that are not classes at all. Designers are encouraged to stick to the fundamental guideline that each class should correspond to a meaningful data abstraction. There are many potential classes (i.e., many nouns); unneeded ones are not central to the solution of the problem at hand. A single method or routine is not a good candidate for a class. In contrast to a routine that performs a particular task, a class should offer a number of services to objects of a certain type (Meyer 1989).

Johnson and Foote (1989) examine the question of when to create a new class and when to add a method to an existing class. Although they caution that their criteria are not absolute, they suggest that a new class be created when:

■ the new class represents a meaningful abstraction for the problem domain,

■ the services it provides are likely to be used by several other classes,

■ its behavior is inherently complex,

■ the class or method makes little use of the representations of its operands, and

■ if represented as a method of another class, few users of that class would invoke it.

The compiler example mentioned previously illustrates the dilemma of implementing behavior as a class versus a method. The compiler's parser might well be modeled as a class or as a method. And, assuming that parser is a method, then it can be difficult to decide which class should contain the parser method.

Predefined class libraries simplify much of the design process and help avoid many of the difficulties in determining what should be implemented as classes and methods. Designers should always look at preexisting classes first, both those supplied with languages and development environments and those that are programmer created. This advice is given with the caveat that additional design time should always be dedicated to making the preexisting classes more general and robust.

Pun and Hilden (1989) caution that two layers of object identification should be brought into design, at least at the conceptual level. These two layers include the application objects and the user interface objects. Application objects are those objects that are not transparent to the user. This is consistent with the Smalltalk model-view-controller (MVC) framework discussed in Chapter 6.

Defining and Organizing Classes

Identifying and defining the objects is only the first step in designing an object-oriented system. Abstraction is the continuing task of the object-oriented designer. After the objects are defined, the next step is to gather common object definitions together in a class abstraction. Classes then relate to one another and form class libraries. Finally, a class library can be refined into an abstract framework useful for creating categories of application. The need for and benefits of abstraction are pervasive in object-oriented system development. And, as previously indicated, no formal methodologies exist.

Defining a class to generate multiple instances of an object offers the first glimpse of the power of abstraction. In Booch's word processor example, directory was identified as an object. If the word processing system supports many users, each user will require a unique directory object. So the class directory is created, and each user's directory is an instance of this class with access to the directory methods.

If the word processing system is expanded to be an office automation system with word processing, time management, and desktop publishing capabilities, then the nature of the object document will change. Word processing, time management, and desktop publishing each has documents with unique characteristics of its own. As illustrated in Figure 7.2, in this office automation system, document becomes a superclass, including instance variables and methods common to all the documents. Special subclasses of document include additional methods and instance variables to support local needs. The time management system, for example, might need a special document subclass called calendar.

As this office automation example illustrates, the ultimate goal of

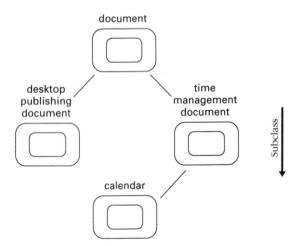

Figure 7.2
Subclasses of the
Class document

object-oriented systems design is to store methods and class data at the highest level of abstraction possible. The higher a method is stored in the hierarchy of the class library, the more subclasses can share it. In this way, reuse is achieved with the largest possible granularity.

Although formal or automated methodologies for refining class hierarchies do not exist, Johnson and Foote (1989) provide one of the few documented rule sets for achieving high-quality design of reusable classes. Their rules are organized into three categories:

- improving standard protocols,

- constructing abstract classes, and

- identifying frameworks.

Standard protocols are the names and behavior of the messages and methods. In order to form a superclass, a set of classes must share a standard protocol. In other words, if the conventions for naming nearly identical interfaces and common sets of operations are not consistent, then the composition process is impeded. Four rules suggested by Johnson and Foote are aimed at improving the quality of standard protocols:

1. Give messages and methods similar or identical names when one class communicates with other classes in order to perform similar operations.

2. Rework any code that explicitly checks the class of an object. Instead, design classes so that a message can be sent directly to an object and be handled properly by methods therein.

3. Reduce the number of arguments by breaking one message into several. This increases the likelihood of messages with similar arguments which should be named identically. Or consider creating a new class that represents a small group of arguments. The threshold for concern is a half dozen arguments or more.

4. Reduce the size of methods. When a method grows too large, it is less likely to be inherited as it is more likely to include "extra baggage." Smaller methods, on the other hand, can be selectively inherited, refined, or overridden. The threshold for concern is a method of thirty lines or more.

Experienced practitioners also suggest that a robust class library should be deep and narrow with several levels of subclassing. Shallow, wide hierarchies suggest the need for design improvement, although finding ways to build composite classes may be difficult. The following rules suggest ways to construct abstract classes:

1. Identify common messages and methods and migrate them to a superclass. This may require breaking methods apart and dividing them between superclass and subclasses.

2. Eliminate from a superclass those methods that are frequently overridden rather than inherited by its subclasses. This will make the superclass more abstract and hence more generally useful.

3. Access all variables only by sending messages. Classes will be more abstract when they depend less on their data representations.

4. Rework subclasses to be specializations. A subclass is a specialization if it inherits all superclass methods and adds new methods of its own. A subclass should always express a superset of its parent's behavior.

Frameworks are the ultimate goal of object-oriented design, as they represent the highest level of abstraction. Frameworks provide a greater leverage to programmers than class libraries because they allow reuse of an entire object-oriented design. Examples of frameworks are Apple Computer's MacApp, Whitewater Group's Actor and NeXT's Interface Builder, all discussed in Part 2. Since frameworks are the ultimate goal in design reusability, their design requires skill and experimentation.

Frameworks are identified by examining large classes and reconsidering how they are factored. The result of different factoring is a collection of class hierarchies, each organized to support particular categories of application. Large classes destroy the reusability of object-oriented systems and generally preempt the evolution of class libraries and frameworks. Johnson and Foote (1989) suggest some rules of thumb for identifying and cultivating the evolution of frameworks:

1. Identify subclasses that all implement the same method in different ways. If a method is always redefined, it must not be an integral part of the superclass. Reconsider where these methods might better be located.

2. Identify and divide classes where some methods access only some instance variables and other methods access only the other instance variables.

3. Send messages to other classes instead of to the class itself. Replace inheritance-based framework into component-based frameworks by replacing overridden methods with messages sent to components.

4. Identify sets of methods combined in a class only to access a common instance variable. Consider migrating one or more methods to other classes. Change methods to pass parameters explicitly. This will facilitate the splitting of classes.

Emerging Methodologies

Current methodologies for object-oriented analysis and design are varied. Some meld the top-down approach of structured analysis with rules of thumb from experienced object-oriented systems designers. Other approaches begin by building a familiar data flow diagram as the initial process of identifying objects. Most approaches are also aided by both paper-based and automated notation systems for representing classes, methods, messaging, and inheritance.

Object-oriented design methodologies are still in their early stages. Like the various object-oriented programming languages, terminology for the object-oriented mechanisms differs among methodologies. Unlike the object-oriented languages, no standard or de facto standard methodologies have been established. Although early attempts have not achieved widespread commercial use, some of these methodologies form the foundation for methods and notation standards of the future. Examples of early methodologies include General Object-Oriented Software Development (GOOD), Hierarchical Object-Oriented Design (HOOD), and Multiple-view Object-Oriented Design Methodology (MOOD). These methodologies were primarily developed for use in the Ada programming environment. GOOD, HOOD, and MOOD are summarized in Wasserman, Pircher, and Muller (1989).

GOOD uses dataflow diagrams in the specification phase to identify abstract entities that become objects in the design phase. HOOD is a derivative of the Booch approach that was originally developed for the European Space Agency. Like Booch's approach, it starts by decomposing the problem into objects and methods from the nouns and verbs used in a textual description. Formalization and organization of the objects is then undertaken using graphics based on Booch diagrams. Further formalization of the object interfaces is then completed, using an

Figure 7.3
Subject Layer for
Coad's Layered
Methodology
(Coad, 1989)

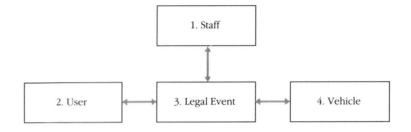

Ada-like Process Description Language. HOOD has no classes or inheritance, making it unsuitable in its current state for full object-oriented analysis and design. MOOD, like GOOD, starts with a structured model, in this case the Ward/Mellor structured analysis methodology. MOOD supports the object-oriented paradigm but requires concurrent processes to be expressed as tasks, an Ada convention, rather than objects.

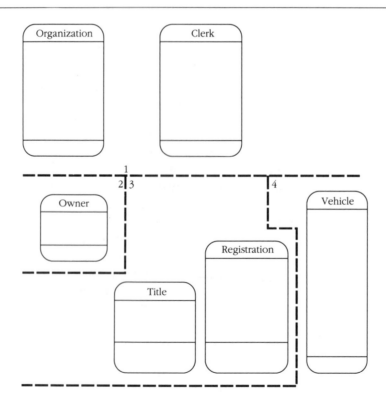

Figure 7.4
Object Layer for
Coad's Layered
Methodology
(Coad, 1989)

The close coupling of these early methods to Ada led to some significant limitations in designing object-oriented systems that were later programmed in more commercially popular languages such as C++. Most notably they tended to be oriented to the Ada definition of an object as a package or a task. Only limited support was provided for inheritance, and the distinction between the definition and use of objects provided little assistance in designing reusable class libraries.

Some, but limited, progress in the formalization of object-oriented design and analysis has occurred beyond the Ada-based methodologies. No formal methodologies exist for the identification of the objects in what is commonly referred to as the analysis phase. Frequently, Booch's method is employed. The classification of the objects in the design phase is supported by a number of methodologies and notation systems. Peter Coad (1989) has set forth a methodology that layers the object-oriented model. First, a subject layer is built. This is used to guide the model reader. The next layer, the object layer, represents an abstraction of the data and its processes. Figure 7.3 shows the subject layer, and Figure 7.4 shows the object layer for a vehicle registration system.

The next layer of Coad's model is the structure layer. The structure layer shows the classification or hierarchy of the objects used in the model. For example, from part three of the Figure 7.4 model, Title and Registration are now subclasses of class Legal Event, as shown in Figure 7.5.

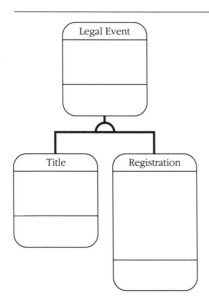

Figure 7.5
Structure Layer for
Coad's Layered
Methodology
(Coad, 1989)

The next layer of the Coad approach is the attribute layer. Coad considers an attribute a data element used to describe an instance of a class. These attributes, such as Number and Fee of Title are shown in the diagram as illustrated in Figure 7.6.

The final layer of Coad's approach is the service layer, which illustrates the methods (or services) of each object, such as Calculate fee and Accept fee of Title. Services are shown in the bottom part of each object in Figure 7.7.

Like Booch's method of identifying the objects and methods, Coad's approach is simple and straightforward in diagramming class structure and methods. Coad's approach is also just a starting point, as it does little to diagram messages, polymorphism, or the complexities of inheritance.

A more recent design methodology, Object-Oriented System Design (OOSD), developed by Wasserman, Pircher, and Muller (1989), extends the early models put forth by HOOD, GOOD and MOOD and provides a more complete notation than Coad. Similar to the earlier methodologies, OOSD relies on some aspects of structured design and attempts to merge the apparent contradiction between it and object-oriented design, namely, top-down versus bottom-up system structuring. OOSD is also less a methodology and more a notation for object-oriented system design. The methodology (or lack thereof) is left to the discretion of the designer. The underlying philosophy of OOSD is that most designs rely

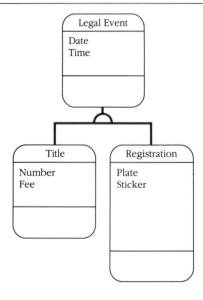

Figure 7.6
Attribute Layer for
Coad's Layered
Methodology

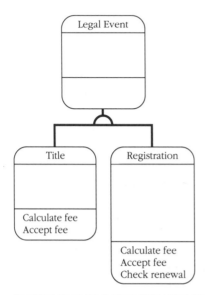

Figure 7.7
Service Layer for
Coad's Layered
Methodology
(Coad, 1989)

on a combination of top-down (structured) techniques for analysis and partitioning of a problem and bottom-up approaches for assembling and building the system. It is often impossible to impose strict design rules on designers and developers.

For the same reasons that programmers have shown a desire to work with hybrid object-oriented languages such as C++, it is likely that systems analysts will prefer tools like OOSD. OOSD provides a bridge from the familiar symbols and processes of structured design. A structure chart is built to assist in the identifying objects. Rules of thumb for object-oriented design, such as Johnson and Foote's, are supported with appropriate notation for classes, methods, messages and inheritance as well as dynamic binding and polymorphism.

In OOSD a class encapsulates methods (called operations) and instance variables (called data objects). The notation provides for explicit representation of a message's arguments (called parameters). OOSD provides ways to illustrate a hierarchy of classes and includes notation for type extension, type specialization, and polymorphism. Central to OOSD is the distinction between definition and reference. Each module of a system is defined once and then reused by reference. As a result, not all elements of a module are reproduced each time the module is displayed. Finally, a distinction is made between *ordinary classes* that are prepared to generate objects and *generic classes* that are capable only of supporting subclasses. The notation system is supported by an automated drawing package supported by a set of underlying design-checking rules.

A simple example illustrates OOSD's object-oriented notations. Consider the class table, as illustrated in Figure 7.8. The table class itself is drawn as a rectangle. The dashed line indicates that table is a generic class. Three methods, represented as boxes along the side of the rectangle, are associated with table: the ability to insert an item, to delete an item, and to search for an item. The arrows are identical to those used in a traditional structure chart. In a structure chart, arrows with an open circle show data passing between process blocks, and closed circles show control information passing between the process blocks. In OOSD, the arrows indicate similar events: arguments to table's messages along with the direction in which they travel. In addition to methods, the generic class diagram shows the names of generic parameters that parameterize any attribute of the class or operation. To specialize table, a value must be set for its size and for the type of rectype records it contains.

Figure 7.9 illustrates a subclass of table, a complex table called cplxtable. While table is a generic class in OOSD terminology, cplxtable is an ordinary class capable of generating an instance or object. Values for instance variables rectype and size specify more precisely that cplxtable shall contain 100 elements (size = 100) that are complex numbers (rectype = complex). Because cplxtable is an ordinary class, it is drawn in OOSD as a solid rectangle. Finally, the solid arrow connecting the two classes indicates that cplxtable inherits from table all methods and in-

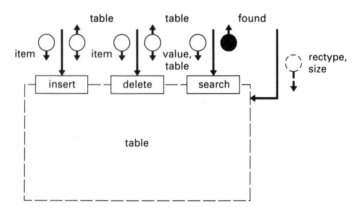

Figure 7.8
Illustration of Class table in OOSD

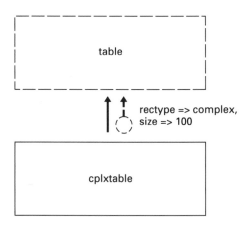

Figure 7.9
Cplxtable Derived
from Generic Class
table in OOSD

stance variables. That is, an object instance of cplxtable will respond to a message requesting that an item be inserted into the table.

OOSD also provides notation for class hierarchies. For example, as shown in Figure 7.10, a symbol table can be defined as a specialization of table. Symbol table inherits the methods and data of table: insert, delete, and search methods, as well as the size and rectype variables. Additional methods, enter block and leave block, specific to symbol table, are added. OOSD's notation of a dashed arrow between the two classes indicates that the properties of table are inherited by symbol table. Both are generic classes, as indicated by the dashed line rectangles.

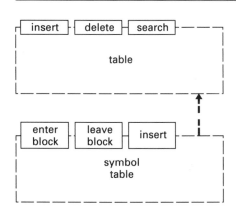

Figure 7.10
Class symbol table
Specialized from
Class table in OOSD

The OOSD notation also supports multiple inheritance. The notation illustrates how the design issue of ambiguity in multiple inheritance is resolved, as shown in the example illustrated in Figure 7.11. The example focuses on the class bh-point, which inherits methods from both history point and bounded point, and indirectly from point as well. A new method, bounds history, is also added. In this example the most abstract class is point, which contains the methods display, location, and move. Bounded point is a specialization of point containing its parent's methods location and display. Bounded point overrides the method move and adds methods min and max. History point is another specialization of point, which inherits methods display and move while overriding location.

The classes responsible for contributing min, max, and display methods are unambiguous because those methods are defined uniquely in the hierarchy. Location and move, however, are not unique. Assume in this example that bh-point inherits the location method from history point and the move method from bounded point. The ambiguity is resolved

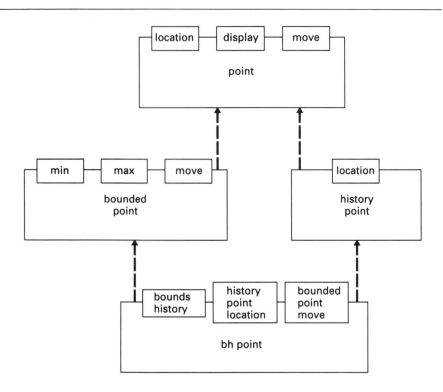

Figure 7.11
Resolving Ambiguity in Multiple Inheritance Using OOSD Notation

and is explicitly noted by naming bh-point methods history point.location and bounded point.move.

The highlighted features of OOSD illustrate its similarity to structured design, plus its additional features for defining classes, including generic definitions, building class hierarchies, and indicating inheritance. In addition, OOSD methodology includes notation for monitors (asynchronous processes), including the event-driven processes found in many real-time systems. For event-driven processes, parallelograms, instead of rectangles, are used to represent classes affected by external operations. The example illustrated in Figure 7.12 shows a buffering monitor that has an internal data object called buffer data, which is affected by two methods: get and put. Buffer contents are passed to and from the buffering task. Solid lines from the get and put processes indicate a direct call. Variations on this notation include a dashed line parallelogram to indicate generic monitors.

In summary, OOSD provides a hybrid notation for combining structured analysis and object-oriented techniques. OOSD diagrams emphasize the definition of generic reusable classes, while relying on the designer to identify classes, messages, and methods from initial specifications. OOSD is an automated system with predefined drawing symbols and extensive design checking for violation of fundamental object-oriented design rules, for example, the issue of inheritance ambiguity discussed previously.

Other notation systems have also been proposed. Shlaer and Mellor (1988) have proposed an analysis methodology and a paper-based notation system called the Information Structure Diagram. It is based on various forms of Entity Relationship Diagrams. The notation is used to describe objects, attributes, and relationships of the model. In this notation, attributes refer to abstractions of a single characteristic possessed

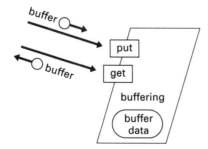

Figure 7.12
Asynchronous Process Notation in OOSD

by instances of an object. Relationships are any pattern of associations between objects.

The Shlaer and Mellor methodology suggests that the analyst construct three formal types of models: an information model, a set of state models, and a set of process models. The information model is represented both graphically and textually and identifies the objects, attributes, and relationships. In the textual representation of the information model, each object becomes a table, and each instance becomes a row in the table. Graphically, the information model shows a global view of each object.

The second type of model, the state model, expands the information model by illustrating the behavior of each object or relationship in the information model. The state model is documented through the use of a standard state transition diagram or a state transition table. The state transition table is an event list or methods list for each object.

The final type of model developed is the process model. In the process model, a dataflow diagram for each method or state is developed. A modified DeMarco diagram is used to document each process.

The Shlaer-Mellor approach is supported by a specific notation system. In Shlaer-Mellor methodology, an object together with its attributes is shown by a box with attributes annotated according to the following rules:

- Prefix any attribute that is part of the preferred identifier with an asterisk.

- Prefix any attribute that is not part of the preferred identifier with a dot or a circle.

- Append an (r) to any attribute that is used to formalize a relationship.

A car object might be represented as shown in Figure 7.13.

Shlaer and Mellor give several rules for assisting the designer in the definition of object attributes:

- Each instance of an object should have exactly one value for each attribute.

- No attribute should contain an internal structure.

- Every attribute should represent a characteristic of the entire object, not just one of its identifiers.

- Every attribute should represent a characteristic of the entire object, and not a characteristic of another attribute.

```
CAR
   *  title #
   *  state
   •  license #
   •  manufacturer
   •  owner (r)
```

Figure 7.13
Object Notation in
Shlaer and Mellor
Form

These rules are familiar to database designers and assure that an object can be represented as a single row in a table with each attribute occupying exactly one cell in the row. For example, if the first rule were broken and an attribute of an object had two values, then those values could not be stored in their allocated location.

Relationships in the Shlaer and Mellor notation are indicated by arrows drawn between the objects. Three types of arrows are used to describe the simple (unconditional) cardinality relationship between pairs of objects. The relationships are as follows:

■ One-to-one, as found between a governor and the state governed.

■ One-to-many, as found between a parent and the children parented.

■ Many-to-many, as found among authors who write books.

Seven conditional and biconditional relationships complete the set. A conditional relationship means that not all instances of an object share the relationship. For example, some books have a single author, and some authors have a single book, and so the many-to-many relationship between authors and books is biconditional. All ten relationships are summarized in Table 7.3. The arrow representing the relationship is an-

Unconditional Forms	← → (1 : 1)	← → (1 : M)	← → (M : M)
Conditional Forms	←C→ (1 : 1c)	C ← → (1c : M) ←C→ (1c : Mc)	←C→ (M : Mc)
Biconditional Forms	C C ← → (1c : 1c)	C C ← → (1c : Mc)	C C ← → (Mc : Mc)

Table 7.3
Relationships
among Objects

notated with the name of the relationship, stated from the point of view of both participating objects. In particular, a verb phrase is placed on the end of the arrow that describes the relationship from each point of view. The notation as illustrated below can be read: "The car owner owns one or more licensed cars." or "A licensed car is owned by a car owner."

For conditional relationships, a "C" is placed near the relationship phrase that is only sometimes true. As shown below, the relationship between a deduction and a paycheck can be read "Deduction is taken on paycheck," and "Paycheck may take deductions."

Shlaer and Mellor also introduce the concept of a correlation table, which is used to model many-to-many relationships. When an associative object arises from a relationship, a diamond is placed on the line representing the relationship, and the associative object is connected to the diamond, as shown in Figure 7.14, which describes the relationship between committees, club members, and committee membership.

The associative object may have one or two arrowheads pointing to the diamond. A single arrowhead indicates that a single instance of the associative object exists for each instance of the association; a double

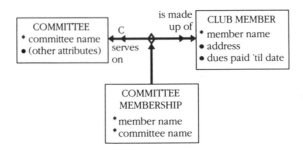

Figure 7.14
Correlation Table
for Many-to-Many
Relationships

arrowhead indicates that many instances of the associative object can exist for each instance of the association. For example, a single license is issued for each legal manufacturer of a drug, but many batches of the drug can be made by each manufacturer, as shown in Figure 7.15.

The Information Structure Diagram methodology also includes notation to denote the case that all instances of one object must be related to all instances of another object. To illustrate this notation Shlaer and Mellor (1989) provide the example of a billing system in which the objects service period and billing group are defined. A service period is defined as a time during which a service is provided and might typically be one month. A billing group is a set of accounts all billed as a unit in a single run. Each account is placed in a single billing group, and every group must be billed in every month. This leads to a many-to-many-all relationship between service period and billing group, which is illustrated in Figure 7.16.

Shlaer and Mellor use the terms subtype and supertype to describe objects related hierarchically. In their notation, a small bar indicates that the object tape mount is the supertype, and operator tape mount and tsar tape mount are subtypes. The notation is illustrated in Figure 7.17.

Shlaer and Mellor recommend numbering the objects and relationships on the Information Structure Diagram, so that the diagram can serve as a graphic table of contents to more detailed textual Object and

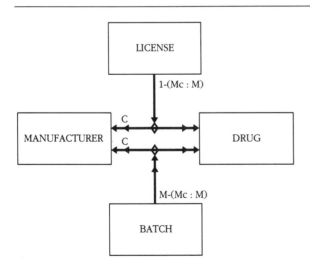

Figure 7.15
Single and Multiple
Instances

Figure 7.16
Many-to-Many-All
Relationships

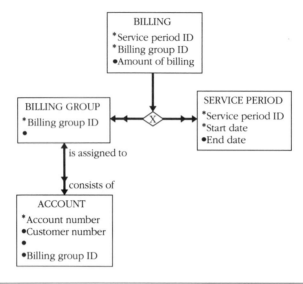

is assigned to

consists of

Relationship Specification documents. Preparing these documents is considered the second step in the Shlaer-Mellor methodology.

In summary, Shlaer and Mellor provide an analysis methodology, a notation system, and a documentation standard for object-oriented system design. The methodology embraces the concept of an object as a record in a database and provides data-analysis strategies for modeling the data. Although it provides the object-oriented designer with a starting point, Shlaer-Mellor methodology fails to account for the vast majority of object-oriented concepts. Unlike Wasserman's OOSD, no new graphic illustrations are provided for object-oriented analysis. Instead, their notation is taken primarily from dataflow diagrams, entity relation-

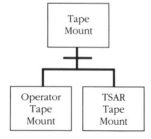

Figure 7.17
Supertype and Sub-
type Relationship

ship diagrams, and state transition diagrams, as found in other structured analysis methods. There is no way to express concepts such as methods or messages, for example. The notion that procedures be encapsulated with data is entirely missing. Finally, the methodology is not automated and relies on paper-based diagramming and unique naming conventions to describe the resulting system.

Other strategies are continually being documented to help designers think in object-oriented terms. One additional example is Class, Responsibility, and Collaboration (CRC) cards (Beck and Cunningham 1989). In this methodology, classes are represented by 4″ by 6″ paper cards, which become the focal point for an object-oriented design review. Each card contains the name of the class it represents. In addition there is a description of the responsibilities (methods) associated with the class, as well as a list of other related classes via message passing. Figure 7.18 shows three CRC cards representing the three central classes in the Smalltalk MVC framework discussed in Chapter 6.

The CRC system is used primarily as a teaching tool and as a methodology for studying the behavior of object-oriented designers. As an

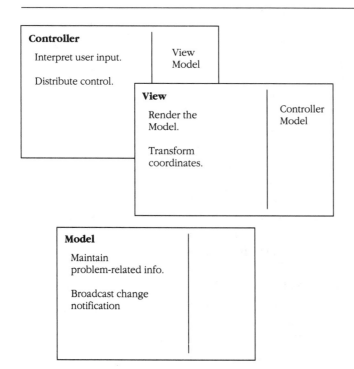

Figure 7.18
CRC Cards Representing the Model-View-Controller Framework (from Beck and Cunningham 1989)

example of the latter, Beck and Cunningham (1989) describe how a design team will lay the CRC cards out on a table in patterns indicating clusters of interrelated classes or lay one card atop another to indicate the control one object has over another. CRC cards are also a memory aid and help experienced and novice programmers communicate with one another about modeling the world with objects.

Summary

With continuing experience, rigorous analysis techniques will emerge to support object-oriented analysis and design. In part these methods will reflect a merging with structured analysis techniques. In larger measure, the methods will reflect a change in analysis strategy necessary to encompass the fundamental mechanisms and challenges of object-oriented system construction. Until then, the design of object-oriented systems will require skill and experience. Rules of thumb, in combination with automated notational systems, will guide the learning process. Several distinct benefits result from the use of an object-oriented design. First, the use of an object-oriented design approach helps insure that the full capabilities of an object-oriented language be utilized. Second, the use of this approach results in both designs and systems that are resilient to change. Finally, an object-oriented design is more intuitive to developers and users alike.

Practitioners agree that the process of object identification and class definition can be learned even by those who begin with a traditional structured systems perspective. Techniques such as Booch's lexical analysis or the CRC cards of Beck and Cunningham will accelerate the process. However, the process of organizing class libraries and designing application frameworks requires much more skill and experimentation.

Automated notation systems that automatically critique a design with proven rules of thumb are likely to provide valuable assistance for the novice system designer. On the other hand, the availability of class libraries and application-specific frameworks will also mitigate some of the design challenges.

Finally, object orientation itself enhances the design process. Because the code lets the design shine through, object-oriented techniques will conquer a problem that has never been overcome in traditional systems development: the inability to impose a design methodology upon the general programming community.

Key Points

- Object-oriented design offers several advantages over structured systems analysis, including less and more reuseable code.

- Object-oriented analysis is primarily a bottom-up process based on increasing abstraction of classes.

- Object-oriented techniques are based on identifying objects, defining and organizing classes; organizing class libraries; and creating frameworks for specific applications.

- No rigorous methodology exists; instead, rules of thumb and notational aids are available.

- Several notation systems, such as Wasserman's OOSD, are available to assist the beginning practitioner.

For Further Study

American Programmer. 1989. Special issue on object orientation. Vol. 2, Nos. 7–8, Summer.
    This special edition includes views of object-oriented analysis and design by the leading authors of both structured and object-oriented methodologies.

Jeffcoate, J., Hales, K., and Downes, V. 1989. *Object-Oriented Systems: The Commercial Benefits.* London: Ovum Ltd.
    This report reviews the analysis and design process.

Martin, J., and McClure, C. 1988. *Structured Techniques: The Basis for CASE.* Englewood Cliffs, N.J.: Prentice Hall.
    Read this handbook for an overview of structured analysis techniques.

Meyer, B. 1988. *Object-Oriented Software Construction.* Englewood Cliffs, N.J.: Prentice Hall.
    Read Chapter 14, "Techniques of Object-Oriented Design," for an experienced practitioner's approach to design—complete with common pitfalls. Although this book is specific to the Eiffel language, Meyer provides many insights into object-oriented design in any language.

Shlaer, S., and Mellor, S. 1988. *Object-Oriented Systems Analysis: Modeling the World in Data.* Yourdon Press Computing Series. Englewood Cliffs, N.J.: Prentice Hall.

Read this novice's guide to object-oriented design for an introduction with a strong structured analysis flavor.

Wasserman, A. I., Pircher, P.A., and Muller, R.J. 1990. "The object-oriented structured design notation for software design representation." *Computer,* Vol. 24, No. 3, March.

Wasserman is a noted guru on design methodology. His company, Interactive Development Environments (IDE), publishes well-written papers on design methodology, as well as provides an automated package for object-oriented design notation. IDE has offered courses on object-oriented structured design.

References

Bailin, S. 1989. "An object-oriented requirements specification method." *Communications of the Association for Computing Machinery,* Vol. 32, No. 5, May.

Beck, K., and Cunningham, W. 1989. "A laboratory for teaching object-oriented thinking." *Proceedings of Object-Oriented Programming: Systems, Languages, and Applications 1989* (OOPSLA '89). *SIGPLAN Notices,* Vol. 24, No. 10, October, pp. 1–6.

Booch, G. 1983. *Software Engineering with Ada.* Redwood City, Calif.: Benjamin-Cummings.

Coad, P. 1989. "Object-oriented analysis." *American Programmer,* special issue on object orientation, Vol. 2, Nos. 7–8, Summer.

Johnson, R. E., and Foote, B. 1988. "Designing reusable classes." *Journal of Object-Oriented Programming,* Vol. 1, No. 2.

Martin, J., and McClure, C. 1988. *Structured Techniques: The Basis for CASE.* Englewood Cliffs, N.J.: Prentice Hall.

Meyer, B. 1988. *Object-Oriented Software Construction.* Englewood Cliffs, N.J.: Prentice Hall.

Pun, W., and Winder, R. 1989. "A design method for object-oriented programming." *Proceedings of the Third European Conference on Object-Oriented Programming (ECOOP).* Cambridge: Cambridge University Press.

Wilson, R. 1987. "Object-oriented languages reorient programming techniques." *Computer Design,* November 1.

Chapter 8

Programming and Maintenance

- **Procedural Programming and Maintenance**

- **Object-Oriented Programming and Maintenance**

- **Object-Oriented Project Management**

- **Development Tools and Environments**
  Browsers
  Inspectors
  Profilers
  Debuggers
  Development Environments

- **Summary**

This chapter provides an overview of the process of object-oriented programming. We shall compare object-oriented programming to traditional programming techniques. In addition, we shall review tools and development environments used to support the objected-oriented programming and maintenance process.

Read this chapter to gain a better understanding of the construction and maintenance of object-oriented systems.

Software engineering, object-oriented or otherwise, remains an iterative process. Since the late 1960s efforts have been made to refine and systematize the way software is developed. Most of these methodologies are based on the traditional waterfall method. The waterfall method divides software development into five stages. In an idealized world, applications are built with a logical progression through each of the following five steps:

Analysis: The external characteristics of the system are defined and described in a requirements document.

Design: The system design is partitioned into subsystems, and the interface and functionality of each subsystem is defined.

Coding: Subsystems are coded and assembled into the complete system.

Testing: Testing is performed to verify that the system does what it is supposed to do.

Maintenance: Software is revised to fit new specifications and correct errors after it is put into production.

This logical progression is illustrated in Figure 8.1.

Unfortunately, the waterfall model does not accurately describe how software is actually developed. The real world of software development does not proceed uniformly from the first step to the last, but instead, at any stage, a step or two backward is typically required before any further progress. Iteration is more the rule than the exception in software development. Problems that surface during testing may require a change to the product design. Users may request a new feature that requires a change to the requirements document. There is nothing particularly procedural or object oriented about this iterative development process, as shown in Figure 8.2. Whether the language being used is COBOL or C+ +, the same steps in the development cycle are followed. Object orientation does not change the cycle.

This model contains many challenges for the traditional programmer. The programmer must understand the problem, build a semantic model of the problem, and finally translate the model into code. Several strategies for addressing these challenges of the programming process have been attempted. Structured programming, popularized in the 1970s, was the most recent attempt to minimize the syntax hurdle by

Figure 8.1
Waterfall Model of
Software
Development

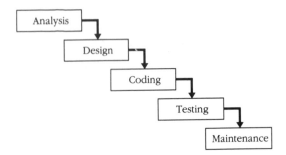

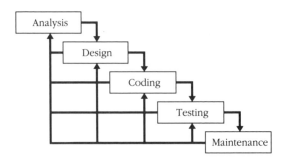

Figure 8.2
Iterative Model of
Software
Development

structuring a program into a semantic view of conditions and while loops. This did help with many of the batch type applications being developed at the time. However, the interactive application requirements of the 1980s outgrew these constraints.

Prototyping tools were another aid that allowed the user and the developer to better understand the problem definition and to build an agreeable solution strategy. To support the prototyping process, joint application development (JAD) sessions became a popular and effective form of user-systems analyst-programmer interaction.

Another attempt at addressing the programming challenges was the emergence in the 1980s of computer-assisted software engineering (CASE) tools. CASE tools automated popular structured analysis approaches, translated design specifications into code structures, and, in some cases, automatically created entire programs. These tools were intended to minimize the risk of translation of the solution strategy into action. Reengineering tools also emerged in this time period to allow previously built software to better address changing user requirements and system configurations.

Structured programming approaches, new approaches for user interaction, and CASE did result in overall improvements in the programming process. Frequently the gains were not easily quantifiable. Less quantifiable gains include more satisfied users, better tools to support traditional programming languages, and less expensive development platforms.

Object-oriented software construction changes the challenges inherent in the programming process. The primary differences between object-oriented and traditional software construction are in the relative difficulty moving between stages of the development cycle, the roles of the programmers, and the importance and variety of tools they use to complete their tasks. A comparison of the traditional and object-oriented paradigms during a typical software life cycle will point out these differences and illustrate the relative merits of the two approaches.

Object-oriented programming differs from conventional, procedural programming in several ways. First, design continues throughout the development cycle. This allows for user involvement and refinement of the problem and solution definition through the entire development cycle. Second, object-oriented programmers spend most of their time reviewing, reusing, and extending existing code, instead of writing new code from scratch. Object-oriented programming has been described as programming the differences. The programmer's job is not the traditional challenge of writing a program to solve the problem, but instead is one of finding an existing set of classes that most closely solve the problem and modifying them accordingly. This mitigates much of the coding challenge present in traditional programming.

Finally, an object-oriented program grows incrementally and evolves smoothly as additional functionality is added. This is in contrast to conventional programming, where progress is marked by infrequent, major changes in both the size of the program and its functionality. Each of these differences affects users, programmers, and project managers alike.

Although the object-oriented paradigm is a significant step forward, object orientation is not an immediate panacea for all programming challenges. Many of the challenges of programming remain the same for both the procedural and the object-oriented programmer. It is of course still possible to write object-oriented code that contains errors. Debugging remains a significant challenge. Testing to assure high quality is still required. Rethinking the original design in the face of implementation obstacles still occurs. There is still a cost associated with realigning old code to a new, better design.

Object-oriented programming is intellectually difficult. Programmers must first understand code before they can reuse it. They must then locate the right reusable classes, methods, and messages. Finally, because object-oriented design and programming are intertwined, programmers must reconsider the design of the software throughout the lifecycle. They will often restructure incorrect or inelegant code several times until the code finally becomes intelligible and reusable.

In the sections that follow, the traditional or procedural approach to programming and maintenance is contrasted with the object-oriented approach. A discussion of the changes in project management follows. Finally, a review is provided of the development tools and environments that aid object-oriented programmers.

Object-oriented programming is not a panacea. It will not serve as a floor wax and a dessert topping under all circumstances. It's just better than the current alternatives.
Deutsch, 1989

Procedural Programming and Maintenance

Procedural programming has been idealized as a linear process in the waterfall model. In practice programmers move forward and back among the tasks of design, coding, and testing. The design stage for the procedural process begins by partitioning the problem into subsystems, such as a print subsystem and a windowing subsystem, each responsible for a related set of tasks. Interfaces to each subsystem are defined. Data that are needed by more than one subsystem are specified. Rules for integrating each subsystem into the full system are established. Each subsystem is further refined into data and procedures, resulting in a set of data definitions and a set of procedures with their interfaces. Coding conventions, specifying, for example, how variables and files should be named and how source code should be documented and formatted, are established and agreed upon by the project team. Subsystems are assigned to the programming team members and a development schedule is established. If the project is large enough, a project member is assigned the administrative tasks such as version control, backups, and library maintenance.

During the coding phase, the programmer faces the difficult task of converting the semantic description in the requirements document to the syntax of the procedural language. The real world is not made up of procedures and data, yet that is what the programmer must convert it into. The resultant semantic gap between the design and the code makes it difficult to understand what the code is supposed to do, and hence difficult for someone at a later data to modify, correct, or borrow it for use elsewhere.

The programmers may also require the services of libraries of routines, such as mathematical algorithms or routines to display windows and dialog boxes. Libraries of procedural routines are typically not very flexible. The libraries may require the programming team to adapt to a set of conventions for parameter passing and data definitions that is different from the project conventions. The libraries may not offer the functionality required by the system and thus require modifications of source code unfamiliar to anyone on the programming team. Some third-party vendor libraries may not even include source code and thus may be completely unmodifiable.

Coding is performed incrementally, each subsystem built up a piece at a time. The programmer continually cycles through four stages during coding, as shown in Figure 8.3. Programmers generally do not share code during the coding phase. Although it is likely that code in other

Figure 8.3
Procedural Pro-
gramming Coding
Cycle

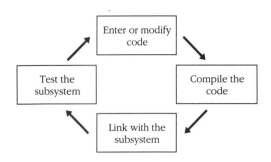

subsystems provides useful functionality, adapting it for reuse is typically more difficult and time consuming than writing new code.

Some tools are available to make the coding process more efficient. The tedious code/compile/link/test cycle is made easier by integrated development environments, which permit the developer to construct and test a program without leaving the environment. These environments provide a uniform interface to editors, compilers, and linkers. Incremental compilers, which recompile only those portions of the code that have been changed, speed the compile/link process, which can be time consuming in large subsystems. Interpreters eliminate the compilation process and allow testing of a program module directly from its source code in just a few seconds.

Errors usually occur at three points in the coding phase. First, the compiler or interpreter identifies syntax errors within a subsystem. These errors are generally obvious enough to be fixed immediately. Second, the linker identifies errors between subsystems. A link error occurs when a procedure in one subsystem attempts to call a procedure in another subsystem with the wrong type or number of parameters. This type of error is often a result of a communication problem between team members and can become a more serious problem as subsystems grow in size and complexity. Third, after the system compiles and links successfully, run-time errors can emerge during system testing. The errors arising at this point are not syntactical. The system runs, but does not perform as it is intended. Correcting run-time errors can be time consuming and may require the use of debugging tools to track down the problem.

As the amount of accumulated code grows, the code typically becomes less malleable. This is because traditional programs separate data and procedures and allow procedures to read and modify data. Over time this separation results in a proliferation of procedure-data depend-encies. These dependencies result in a greater need for tracking, com-municating, and verifying changes, as a change in one part of the program can cause unforeseen consequences elsewhere.

Testing of the system is performed iteratively with the coding phase. At intervals dictated by the project schedule, selected subsystems are integrated, and integration testing is performed. This unit testing is per-formed to ensure that the system is satisfying the requirements specified at the analysis stage.

The last stage in the life cycle is maintenance. Software must contin-ually be revised to remove defects, add new requirements, improve per-formance, and accommodate new hardware or systems software. As software is extended, the original structure of the system frequently de-teriorates. Modification alters originally clean designs. Fix is made upon fix. Data structures are altered. Members of the original programming team disperse. Formerly current documentation becomes outdated. The software grows steadily larger and more error-prone. The programs be-come difficult and expensive to modify.

In summary, procedural programming is accomplished by decom-posing functionality into small blocks, writing the code, assembling the blocks, and debugging the result. As programs grow in size and com-plexity, the conventional approach begins to stall. These dependencies among procedures and data make code difficult to debug, extend, share, and maintain.

Object-Oriented Programming and Maintenance

Like conventional programming, object-oriented programming begins with a design. The object-oriented design process, discussed in Chapter 7, provides programmers with a blueprint that identifies the key classes. Descriptions of class behavior suggest messages and methods. The de-sign may also specify a class hierarchy or framework. In the process of constructing classes and methods, programmers flesh out the details not specified in the design. More importantly, they discover ways to im-prove the design by, for example, reorganizing methods within a set of classes, moving some methods higher in the class hierarchy so that they can be shared more widely, or even rethinking the classes themselves to achieve a more flexible and elegant design.

Object-oriented programming blurs the distinction between design and coding. Design and coding differ only in their levels of abstraction.

During design, it is proper to leave some details unspecified, while during coding it is imperative that details be expressed fully. In moving from design to implementation of the code, new objects are introduced that do not necessarily correspond to real-world entities. This is a natural process that reflects lower levels of implementation detail. The more abstract levels of a design still closely model elements in the application domain.

During the coding stage the object-oriented programmer cycles through the same code/compile/link/test steps as described earlier for the procedural programmer. However, the details of object-oriented code development and enhancement differ from the procedural coding practices. To illustrate the process of object-oriented programming and to contrast it with procedural programming, consider how a programmer might implement a visual gauge that appears in a window on the screen and shows both an exact digital value and an analog indication of the value. This example is modified from Stefik and Bobrow (1987).

As specified in the design phase of the gauge, the class Digital-AnalogGauge will create objects that respond to a message providing a value to be displayed, a valid range for values, and a title for the gauge. Figure 8.4 shows how the display will look when provided with a value of 100, a minimum value of 50, a maximum value of 150, and the title Total Weight. In addition, the programmer is advised that a potentially useful class in the class library is Rectangle. In summary, the design identifies the class to be written, its desired behavior, and a likely place in the class library from which to start.

As this example illustrates, implementation of an object-oriented program rarely begins with a blank piece of paper. Most object-oriented languages are accompanied by class libraries that provide low-level functionality, for example, input/output routines, graphic primitives, and essential data structures. Class libraries may also provide frameworks such as the Model-View-Controller (MVC) framework for building graphical

Figure 8.4
A Digital and
Analog Gauge

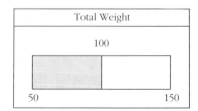

user interfaces, as discussed in Chapter 6. In addition, classes can be imported from previous development efforts, stripped of the functionality not relevant to the new application, and reused. Lastly, the starting point can be classes developed for a prototype of the system. In all these cases, development does not begin from scratch.

In the example of DigitalAnalogGauge, the existing class Rectangle provides a starting point. A digital analog gauge can be thought of as a rectangle with additional properties, such as a heading, a digital display, and an analog display. DigitalAnalogGauge becomes a natural candidate for a subclass of Rectangle.

One of the primary activities of object-oriented programming is the construction of subclasses. A pervasive programming strategy is stepwise refinement by specialization. By deriving subclasses, object-oriented programmers model, in classes, the most general concepts of the problem. Special cases are handled by more specific subclasses. Subclasses refine existing classes by adding new instance variables, adding new methods, and changing existing methods.

To build a digital analog gauge, then, the programmer must construct a subclass that extends the behavior of Rectangle. As a first step, the programmer may decide to implement and test a subclass called DigitalGauge, which is a subclass of Rectangle with added functionality. DigitalGauge will produce a display containing a title and a numeric value, as shown in Figure 8.5. DigitalGauge inherits coordinate data from Rectangle. In addition, DigitalGauge contains instance variables to store a title and a value, and two methods. One method shows the digital value and the other method shows the rectangle plus its title.

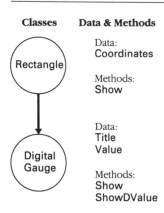

Classes   **Data & Methods**

Rectangle

Data:
Coordinates

Methods:
Show

Digital Gauge

Data:
Title
Value

Methods:
Show
ShowDValue

Figure 8.5
DigitalGauge is a
Subclass of
Rectangle

In the example a subclass inherits all data and overrides one method from a parent class. The programmer augments functionality with additional methods and data. The programmer can also modify the parent class or insert an intermediate class in order to better factor functionality among the classes, as the example goes on to show.

There are alternatives to consider before proceeding to the next step in programming the digital analog gauge. One alternative is to create a second subclass of Rectangle called AnalogGauge, and then to construct a subclass of both AnalogGauge and DigitalGauge to solve the problem at hand. However, if AnalogGauge is derived from Rectangle, it will need to duplicate DigitalGauge's title and value data. This duplication can be eliminated if, instead, an intermediate class called Gauge is formed from which DigitalGauge and AnalogGauge are then derived. This alternative is superior because it provides a more economical representation, as shown in Figure 8.6. Gauge is inserted in the class hierarchy. Title and value data, as well as the Show method, are hoisted from DigitalGauge to Gauge. DigitalGauge is modified to be a subclass of Gauge.

Several points are illustrated at this step of the example. First, the programmer continues to refine the design and rethink the nature of the classes that best factor the problem. Because of the encapsulation of data and procedures, poor designs appear flawed more quickly. In this case the need to store the same data twice signaled the need for an intermediate class. As we have undertaken the coding phase of

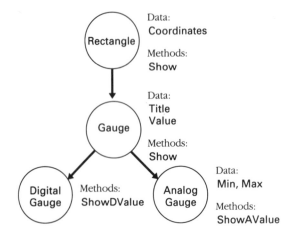

Figure 8.6
Gauge Is Inserted
in the Hierarchy

object-oriented software construction an important difference from procedural development is evident. The departure from subroutines common in procedural programming is fundamental in making the shift to object-oriented programming. According to Verity (1987), objects are quite different from traditional subroutines. The differences are as follows:

1. Objects reflect a deeper abstraction.

2. Objects respond only to certain strictly defined messages passed to them.

3. Objects receive messages and take full control of the system until it passes control to some other object via another message. In contrast, traditional subroutines eventually pass control back to the main routine.

4. Objects interface to other objects in a clearly defined manner and cannot be subverted. For example, a Smalltalk program cannot jump suddenly into the middle of an object in the way that a wayward FORTRAN program might mistakenly activate code deep within a subroutine.

Now that the class hierarchy and organization of methods and instance variables are defined, all the functionality is in place for creating and displaying both analog and digital data. The functionality is gathered together by defining DigitalAnalogGauge as a subclass of both DigitalGauge and AnalogGauge. A method called ShowValues is added to this class, which is implemented by sending messages to invoke the ShowAValue and ShowDValue methods in succession. The final class hierarchy is shown in Figure 8.7.

As the gauge example illustrates, object-oriented programming is the process of locating relevant parent classes, deriving subclasses, and adding or modifying methods and data. Appropriate organization of the class hierarchy and abstraction of methods is the fundamental design and coding strategy. Classes are added to a body of existing code. Methods and data are moved around among classes until the twin goals of functionality and reuse are met. Factors such as lines of code per method, number of methods per class, depth of the class hierarchy, number of method users per class, average number of message sends per method, and total lines of code reused are the primary considerations in the iterative coding process as it applies to object-oriented programming.

Figure 8.7

Multiple Inheritance
for DigitalAnalog-
Gauge

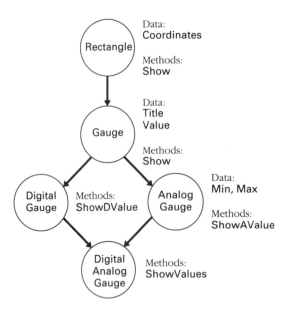

Software reuse mechanisms such as inheritance make consistency easier to maintain. This applies to coding conventions hidden within the software as well as those that are visible to users. While constructing a budget development application, for example, users would like to be able to set a quantity and a multiplier for a variety of situations, such as head count multiplied by a benefits fee, or units multiplied by price, leaving the application to propagate the resulting total. A class defining a generic dialog box to consistently handle all quantity and multiplier situations could be developed. This class could then be subclassed to encompass more specific situations such as the two just mentioned.

Errors in object-oriented programs are also less costly because they are likely to affect smaller, encapsulated bodies of code. Errors in coding a method are encapsulated within a class. Message-handling errors, those errors that occur in passing information between objects, are more easily resolved since the exact boundary between communicating objects is clear.

To take advantage of the benefits of object-oriented software construction, programmers must understand how class libraries are arranged. The good programmers are those who know best how to take advantage of the existing class libraries. Programmers will be measured by how closely they can match an existing library class to the new problem, and by how little extra code they have to write. This is in contrast with the traditional coding practice of estimating and rewarding progress by counting the number of lines of code produced.

Class producers, that is, programmers who add new classes to the class library for others to use, must provide clear documentation of their work. Documentation increases the value of classes, making them more likely to be reused. This is essential for class consumers, that is, programmers who use existing classes to create applications, to be motivated to use the class library.

Object-oriented code remains malleable throughout its entire lifetime if the object-oriented construction approach is followed. When adding a new feature, the object-oriented programmer does not rush to code, but instead first looks to see what classes are already available and how the new feature will fit into the existing class hierarchy. This often leads to design review meetings, where programmers request and recommend changes to the existing code base so that their new features will be better accommodated. These meetings typically resolve issues at a relatively high level of abstraction. Programmers are mainly interested in the methods provided by objects, not in the internal details of how those methods are coded. Object responsibilities are defined, methods are apportioned among them, and interfaces are adjusted and agreed upon. A document from these meetings might consist of a drawing showing the agreed-upon relationships of objects and which methods each will supply.

Figure 8.8 illustrates a typical working paper from a software project at Pillar Corporation, showing how a group of objects will communicate with each other to update a window after an edit to the database. Only the information needed by other programmers is illustrated: object names and the sequence of messages required to carry out the update. Implementation details, such as names of instance variables or method code, are suppressed.

Once the restructuring of existing classes and methods has been agreed upon, the addition of the new feature is often a fairly trivial task. In fact, after a review of existing code, the programmer often discovers that the new feature is mostly provided by an existing class that requires only a modest change or extension.

Hybrid object-oriented languages, such as C++, ease the transition to object-oriented software construction by allowing programmers to mix existing procedural code with object-oriented constructs. Programmers have the option of converting these libraries to object-oriented libraries by building an object-oriented layer around the functions and

Figure 8.8
Typical Object-Oriented Software Project Working Paper

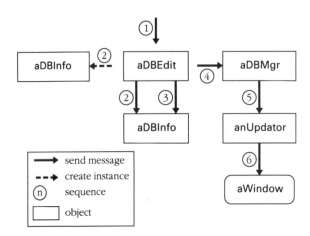

converting procedure calls to message calls. For example, Pillar Corporation took advantage of the existence of commercial procedural libraries for data storage and graphical image display. Pillar converted these two libraries to class libraries compatible with their object-oriented language and, in addition, removed some of their idiosyncrasies, making these libraries more generally useful to the project.

Debugging an object-oriented program is not very different from debugging a procedural program. The object-oriented programmer needs to know why an object did not receive an expected message or why a particular method did not get used, just as the procedural programmer needs to know why a procedure did not get passed an expected parameter or why a procedure did not get called. Both programmers will try to fix their respective bugs by browsing through source code, setting breakpoints, and tracing program execution line by line.

The differences in the paradigms, however, do result in somewhat different approaches. Tracing the flow of control in an object-oriented program is generally more complex than in a procedural program. Object-oriented programs typically have their functionality spread over a greater number of smaller modules, resulting in more steps in and out of modules than in traditional programs of nested subroutines. On the other hand, thanks to the appropriate distribution of behavior among objects, the object-oriented programmer usually has a better idea where an error can be found when it does occur.

Object-oriented debugging requires the programmer to keep track of some extra relationships that do not exist in a procedural program. For example, there is no equivalent in the procedural world to the concept of inheritance, nor do traditional languages have the additional complexity of polymorphism, with multiple method implementations for the same message. This can complicate the object-oriented debugger's task and certainly requires extensions to debugging tools.

Object-oriented languages and programming techniques do not eliminate the need for maintenance of implemented systems. Users and applications will always require new functions, errors must always be corrected, and new hardware and system software must always be accommodated. But object-orientation can lessen the severity and expense of the maintenance process, in two primary ways. First, an object-oriented program will save the maintenance programmer time understanding the existing code. A properly written object-oriented program consists of a set of class definitions arranged in a hierarchy. Each class definition consists of an external interface, the messages its objects accept, and an internal implementation, the instance variables and methods. The maintenance programmer need read only the class messages to get an understanding of each class' behavior. Implementation details can be ignored until they become necessary. A study of the program's class hierarchy gives a visual overview of the total functionality of the program and how its parts fit together without actual looking at the code. Some of the classes may come straight from the language's or development environment's class library, in which case they will be already familiar to the programmer. New subclasses need only be understood in how they differ from their parents.

Object-oriented development environments and tools make this examination of existing code an efficient and systematic process. This process of browsing through the program's source code at the class level is in fact the same process the programmer undergoes in creating a new program by browsing through the class library for candidate classes to incorporate and modify. Maintenance consists in incremental changes to the program's classes, just as creating the program consisted of incremental changes to the class library. Maintenance is, in fact, a continuation of program creation, instead of an entirely new process.

A second reason that the maintenance difficulty is lessened is the modular structure of an object-oriented program. Data in an object-oriented program are encapsulated in objects, and the only way to access or change data is through the messages that are sent to objects. This simplifies the process of finding out what caused data to go bad. Only the object's messages need be examined to identify which caused the problem. Furthermore, new classes of objects can be added without worrying about their effect on existing classes.

In summary, object-oriented programmers spend proportionally more time inspecting, understanding, and extending existing code than their conventional counterparts. Although the initial design suggests likely classes, the object-oriented programmer reconsiders the design all through the implementation process. The process of coding consists primarily of deriving subclasses, adding methods and data, and moving methods and data among classes. The focus on reuse increases the need for communication among members of the programming team. Finally, maintaining object-oriented software is simplified by the increased modularity and clarity of the code.

Object-Oriented Project Management

Managers of software projects based on object-oriented techniques will need to adjust their overall management approach, particularly their performance measurements. Incentives for object-oriented programmers must focus on the goal of software reuse and not on code quantity. The object-oriented paradigm also suggests new ways to encourage or enforce coding and product consistency. Finally, the building of class libraries and application frameworks is a critical success factor deserving much of the managers' attention.

Managers must learn new ways to measure and track productivity. Even for conventional programming, the number of lines of code has been an inadequate measure of programmer productivity. For object-oriented programs, lines of code will become either an entirely inappropriate metric or a metric inversely related to the productivity. There is not yet a consensus on what metrics are appropriate to measuring object-oriented software productivity. One typical set was developed to help measure the software progress for the Hewlett-Packard Vista project (Kraemer 1989). As Table 8.1 shows, the metrics follow the phases of the waterfall model. Many of the measures, for example, cumulative engineering months and link success rate, are not specific to object-oriented programming. Other measures, such as methods planned and object classes tested, although unique to the object-oriented development process, have corresponding measures within procedural programming, for example, data types planned and procedures tested.

Analysis Phase	Design Phase	Coding Phase	Testing Phase
Cumulative engineering months	Number of object classes designed and engineering months to design object classes	Number of object classes coded and engineering months to code object classes	Defects found, resolved
	Number of methods designed and engineering months to plan methods	Number of methods coded and engineering months to code methods	Cumulative defects versus cumulative Q/A hours
		Compile and link success rates	Defect finding rate
			Estimated Q/A hours remaining
			Unresolved defects by severity

Table 8.1
Software Metrics by Life Cycle Phase (after Kraemer 1989)

As managers gain experience in tracking object-oriented development, new metrics will undoubtedly arise. Managers also need to reconsider with care the incentives they set for programmers. The programmer who derives a new class with the least effort should be rewarded.

Similarly, the software engineer who can refine a class hierarchy to make it a stronger application framework will be in high demand. The factors that contribute to high-quality designs and programmed solutions are likely candidates for performance evaluation. As previously discussed in Chapter 7 and in this chapter, these factors include:

- Lines of code per method.

- Number of methods per class.

- Number of method users per class.

- Average depth of the class hierarchy.

- Average number of message sends per method.

- Length of time since a class was modified.

- Lines of code reused.

It is important for both the manager and the development team to understand the flexibility of the object-oriented process before defining the product specification. Otherwise, they might not consider features that would be difficult to provide with a traditional implementation. Managers have come to believe that rapid or radical changes in functionality are difficult to achieve. Because of the proliferation of procedure-data dependencies, the difficulty of change ordinarily increases sharply with the amount of code. In addition, code reuse is problematic. A programmer typically wants to reuse an existing piece of code, except for one or two minor changes. But making the minor changes can be expensive. The programmer must have possession of the source code and understand the whole program well enough to make a change that does not modify other functionality or introduce any new bugs. As managers have come to expect, the difficulty of satisfying these requirements discourages programmers from making changes to a product, even if these changes would result in real improvements.

For object-oriented programs, however, significant flexibility remains throughout the coding process. Instead of one giant collection of interdependencies, object-oriented programs consist of a collection of objects loosely coupled by messages. As a result, complexity grows much more slowly as the program grows. Because of the modularity and clean interfaces of objects, neither users nor programmers need be discouraged from making suggestions and changes, even significant ones, throughout the development process. Often, design changes result in significant extensions to the program's original feature set. Managers should be prepared for increasing functionality and flexibility as a by-product of the object-oriented approach.

This increased flexibility requires increased discipline from the programming team. As new design ideas can easily be incorporated during the development process, the temptation is strong to deviate from established specifications. Managers must learn to recognize and control design deviations, so easily realized by programmers, that can cause significant problems for the writers, testers, and other members of the full project team.

A high level of cooperation among members of the programming team is also required to achieve the benefits of object-oriented programming. Not only must they write code that works, they must also make the individual components of the code reusable. This requires a great deal of sharing; programmers are expected to read others' code and show their own code to others.

Some developers encourage design for reuse by dividing programmers into two groups: class programmers and application programmers. Class programmers have long-term ownership of their classes and are encouraged to polish and enhance them for reusability in different applications. Application programmers are concerned with delivering the solution as quickly and efficiently as possible. Application programmers can reduce the component count in their application by asking the class programmers for more generalized classes or frameworks.

Managers are also wise to focus their attention on the evolution and documentation of the class library. Object-oriented class libraries should be readable and understandable to manager and engineer alike. Managers must recognize the importance of the class library as a corporate resource for the development of later versions of the current system or for entirely new systems.

Development Tools and Environments

The dependence on tools does not change for object-oriented software construction. The programmer needs quick access to code, the ability to navigate through class hierarchies, and rapid compilation of classes and methods. Incremental compilations are a must. In addition, because of the tremendous amount of communication between objects in the form of messages, performance tuning is frequently required.

The principal tools for object-oriented software development and maintenance are browsers, inspectors, profilers, and debuggers.

Browsers

One of the advantages of object-oriented languages over traditional languages is the existence of class libraries. Class libraries are aptly named. They are valuable repositories of information to be studied, used, and enhanced by developers. Having predefined classes reduces the need for repetitive coding of low-level constructs, as well as enforcing standards on high-level constructs such as window styles. The use of classes, however, diverges from the familiar experience of programmers used to scanning program listings and tracing the flow of control in the program's logic. Programmers must instead learn to navigate among the classes in the system.

Browsers are interactive programs that permit navigation through class libraries. Browsers are a concrete example of object-oriented programming as programming by looking around. A browser typically shows the following information:

- Relationships among classes,

- Messages and methods for a class,

- Variables for a class,

- Senders of a message,

- Implementors of a message, and

- Implementation code for a method.

A browser can also provide templates for defining new classes, methods, and messages, and for modifying existing ones.

The first browser was developed for the Smalltalk environment by Larry Tesler of the Xerox Palo Alto Research Center, and it was later enhanced by Dan Ingalls. A modern successor to the Smalltalk browser is Objectworks for C++ from ParcPlace Systems. Objectworks for C++ consists of a series of tools for the C++ programmer. Figure 8.9 shows the source code browser examining the inheritance structure of a C++ program and, in particular, a method called myshape(point,point). This method belongs to the class myshape, which is itself a subclass of

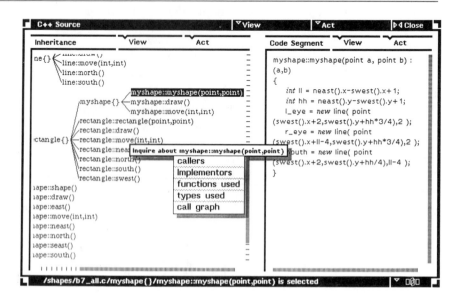

Figure 8.9
A Source Code Browser from Objectworks for C++

rectangle. The view on the right shows the source code for the selected method. Changes can be entered in the source code.

Other tools, such as GOOD (Graphics for Object-Oriented Design) for the Eiffel development environment from Interactive Software Engineering, provide graphical views of classes. Starting with a class, GOOD will display all of its ancestors (shown connected by single lines) and clients (shown connected by double lines). Figure 8.10 is a screen from a representative GOOD session.

Inspectors

Inspectors for procedural languages are used to view and change the values of data while stepping through a program's execution. Inspectors for object-oriented programming are used analogously to examine and

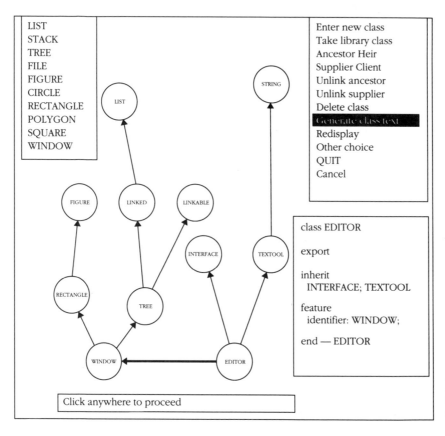

Figure 8.10
Screen from an Eiffel GOOD Session

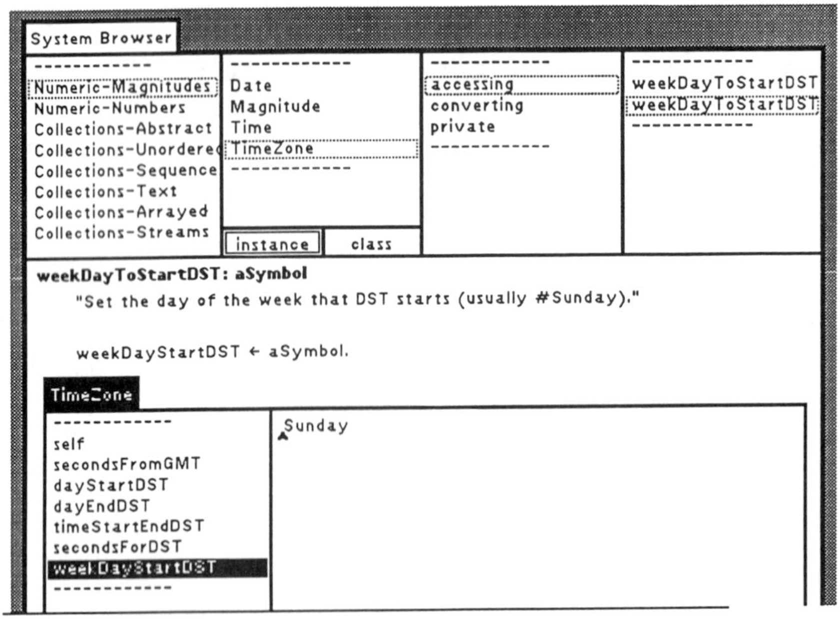

Figure 8.11

Inspecting the Instance Variables of Class TimeZone

```
┌─────────────────────────────────────────────────────────────────────────────┐
│ System Browser                                                                │
│ ------------    ------------    ------------    ------------                  │
│ Numeric-Magnitudes  Date       accessing       weekDayToStartDST             │
│ Numeric-Numbers   Magnitude    converting      weekDayToStartDST             │
│ Collections-Abstract  Time      private         ------------                 │
│ Collections-Unordered  TimeZone   ------------                               │
│ Collections-Sequence  ------------                                           │
│ Collections-Text                                                            │
│ Collections-Arrayed                                                         │
│ Collections-Streams    ┌─────────┬────────┐                                  │
│                        │ instance │  class │                                 │
│                        └─────────┴────────┘                                  │
│ weekDayToStartDST: aSymbol                                                    │
│     "Set the day of the week that DST starts (usually #Sunday)."             │
│                                                                               │
│     weekDayStartDST ← aSymbol.                                                │
│ ┌───────────────┐                                                            │
│ │ TimeZone      │                                                            │
│ ├───────────────┬──────────────────────────────────────────────────────┐   │
│ │ ------------  │ Sunday                                                 │   │
│ │ self          │                                                        │   │
│ │ secondsFromGMT │                                                       │   │
│ │ dayStartDST   │                                                        │   │
│ │ dayEndDST     │                                                        │   │
│ │ timeStartEndDST │                                                      │   │
│ │ secondsForDST │                                                        │   │
│ │ weekDayStartDST │                                                      │   │
│ │ ------------  │                                                        │   │
│ └───────────────┴──────────────────────────────────────────────────────┘   │
└─────────────────────────────────────────────────────────────────────────────┘
```

edit the values of an object's instance variables. One example of an inspector for both procedural and object data is the Watch window for the Turbo Pascal 5.5 debugger (Borland International 1988) described later in this chapter.

A second example of an object-oriented inspector is found in Objectworks for Smalltalk-80. As shown in Figure 8.11, the programmer has located the current value for an instance variable of class TimeZone called weekDayToStartDST. The system browser, shown in the background, is used to inspect the definitions of classes, messages, and methods. The inspector opens a window labeled TimeZone and provides a list of TimeZone's instance variables. When an instance variable is selected on the left, its current value appears on the right.

Profilers

The principal tool for analyzing a program's performance is called a profiler. A profiler tells where a program is spending its time. With this information, the developer can identify those parts of a program that require performance tuning. Profilers for object-oriented languages differ only slightly from their procedural counterparts. A profiler for a traditional program typically produces a report identifying how many times each procedure of the program was called and what percent of the total time was spent executing each procedure. A profiler for an object-oriented program provides the same type of information but based on message sends instead of procedure calls. For example, the Smalltalk environment provides a profiler called Spy, which can analyze a block of code and issue a report of the sequence of messages sent and the percentage of time taken up evaluating each. The profiler for the Actor language from the Whitewater Group produces an equivalent report listing the number of times that each method was executed during the program's execution. Methods that are called many times are thus identified as candidates for performance optimization.

Debuggers

Debuggers allow controlled execution and examination of a running program. Much of the power of any debugger lies in its ability to view the program under test in different ways. Object-oriented debuggers provide views of nonprocedural program elements and relationships, such as classes, class-subclass relationships, and message-method connections. In other respects, their capabilities do not differ much from procedural debuggers.

The Smalltalk/V debugger from Digitalk, Inc. (Digitalk 1989), shown in Figure 8.12, is a good example of a modern object-oriented debugger. The top left pane serves two purposes: presenting a walkback and listing breakpoints. If the walkback button is pressed, the upper left pane contains a list of messages sent, with the most recent message listed first, making it easy to trace back in time what the program has been doing. When a walkback line is selected, the other panes contain related information. If the breakpoints button is pressed, the upper left pane contains the class name and method selector for all methods that have breakpoints set. When a breakpoint is selected, the pane below displays the source code for the selected method. Setting a breakpoint in a method causes executions to stop when the method is entered. The two panes on the top right serve as an inspector for the receiver, arguments, and temporary variables of the selected method. The pane on the left of the two contains self, representing the receiver, and the names of all arguments and temporary variables. The pane on the right displays the value of the selected variable.

The button bar just below the little bar of the Debugger window contains three more buttons related to debugging: hop, skip, and jump.

Figure 8.12

Smalltalk/V Debugger
Window

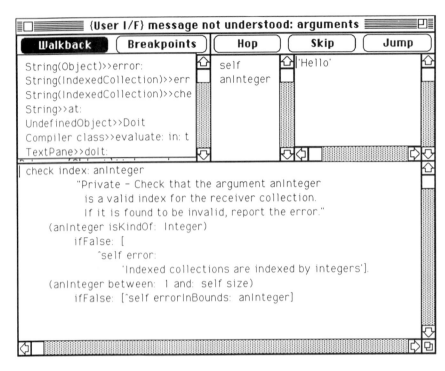

Hop executes the next expression in the running program. Skip executes the next expressions in the selected method or up to the next breakpoint, whichever comes first. Jump executes up to the next breakpoint. The debug menu has commands for resuming normal execution and adding and removing breakpoints.

A debugger for a hybrid object-oriented language must provide functionality to permit the debugging of the procedural constructs of the language as well as its object-oriented extensions. In many cases, hybrid language debuggers have evolved from their procedural language forbearers. The debugger for Turbo Pascal 5.5 (Borland 1988), for example, is a version of the original Turbo Debugger enhanced to support the object-oriented features of Turbo Pascal 5.5. These additions are stepping and tracing method calls and examining object data; they are exactly analogous to stepping and tracing Pascal procedure calls and examining Pascal records. In addition, the Turbo Pascal 5.5 Debugger provides a window for examining class hierarchies. Figure 8.13 illustrates its use within the Turbo Pascal integrated development environ-

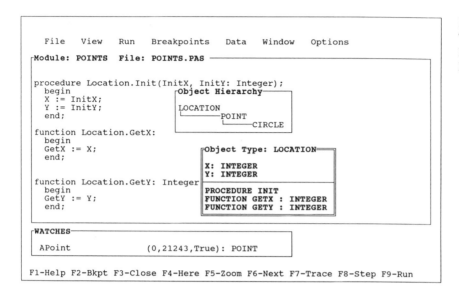

Figure 8.13
Turbo Pascal
Development
Environment

ment. The large window shows the code for three methods of class Location. Overlaying this window are two smaller windows, the upper one showing the hierarchy of classes within the application, and the lower one showing the instance variables and messages for class Location. Below is a window showing the current values of the instance variables for the object APoint of class Point.

A variety of other tools are also available. Eiffel, for example, provides tools that offer more abstract views of the software. These include a class abstracter (short) and a class flattener (flat).

The tool short offers simple but useful means for taking a class and automatically producing interface documentation. Included in this output will be the text of the class, exclusive of any implementation detail and any nonexported feature—a bit like the specification part of an Ada or Modula-2 module, but produced by the computer rather than the programmer.

When a class has been defined through one or more levels of inheritance, it will often be difficult to understand the class by merely viewing it in isolation. This is because the definitions for many of the class's components can be found only by examining its ancestors. Such detailed information cannot be obtained just by using the short command. The Eiffel class flattener addresses this problem by producing as output a flat version of the class in which it is shown as a self-contained module, without reference to any ancestor. This means that all inherited components are copied into the output class, and that the inheritance class is removed. For clients of the class, the resulting flat version is functionally equivalent to the original. By inserting the output of flat into short, programmers can obtain a complete interface for a class providing the same type of information for inherited features as for features declared in the class itself.

Development Environments

Software development environments help programmers construct systems by integrating the tools they use and by managing many of the housekeeping tasks associated with programming. Development environments simplify the process by providing uniform conventions for viewing, editing, and testing codes. Windowing capabilities of these environments satisfy the programmer's information needs by displaying multiple views of interest simultaneously. Graphical development environments provide more meaningful ways to display relationships and interactions among a program's parts. They also permit project managers to track progress by providing the managers with direct access to the current state of the project.

Some development environments specific to object-oriented user interfaces have been discussed in Chapter 6. These environments, such as the Whitewater Group's Actor, are based on a refined class library specific to the user interface component of software construction. Overall application construction environments for hybrid object-oriented languages such as C++ and object-oriented Pascal are fairly new. In contrast to the Smalltalk development environments, the hybrid language development environments are generally extensions to the environments for the traditional language. An example of a development environment for object-oriented Pascal, Turbo Pascal 5.5 from Borland International, is shown in Figure 8.13. Another example of a development environment for a hybrid object-oriented language is Objectworks for C++, shown in Figure 8.9. Objectworks provides an environment for the creation and management of C++ programs and projects, and has such features as:

- incremental compilation and linking,

- access to code by class and hierarchy,

- graphical representation of inheritance, including multiple inheritance,

- object inspection that provides inspection and alteration of objects at run time,

- an interactive source-language debugger, and

- a context-sensitive inquiry and explanation facility to aid in the reading and debugging of code.

Another integrated environment, discussed by Microsoft Corporation, is referred to as Microsoft's Application Factory. The Application Factory, which represents Microsoft's view of the future programming environment, would be an integrated environment for supporting object-oriented program construction. This environment is described as including:

- tools for creating and manipulating objects including combining, linking, and browsing;

- a visual programming environment designed for constructing application objects, user interface objects, and persistent objects; and

- a shell for supporting both object-oriented and traditional programming.

The Factory would be the tool-rich workbench for developers, but another level of programming tools would most likely be available for entry-level programmers and end users. This novice level of programming tools, labeled by Microsoft as the Application Framework, could include:

- subclassed generic application skeletons,

- a visual programming environment that would be a subset of the development workbench tools including object viewing and manipulation tools, and

- run-time libraries to provide a higher level of encapsulation for system services.

This advanced development scenario described by Microsoft will be based around a central repository that Microsoft refers to as a Global System Cache (GSC). The GSC would maintain a database that stores all the details related to a given software project and would allow programmers to manage access to the visual and object tools provided by the application developer's workbench, to the system object manager and the object-oriented file system (OOFS) and to other tools such as the

Figure 8.14
Proposed Microsoft
Object-Oriented
Programming
Environment

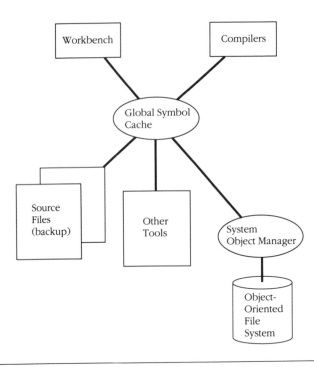

object-oriented language compilers and debuggers. Figure 8.14 summarizes the Application Factory model.

Summary

The programming process, whether procedural or object oriented, involves an iterative process throughout the series of development phases. Programming within the object-oriented paradigm makes this process smoother and more rapid. This increased flexibility carries with it the additional responsibility of team members and their managers to monitor changes and keep from straying too far from the original design.

The object-oriented programmer reconsiders the design all through the implementation process. Appropriate organization of the class hierarchy and abstraction of methods is the fundamental design and coding strategy. Methods and data are moved around among classes until the twin goals of functionality and reuse are met. Factors such as lines of code per method, number of methods per class, depth of the class hierarchy, number of method users per class, average number of message sends per method, and total lines of code reused are the primary considerations in the iterative coding process as it applies to object-oriented programming.

Successful object-oriented software construction requires a high level of cooperation among members of the programming team. Because software reuse is a primary goal, programmers must understand that a large part of their time will be spent reading other people's code for possible reuse. Similarly, a large part of their coding effort will be spent writing code so that it can be easily reused by others.

Managers should understand that traditional metrics for measuring performance are not necessarily applicable to the object-oriented process. Managers must understand the importance of reusable code and encourage its development.

Like traditional software development, tools play an important role in object-oriented programming. The principal tool for object-oriented software development is a browser, which permits navigation through class libraries. Additional tools, including inspectors, profilers, and debuggers, differ little from their procedural counterparts. Also similar to conventional programming are development environments that combine tools with class libraries and frameworks.

Key Points

- With object-oriented programming, design continues throughout the development process.

- Object-oriented software constructions stress review, reuse, and extension of existing code through the use of class libraries and frameworks.

- Software reuse mechanisms, such as inheritance, make consistency in object-oriented programs easier to maintain.

- Unlike procedural programming, object-oriented code does not become less malleable as the system grows in size or complexity.

- The modularity and clean interfaces of objects facilitate flexibility in the program functionality throughout the life of a system.

- The programming challenges of debugging and testing remain with object-oriented programming. However, a variety of improved tools such as browsers, inspectors, and profilers mitigate the debugging difficulties.

■ New metrics are required to determine the productivity of object-oriented programmers. These new metrics are based primarily on building reusable classes.

For Further Reading

Borland International. 1989. *Turbo Pascal Version 5.5 Object-Oriented Programming Guide*. Scotts Valley, Calif.: Borland International.
    The guide provides an introduction to the primary concepts of object-oriented programming for the programmer making the transition from procedural programming.

Franz, M. 1990. *Object-Oriented Programming Featuring Actor*. Glenview, Ill.: Scott, Foresman, and Company.
    Provides a comprehensive overview of an object-oriented development environment.

Goldberg, A. 1984. *Smalltalk: The Interactive Programming Environment*. Reading, Mass.: Addison-Wesley.
    Contains an in-depth description of the Smalltalk development environment.

Meyer, B. 1988. *Object-Oriented Software Construction*. Englewood Cliffs, N.J.: Prentice Hall.
    Discusses issues of reusability, reliability, and maintenance.

References

Deutsch, L.P. 1989. Comment made during a panel discussion at OOPSLA '89, October, New Orleans.

Digitalk. 1989. *Smalltalk/V Mac. Tutorial and Programming Handbook*. Los Angeles, Calif.: Digitalk, Inc.

Kraemer, T. 1989. "Product development using object-oriented software technology." *Hewlett-Packard Journal*, August, pp. 87–100.

Stefik, M., and Bobrow, D. 1986. "Object-oriented programming: Themes and variations." *AI Magazine*, Winter, pp. 40–62.

Verity, J. 1987. "The OOPS revolution." *Datamation*, May 1.

Chapter 9

Emerging Applications

- **Benefits of Object-Oriented Applications**
    - Greater Flexibility
    - Transparent Integration
    - Increased Ease of Use

- **Functionality of Object-Oriented Applications**
    - From Processing to Simulating to Realizing
    - From Centralized to Distributed Computing
    - From Text and Graphics to Multimedia
    - From Objectlike to Object Oriented

- **Examples of Object-Oriented Applications**
    - Computer Aided Software Engineering
    - Computer Aided Instruction
    - Computer Integrated Manufacturing
    - Computer Aided Publishing
    - Visual Programming Environments

- **Future Trends in Object-Oriented Applications**

- **Summary**

This chapter examines an emerging category of applications that are object oriented. We shall identify benefits that users will gain from object-oriented applications. We shall explore the functionality of object-oriented applications and contrast them with applications that are conventional or objectlike. We shall describe object-oriented applications as they appear in application areas such as computer aided design, computer aided software engineering, and computer integrated manufacturing. Finally, we shall speculate about future applications enabled by object-oriented techniques.

Read this chapter to see how object-oriented concepts apply to current and future applications.

Benefits of Object-Oriented Applications

The 1980s delivered many new applications to the computer user. No longer was application software delivered as a predefined set of functions to solve a specific problem. Instead, applications were delivered as a set of tools to solve a large class of problems with the ultimate specifics of the application solution defined by the user. Spreadsheets, databases, and word processors are the most common examples of such application frameworks. The complete list of such tool-oriented applications, however, is quite lengthy and encompasses computer-aided design and desktop publishing among others.

With these applications basic functionality is still delivered as programmed functions with extensibility allowed through user-oriented programming languages usually in the form of macros or scripts. The emergence of standard applications used by millions of end users also facilitated functional extensibility through the creation of a ready-made market for add-on products. This constantly expanded the functional choices available for these application frameworks.

The 1990s should usher in applications with even greater flexibility, transparent integration, and, at the same time, increased ease of use. As discussed in Chapter 1, these applications will benefit not only from enhanced computing power but also from new development technologies with object orientation playing a strong role. The benefits of object orientation delivered to the professional programmer using object-oriented languages have already been described in Chapter 4 and Chapter 8. The benefits of object orientation take on a different form for application users. Although users do not want to share and reuse portions of C++ code, they do want to tailor and extend their applications so that they can perform work quickly and easily.

Greater Flexibility

Generally speaking, today's applications provide users with a finite set of fixed functions. The cell of a spreadsheet, for example, can contain a number, some text, or a formula, and that is all. With object orientation, the concept of a spreadsheet will be extended to be a rectangular array of objects that are instances of classes defined by the user. One class of cells might actively publish their values to other applications; another class of cells might be tailored to accept graphics or to store audio information rather than just numbers and text.

Object-oriented applications will allow users to adapt and tailor functionality to personal needs and preferences. Today, traditional applications allow procedures to be stored for repeated execution. Examples of such user-programmable applications include spreadsheet programs with macro languages and Apple Computer's Hypercard with its scripting language. Some current applications have objectlike behavior and allow icons and their attendant behavior to be cut and pasted from one application to another. Object-oriented applications will provide even greater user programmability and flexibility. Rather than merely replaying keystrokes to exercise built-in functionality, users will be able to extend the functionality of the application itself.

Transparent Integration

Object-oriented applications will provide users with live integration of information, while at the same time easing the sharing and navigation of data across applications. Currently, sharing data across applications typically means converting live data from one application into a static form the other application can accept, and then moving the data between the applications using a data exchange mechanism included with the application. For example, a project plan prepared with a project management package can be moved into a proposal, but the resulting plan data are static. Changes to the original project plan are not propagated automatically through the proposal. Detailed planning information that underlies the chart has been left behind. Changes to the plan must be entered into the project management software, and the updated plan must again be exported to the proposal.

Object orientation provides stronger mechanisms for integrating information across applications. The concept of encapsulation that aids professional programmers in building reusable code modules will also aid users in sharing information among applications. Rather than copying raw data and then reapplying new procedures—for example, copying from the spreadsheet and editing with the word processor—applications will share objects that contain both data and methods. With object orientation, project plans and spreadsheet tables will be published rather than pasted in other documents, enabling the procedures for managing information to move along with the data.

Increased Ease of Use

Perhaps the greatest benefit of object-oriented applications is the ease of use delivered to the end user by the increasing similarity between the problem at hand and the solution developing on the computer. Object-oriented applications reflect the user's view of the world. With object orientation the user views a model of the problem and the solution. This model is usually populated with familiar entities such as event calendars, PERT charts, story boards, and telephone directories. This combination of the graphic world and object orientation allows the user to interact with an application much the same way he or she would interact with the real world. The event calendar can query other managers' event calendars to make sure that meetings are scheduled, and then it can publish itself for distribution. The company's employee telephone directory can be linked to the human resources database so that a change in personnel automatically updates the telephone directory.

In general, users of object-oriented systems will assemble their applications to contain the central elements of their work, such as calendars and telephone directories, and configure these elements with behavior specific to their needs. Object-oriented applications hide the actual program and programlike approaches to using and extending the application. Instead of learning a macro language or scripting language, the user begins with a set of objects and models the application to meet the unique characteristics of the problem at hand. As explained in previous chapters, dependence on an application framework or a generic class library is critical to providing such a modeling capability. But, given an adequate framework, the user is encouraged to model an exact application fit through the capabilities of the object-oriented environment.

In the past, application software was available only for generic tasks, and a programmer or a programmer's tool was needed to tailor an environment for a particular user's needs. In the 1990s, users will be able to tailor applications precisely to their needs and build unique environments to accelerate their work without calling on programmers.

Functionality of Object-Oriented Applications

Object-oriented applications will inspire users to think differently about the nature of computing. Programs in an object-oriented environment will be transparent. Object-oriented frameworks will facilitate simulating and constructing user-specific solutions. Objects will be shared in networking environments to distribute information within a work group or to parcel out tasks for distributed processing.

From Processing to Simulating to Realizing

Applications have traditionally been viewed as programs that process data. In a manner akin to manufacturing, the user moves data from one process to another on the way to a final result. More recently, applications began to simulate possible solutions. Spreadsheets, for example, with their ability to quickly reflect changes in assumptions, simulate the process of many accounting applications and make it possible for users to try out alternative scenarios easily. Another example of a simulation approach to problem-solving can be found in an integrated desktop publishing environment. Desktop publishing applications maintain an accurate view of a document as if it were printed on paper. More recently animation and full motion video are encouraging simulation as a new form of applications in many domains. Rather than maintaining independent, intermediate results and imagining how they fit together, users of simulation software can see the solution as it develops.

Today's applications are progressing beyond processing data and simulating solutions to realizing results. Realization means that a user can select the final solution to a problem from choices generated by simulation. In the case of desktop publishing, a final solution is realized simply by taking a snapshot of the work in progress when it is deemed acceptable. No subsequent processing steps are required by the user.

While desktop publishing applications allow users to simulate and realize a solution, many applications do not. The multimedia environment necessary to support simulations may encompass synchronization of many components, including graphics, text, sound, and video. Traditional approaches to programming such complexity of datatypes and interrelations have been explored in previous chapters. The traditional approach of a set of master procedures controlling the calling of subroutines cannot handle these application requirements. Many applications are candidates for simulations. Facilities management is one such example. For instance, when active objects to which behavior can be ascribed are available, they might be used to simulate traffic patterns in a building by visitors and staff. Once the patterns that promote an even flow of people around the building are identified and tested, a successful floor plan can be printed.

Some simulations may be more dynamic and fully utilize the capabilities of object orientation. One example of such a possible simulation is in Maxis' Sim City application. Sim City is a game that allows the player to simulate city planning components including zoning, budgeting, traffic patterns, and environmental components. Most of the elements are visually expressed. Sim City contains algorithms for over ten spatial arrays for the data components, as well as over 300 objects. To the user the system appears almost unpredictable as the simulation is conducted and the objects interact. Albeit a game, Sim City is representative of a typical object-oriented simulation application. It visually presents complex interrelationships of data with about half the programmed code of a procedurally oriented application, allowing the application to run on an economical personal computer.

Realization is achieved by better integrating the software model with the world around it. For example, computer-aided publishing is realized when the text, diagrams, and color displayed on the screen are identical to the finished printed page. Computer-integrated manufacturing is realized when robots, sensors and controls are actually connected to the models running on the computer. The results of a successful computer-integrated manufacturing simulation becomes reality when instructions are downloaded from the computer to the flexible transport and tool machinery on the shop floor.

From Centralized to Distributed Computing

Until recently companies had two basic choices for their computing environments. They could centralize their data and programs in a single large computer and share those resources via terminals, or they could distribute their resources among personal computers running independent of the larger computer on every employee's desk. Each choice had obvious advantages and disadvantages. Today there are more options. Networks can interconnect computers and workstations to provide storage, processing, display, and communication services in a distributed computing environment, offering the best of both worlds. The challenge is that, to cooperate, these machines must share information. One way of accomplishing this is to develop standard protocols and formats. If all machines expect the same data and can execute the same algorithms, then computing can be distributed. Practically speaking, however, computing environments are more often heterogeneous. Not all applications conform to the same protocols or even support the same operating environments. With such heterogeneity, interoperability enabled by identical storage of data and execution of procedure is virtually impossible.

In a distributed computing environment, object-oriented techniques make cooperation easier by changing the nature of the information that is shared. A module that contains both procedures and data is intrinsically better suited for cooperation. Object-oriented systems allow applications to have active agents that perform not only well defined tasks such as computations or sorts, but even manage resources. Object-oriented approaches will allow for building agents that perform the complex cross checking and behind-the-scenes monitoring necessary to support cooperative processing challenges, such as integrity, redundancy, and changing resource conditions. This functionality will likely become standard components of distributed database applications, as well as object-oriented groupware appplications, such as electronic mail or group scheduling. Object servers, probably implemented with object-oriented databases and akin to today's data servers, will provide storage. Standards are still necessary to bridge the class libraries of various vendors, but with object orientation there is a reduction in the standards' complexity. An initial attempt to begin setting standards for object exchanges has been made in the Object Management Group led by Hewlett-Packard (Rymer 1989).

From Text and Graphics to Multimedia

Computing technology has moved from character-based displays to graphical user interfaces that communicate with icons and pointing devices in addition to keyboards and text. In the next generation, computing machines will support an even broader array of media, particularly full-motion video and sound including voice. Higher definition displays will be accompanied by new input devices, such as electronic styluses and spatially sensitive gloves.

Such multimedia capabilities allow computers to be used in new and interesting ways. Combined with the high-volume storage capability of optical media, multimedia computers will provide computer-based training with vivid imagery and the ability to browse large knowledge repositories. A mechanic learning to repair a new car model, for example, will be able to observe an animation of a master mechanic performing disassembly and diagnostic procedures. In addition, the apprentice can electronically browse information previously stored in parts catalogs and shop manuals.

To build multimedia applications, programmers must manage new types of data. Object-oriented operating systems and interfaces will help programmers to store and access multimedia data because object orientation localizes data as a part of the definition of an object. In addition to storing and accessing characteristics, multimedia data are displayed in a variety of different ways. Varying display methods with media fits well with the object-oriented perspective. Since objects encapsulate both data and methods, responsibility for displaying and editing a module of voice or video data resides with those data.

Multimedia applications also demand a high level of interactivity. Audiences will be responding to sights and sounds in real time. Application developers will be editing sequences of audio and video information and interlacing it with other media. The ability to propagate change through a hierarchy of objects provides the animator flexible editing capability. The combination of a visual environment populated with objects modeling the real world eliminates the need for the user to learn scripting or macro languages. The power of object-oriented tools and methods to handle complex constellations of data will be essential to the success of multimedia computing. In essence the computing environment becomes a soft studio for users and programmers alike.

An example of such a visual modeling approach can be found in MacroMind's Director, an application that provides users with control over the content of a presentation by direct manipulation of images, sound, and sequence. Figure 9.1 shows one of Director's screens. In this example, the author has created a sequence of three images, US Map 1, US Map 2, and Railmeet, and provided timing delays for two of these images with the watch icons. Different dissolve methods link together segments of the scene. The control panel at the bottom of the figure, modeled after the controls of a video tape player, is used to preview the results. Thus, Director provides a software alternative to the film cutting room.

From Objectlike to Object Oriented

Object orientation is new and its acceptance incremental. Thus, applications in the early 1990s will typically be objectlike rather than object oriented. Objectlike applications provide users with some, but not all, of the capabilities of object orientation. For example, objects may be available for the user to move, activate, and copy, but not to change. Objectlike applications fail to provide users with the flexibility provided by access to frameworks and class libraries. They do not provide the means to create new classes of objects, nor to easily modify the behavior of existing objects.

Apple Computer's HyperCard is an objectlike application. A HyperCard button can be cut and pasted, and the button's behavior travels with the icon. It is not possible, however, to modify the behavior of all buttons by modifying a parent class, nor is it possible to create a new button through the object-oriented paradigm of subclassing. Instead, a new button is created by copying an existing button and editing its script.

HyperCard and other objectlike applications exemplify a trend to provide objects on the outside of an application. Although the interface provides icons or objects that can be directly manipulated by the user, the application is implemented in conventional code. Users have no access to the application's class library because the library does not exist.

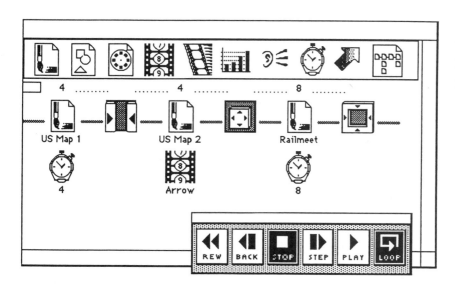

Figure 9.1
Sequencing by Direct Manipulation with MacroMind's Director

Since the underlying software does not provide inheritance mechanisms, objects on the surface lack inheritance as well. Imagine also the task of a graphic designer setting a common style for diagrams in a word processing document. A master template is prepared with proper line thickness and shadowing. Once drawn, the object can be replicated to prepare a series of templates. Replicates retain the line thickness and shadowing of the master but perhaps differ in size. The weakness of an objectlike draw program is revealed when the artist decides to change the master template. Line weight for the master template can be adjusted easily. Unfortunately, this change to the template is not reflected automatically in its replicates.

Applications with objects solely on the outside fall short of providing users with a rich and flexible object-oriented environment. Without access to a class library and inheritance mechanisms, users are deprived of one of object orientation's most powerful capabilities—abstraction. Instead of being able to extract common behavior from a set of objects and to represent it in a parent class, users of objectlike environments are forced to replicate behavior by using copy or transfer routines.

Object-oriented drawing programs have carried the object model further. Objects in these programs can be stretched, compressed, reshaped, and, in the case of three-dimensional drawing programs, assembled or dismantled into component polygons. These object-oriented programs permit the creation of multiple copies of a master object which are automatically reshaped when the master is changed. 3-D drawing programs also allow objects to retain additional behavior such as casting shadows.

Silicon Beach Software's Super 3D supports object orientation both programmatically and in the user's view. In this application five basic objects are defined in the Shape Library; points, lines, polylines, polygons, and text. A shape is formed by combining thorough inheritance sets of these objects to form a larger object or shape. Objects in these shapes are hierarchical to facilitate efficiency in performance and use of memory, to support subsequent editing and to provide animation. An illustration provided by Silicon Beach (1989) is that of preparing a model of a wagon. In this model the wagon is the parent, the bed and axles are the children, and the left and right wheels are the children of the axles. To define the model only the relationships between the objects in the parent-child hierarchy need to be defined. Animation and modeling are facilitated as the wheels move relative to the axle, and the axles move relative to the wagon. With this object-oriented approach, editing of the model is also facilitated, as change is propagated through the hierarchy.

Object orientation and its benefits can be ascribed to many potential applications. For example, Pillar Corporation has developed an object-oriented approach to a budgeting application. The application requires a parent model to be defined for an organization's budgeting process. Child models for each department maintain the fundamental framework of the parent to allow for ultimate consolidation, but facilitate the specific requirements of each department's budgeting process. The framework defined by the Chief Financial Officer was imposed without compromising the flexibility required by each department through the process of subclassing.

In the Pillar application, each entity in the budgeting process (for example, cost centers, accounts, users, and line items) is an object. Each object has sole possession and control of information particular to it, such as its name and how to calculate itself. This results in a clean separation of functionality amongst entities, and provides the user with great flexibility in changing the characteristics of the entities.

Figure 9.2 shows a budget report consisting of individual expense line items. The reference to the Travel and Entertainment account for the General Travel line item was selected by clicking on the Travel and Entertainment object in the Choices for Acct # list. This caused the account object to associate its name and number with the General

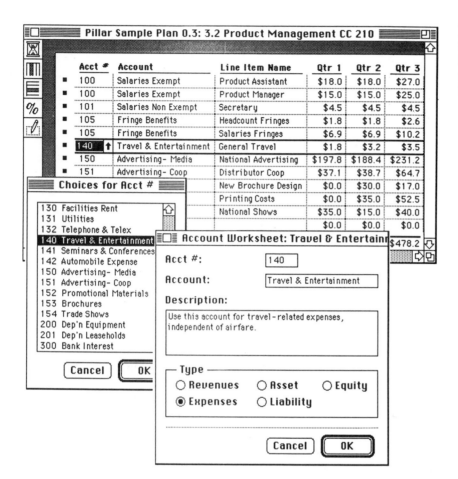

Figure 9.2
Object-Oriented
Budgeting Applica-
tion Developed by
Pillar

Travel line item. The account object in turn was created using the Account Worksheet. Revision of the account numbering scheme is straightforward because the knowledge of an account's number resides with the account object.

As object orientation becomes more commonplace, applications will be object oriented both on the outside and on the inside. Applications with an object model throughout will provide users with the full power of object orientation.

In the early 1990s few applications may qualify as fully object oriented. The primary reason is that object-oriented techniques must first be assimilated by professional programmers and accepted by corporate programming departments. Application development environments that provide objects on the inside have only recently arrived in application development shops.

Examples of Object-Oriented Applications

Not all application areas will be affected equally by object-oriented techniques. Object orientation is favored for applications where the relationships among elements in the data carry the key information. Object-oriented applications capture the relationships among data, while traditional applications perform procedures on already organized data. Engineering and technical applications are examples of applications that handle complex data types and capture the structure of the data. As discussed in Chapter 5, examples of such applications include mechanical and electrical computer aided design (MCAD and ECAD). These applications have always used complex forms of data, representing such phenomena as three-dimensional images and VLSI circuit designs. Currently these applications store their data in application-specific file structures. The data intensiveness of these applications is not only in the large amount of data that need to be programmed but also in the complexity of the data themselves. In these design-based applications, relationships among elements in the data carry key information for the user. Functional requirements for complex cross references, structural dependencies, and version management all require a rich representation of data.

As described in previous chapters the basic tenets of object-orientation can deliver benefits to programmers. In many cases these benefits are not as obvious to users. Applications developed for static domains, such as mathematical formulas, do not necessarily require the management and exploration by the user of complex datatypes and their interrelationships. Some applications derive obvious benefits in not only programmability, but also usability. Applications in the following categories are classic candidates for enhancement through object orientation:

- Computer aided software engineering (CASE),

- Computer aided instruction (CAI),

- Computer integrated manufacturing (CIM),

- Computer aided publishing (CAP), and

- Visual Programming Environments.

The influence of object orientation on these categories of emerging applications will be examined in the sections that follow.

Computer Aided Software Engineering

CASE products automate stages in the software development life cycle. First, analysis and design tools assist programmers in diagramming and documenting software requirements. Code generators then translate requirements into actual computer code, for example, lines of COBOL or C++. Reverse engineering tools help programmers to extract repository descriptions from existing code. Finally, CASE tools generate documentation of the code.

At the heart of a CASE product are the complex data structures that represent the software under construction. These high-level descriptions are stored in a repository or dictionary. Repositories contain a description of each software module and how that module relates to other modules. The description is rich enough to support a visual display of the software's design, such as a dataflow diagram, as well as to support a code generator that can write a complete and executable program. Figure 9.3 illustrates the central role of the CASE repository.

Object orientation provides an enriched architecture for building repositories (Dyson 1989). For example, CASE repositories need to store descriptions that are related hierarchically. In the object-oriented paradigm, general descriptions are stored as classes. Subclasses provide a framework of useful programming components. Objects are created to model a particular program. The repository contains only the differences between a particular object and its more generic parent classes.

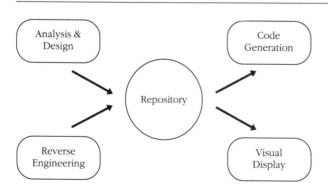

Figure 9.3
The CASE
Repository

Methods and messages provide useful mechanisms for activating code descriptions stored in the repository. Each object will know how to display itself, whether as a portion of the structure chart on the screen or as a few lines of COBOL code. When one module depends on a companion module, a message can be dispatched to activate the companion.

Put slightly differently, with object-oriented techniques, modern programmers will simulate the behavior of a software application. At any point, the CASE product can realize a final result. The simulation is also likely to occur across several computing platforms. The design can be simulated on a workstation and the code that is realized can be ported to a mainframe.

Computer Aided Instruction

Computer aided instruction (CAI) applications use computers to provide training. These applications were often called automated page turners because they did little more than provide an electronic presentation of static information stored in workbooks and textbooks. Later, authoring languages were created that allowed developers to sequence instructional modules depending on the responses of the learner. This allowed fast learners to move rapidly and those failing to prove competence to be guided to remedial lessons. These more sophisticated tutoring programs were referred to as Intelligent Computer Aided Instruction (ICAI) and aimed to provide the judgment that a human tutor might make when interpreting a learner's error. Finally, with the arrival of random-access storage of audio and video data, CAI applications can include these media with screen-based instruction.

CAI applications will profit from object orientation for several reasons. CAI applications typically involve manipulating several categories of information simultaneously. Subject matter must be stored so that it can be browsed and the interrelationships among topics and terms explored. In addition, the sequence of instruction must be represented along with branching and entry points for relocating learners in the learning sequence. Finally, the student's current state of understanding must be monitored.

As illustrated in Figure 9.4, this scheme is analogous to the model-view-controller (MVC) paradigm discussed In Chapter 6. The Tutoring Model functions as a coordinator, with a role similar to that of the Controller in an interactive user interface application. The Student Model maintains information on the student's capabilities and progress. The Domain Model contains the subject matter to be presented.

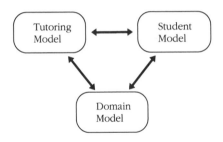

Figure 9.4
The Three Models
of CAI

In addition, new CAI applications will support multimedia, such as full-motion video, to provide learners with vivid and realistic sources of information. This complexity fits well within the visual orientation of object-oriented applications as previously illustrated in MacroMind's Director application, Figure 9.1.

Several characteristics of object orientation will leverage the work of CAI designers. Objects provide a convenient way to model complex subject matter. Active objects representing key elements of the instructional domain can interact with one another to provide the backbone of an environment where students can test their ideas. Early CAI programs were able only to generate and test mathematical problems. In the future ICAI programs will generate and test symbolic problems.

One of the early demonstrations of simulation-based learning in an object-oriented environment was developed at Xerox Palo Alto Research Center in a marketing game called Truckin' (Stefik *et al.* 1983). The game is played by writing a set of business rules for a fictitious company. Several players create companies with different business strategies, and the businesses flourish or fail as the the objects message each other and react to messages from the environment.

Many new applications in the business presentation, educational, and entertainment categories have demonstrated the value of object orientation. For example, the media laboratories of Apple Computer have demonstrated how object-oriented environments can support the intermingling of high quality audio and visual data to produce musical appreciation courseware that accesses musical CDs and political history courseware that browses video CDs.

Computer Integrated Manufacturing

CIM applications provide tools for managing complex manufacturing information such as incoming orders, the implication of orders on both financial and engineering goals, and the status of a factory containing a variety of machines. The application division of Servio-Logic Corporation, for example, has prototyped a set of tools for capacity planners called CIMulators. Servio-Logic Corporation believes that such applications will be increasingly useful when data can be captured, stored, and applied with object-oriented techniques.

The CIMulator toolkit contains a capacity plan manager based on an object-oriented data representation. The interface is a special implementation of a browser that has been tailored for capacity planning. Browsers, as discussed in Chapter 8, provide navigation support for programmers and users who need to locate and modify the contents of classes and subclasses related hierarchically. This browser allows the capacity planner to modify plans and keep track of earlier versions of plans. In addition, the browser can inspect databases showing available machines, the status of raw materials, or the backlog of orders.

Products like CIMulator illustrate how object-oriented techniques will affect applications in the area of computer integrated manufacturing. Object orientation provides support for browsing and managing complex, interrelated sets of data.

Computer Aided Publishing

The publishing industry is moving rapidly toward a goal of making document components reusable and portable. The challenge is very similar to challenges faced by programmers. In the case of publishing, authors would rather not maintain lines of text and would prefer to assemble units of text. In addition, these logical units must be represented in such a way that they can be displayed in a variety of different media.

In moving toward the paradigm of object-orientation, the publishing industry has developed a language called standard generalized markup language (SGML) with which to describe textual units. Gilbane (1989) calls these units logical objects. Logical objects are units of text that can be reused because they are independent from any particular document or medium. A unit of text carries with it structural identifiers without specific commitment to form. For example, a unit of text is stored as a three column table, but the width of the table, the font, and the thickness of the column rules remain unspecified. Information stored once as an SGML three-column table might appear in a scrollable window as part of an on-line help system, in a bound reference manual typeset in helvetica, and in a loose-leaf users guide printed in a typewriter font. Text stored as logical objects can thus be assembled in different ways, published with different specifications, and printed in a variety of formats and media.

Form   Structure

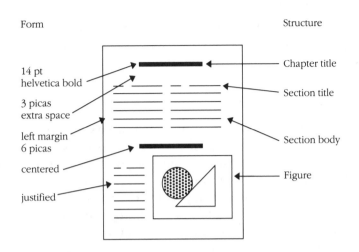

14 pt
helvetica bold

3 picas
extra space

left margin
6 picas

centered

justified

Chapter title

Section title

Section body

Figure

Figure 9.5
Document Structure versus Document Form

Logical structure is a more flexible description of a document than the traditional specification of form. As Figure 9.5 shows, form has traditionally consisted of exact specifications for the printing of a document. Logical structures such as paragraphs and displays do not necessarily encode all of the details. The purpose of SGML is to provide a language for describing structure. Decisions about form are deferred until it is time to publish. Text marked for emphasis may appear in reverse video on a computer screen, underscored on a line printer, and in italics on a laser printer.

SGML encourages an object-oriented view of information, as shown in Figure 9.6. A structural object contains information about paragraphs, titles, tables, and other logical units, Content objects, on the other hand,

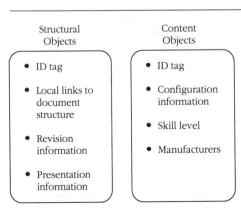

Structural
Objects

- ID tag

- Local links to
  document
  structure

- Revision
  information

- Presentation
  information

Content
Objects

- ID tag

- Configuration
  information

- Skill level

- Manufacturers

Figure 9.6
Objects as Defined by SGML

contain the subject matter. Logical units can be printed with different structural characteristics. By factoring the document in this way, flexibility is maintained.

Visual Programming Environments

Programming by direct manipulation has appeared in several applications. One context is in spreadsheet applications, in which users are able to select formulas from a menu and mark an area of a spreadsheet to be processed by the formula rather than by typing in instructions. Such direct manipulation of visual information is much easier than entering parameters and equations. Spreadsheets and word processors have allowed users to program in limited but meaningful ways. In the future, users will find that they have even more control over the software they use.

Some object-oriented applications provide general-purpose visual programming environments for the construction of entire applications. As shown in Figure 9.7, the Prograph environment from TGS Systems allows users visual access to a class hierarchy, the methods associated with a class, and the inner structure of a method. In this example, class menu is selected from the class library, which appears in the background. Methods associated with class menu are also shown, and the

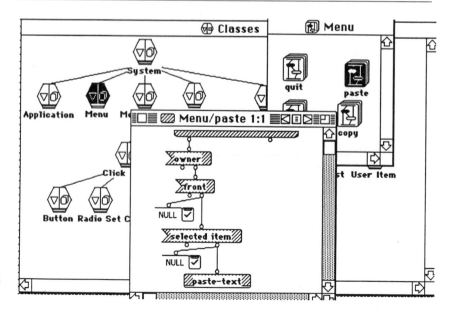

Figure 9.7
Visual Programming in Prograph

inner structure of the paste method is in the foreground. Users can manipulate the diagram of the paste method, and in doing so, they modify the underlying code. The Prograph environment also supports a debugging facility that allows users to view the execution of methods via a familiar dataflow diagram.

Products like Prograph are still primarily targeted to users with a programming background. In the coming years, however, visual programming environments will be pervasive and will most likely be included with applications constructed from class libraries.

Future Trends in Object-Oriented Applications

In the 1990s object-oriented applications will most likely gain in both presence and popularity. Several trends will drive the increased availability of object-oriented applications.

■ Class libraries and application frameworks will appear in the marketplace replacing today's stackware and macros. These libraries will be delivered as part of the actual applications and as aftermarket add-ons. User accessibility to the libraries will allow construction of special-purpose applications by assembling and tailoring classes. Interfaces to the applications and the libraries will be visual, with most programming accomplished by directly manipulating icons.

■ Information access will be transparent across applications and environments. Just as today's writers expect to see on the screen an exact replica of work in progress, tomorrow's professionals will expect to move freely among all varieties of data and media.

■ Applications will increasingly be viewed as models of real world environments and events. Object orientation will encourage this view and will facilitate the management of the synchronization of a multitude of datatypes. Approaching an application as a model will also result in the use of simulations for an increasingly large number of applications.

Summary

Object orientation is a required and natural paradigm for many familiar applications. These classic applications, typically in the design area, require the user to view not only specific data elements but also the interrelationships of the data elements themselves. Many other applications already provide objects on the exterior of the application. Although these objects are easy to copy and manipulate, they cannot be modified and adapted in a fully object-oriented manner. Applications supporting object orientation will allow users to access and tailor elements of the underlying class library. Future applications will likely provide complete visual programming environments.

Key Points

- Object-oriented applications will enable users to model the application closer to the real world environment. Users can then simulate and realize solutions to their problems.

- Early applications will provide objects on the outside that users can manipulate but cannot change. Later applications will expose objects on the inside that users can modify with the full power of object orientation.

- In the 1990s, object-oriented applications will set a new standard for software flexibility and power. Users will program by accessing frameworks and class libraries.

For Further Reading

Bryan, M. 1988. *SGML: An Author's Guide to the Standardized Generalized Markup Language.* Reading, Mass.: Addison-Wesley.
   This guide describes the evolution of object orientation as it applies to document-based applications.

Dyson, E. 1989. "Object-oriented database roundup." *Release 1.0,* September 22. New York: EDventure Holdings Inc.
   As object-oriented applications appear in the 1990s, they will be faithfully dissected and evaluated in Esther Dyson's newsletter. Look to Release 1.0 for a reliable analysis of what is new and what it means.

Friedhoff, R., and Benzon, W. 1989. *The Second Computer Revolution: Visualization.* New York: Harry N. Abrams, Inc.
   This book provides a background on the supporting technologies of visualization and provides many examples of visual thinking with computer applications.

OOPSLA, the Association for Computing Machinery's Conference on Object-Oriented Programming Systems, Languages, and Applications.

Contact the ACM for more information about OOPSLA, an annual conference focusing on object-oriented applications.

References

Gilbane, F. 1989. *An Update on CALS Publishing Issues.* Seybold Computer Publishing Conference, September, San Francisco.

Rymer, J. R. 1989. "Objects at floodtide: Object orientation permeates new development." *Patricia Seybold's Office Computing Report.* 12(6), June.

Silicon Beach Software. 1989. *Super 3D User Manual For Macintosh.* San Diego, Calif.: Silicon Beach Software.

Stefik, M., Bobrow, D. G., Mittal, S., and Conway, L. 1983. "Knowledge programming in LOOPS: Report on an experimental course." *AI Magazine* 4(3).

Part 4

Appendices

- **Glossary**

- **Collected References**

- **Index**

Appendix A

Glossary

- ■ **Terms**

- ■ **Acronyms**

This appendix provides a brief definition for the technical terms and acronyms used in the book. The complete definition of a term and its relationship to object orientation will be found in the body of the book.

Check this appendix to confirm the meaning of technical terms related to object orientation.

Terms

Abstraction: the process of creating a superclass by extracting common qualities or general characteristics from more specific classes or objects.

Active object: an object that monitors events occurring in an application and takes action autonomously. Sometimes called an agent or demon.

ACTOR: an object-oriented programming language with a Pascal-like syntax from the Whitewater Group of Evanston, Ill.

Ada: a Pascal-based high-level programming language developed as standard for the U.S. Department of Defense.

Agent: *See* Active object.

ALGOL: ALGOrithmic Language. A general-purpose, high-level programming language introduced in the early 1960s.

Algorithm: a set of steps in a specific order used to solve a problem, such as a mathematical formula or a series of instructions in a program.

Algorithmic: based on algorithms.

Assembly language: a hardware-dependent language that is one level above machine language. The assembler program translates each statement in assembly language into one machine instruction.

Assertions: *See* Triggers and assertions.

Attribute: a property or characteristic of an object.

Binding: the process of weaving a program together to resolve all the connections among its components. Static, or early, binding resolves these connections before the program is run. Dynamic, or late, binding occurs while the program is running.

Black box: an engineering metaphor that describes a device whose inner components are unknown to the user. Objects are like black boxes in that their inner workings are concealed from users and programmers.

Browser: a tool supplied with the programming language that lets the programmer view the hierarchy and edit code in object-oriented languages.

Byte: the common unit of storage equivalent to 8 bits or a single character, such as a letter of the alphabet or a single digit from 0 to 9.

C: a high-level programming language originally developed by Bell Laboratories.

C++: an object-oriented superset of the C Language written by Bjarne Stroustrup at AT&T's Bell Laboratories. The term C++, coined by Rick Muscatti, means "more than C."

Cache memory: (1) a reserved section of main memory (RAM), or (2) an independent bank of high-speed memory that acts as a buffer between main memory and the CPU to improve performance.

Caching: retaining data in cache memory for rapid access.

Call: a statement in a program that references an independent subroutine or program. After it finishes processing, the called routine or program returns back to the calling program.

Calling program: a program that initiates a call to another program. *See* Call.

Capsule: a term used by Metaphor Computing Systems describing a series of defined operations saved in a procedure. Capsules can call other capsules and can be public or private. Similar to an object in other systems, but without inheritance.

Child: *See* Parent-child.

Child class: *See* Subclass.

Class: the description of a set of nearly identical objects that share common methods and general characteristics.

Class library: a collection of generic classes that can be adapted and tailored for a particular application.

Client /server: a relationship between machines in a communications network. The client is the requesting machine; the server is the supplying machine.

Clipboard: a reserved segment of memory used for temporary storage of data (text or graphics) that have been copied from one document in order to insert them into another. Sometimes called a paste buffer.

Clustering: the storing of objects contiguously on a disk for efficient accessing.

Compiler: a software program that translates a programming language into the machine language the computer understands.

Concurrency: the ability of a running program to do two or more different things at the same time.

Concurrent language: a language that supports the simultaneous execution of multiple objects, usually on parallel architecture hardware.

Cut and paste: an operation that moves text or graphics from one part of the document or file to another.

Data flow diagram: a diagram that illustrates the movement of data as well as any manual and computer processing that is done to it.

Data integrity: the state of data that have been protected from accidental erasure or uncontrolled change.

Database: a collection of data that are stored and managed electronically.

Database management system (DBMS): a set of software programs that control the organization, storage and retrieval, security, and integrity of a database. There are typically three components to a DBMS: a data definition language that describes the data, a data manipulation language that describes what you want to do with the data (e.g., create, update, delete), and a data control language that describes who can access what, when, and where.

Database server: a stand-alone computer in a local area network that holds and manages the database. Operations such as retrieval of records are performed in the server computer. This is in contrast to a file server, which acts as a remote disk drive and requires that large parts of the database be transmitted to the user's computer for such operations.

DB2: a mainframe-based relational database management system from IBM.

Debug: to locate and repair software errors in a program's logic or to correct hardware by locating and repairing errors in circuit design.

Debugger: a program that enables users to correct software errors by examining and changing memory content and starting or stopping execution at a predetermined spot or "breakpoint."

De facto standard: a format or language that is in widespread use but which has not been officially sanctioned by a standards organization, such as the American National Standards Institute (ANSI). *See* ANSI.

Demon: *See* Active object.

Derived class: a subclass in C++. *See* Subclass.

Digital signal processing: a set of techniques that operate on signals generated from a wide range of sources to analyze, break apart, and convert them into digital form.

Display PostScript: a display language from Adobe Corporation that translates elementary commands in an application program to graphics and text elements on screen. The screen counterpart of the PostScript printer language. *See* PostScript.

Distributed database: a database that is geographically dispersed and physically stored in two or more computer systems and then managed and controlled as a single collection of data.

Distributed processing: a system of computers connected together by a communications network with each computer system handling its local workload and the network supporting the system as a whole.

Dynamic binding: the implementation consequence of inheritance and polymorphism. As an object-oriented program runs, messages are received by objects. Often the method for handling a message is stored high in a class library. The method is located dynamically when it is needed and binding then occurs at the last possible moment. *See* Binding.

Early binding: static binding. *See* Binding.

Eiffel: an object-oriented language derived from Smalltalk and developed by Bertrand Meyer.

End user: an operator of a personal computer or workstation or a user of the computer's output.

Encapsulation: the bundling of methods and instance variables within a class or object so that access to the instance variables is permitted only through the object's own methods.

Extensibility: the ability of a program or system to be easily altered so it can deal with new input classes.

Event-driven: similar to real-time programming, an event-driven program has a dispatch loop as the highest level of organization. The loop responds to all user actions, allowing the user to have complete control of the interface with the underlying program ready to respond whenever action is appropriate.

File server: in a local area network, a computer that stores the programs and data files shared by the users connected to the network.

Finder: *See* Macintosh.

Flavors: an object-oriented extension to LISP. Flavors was developed at MIT. *See* LISP.

Framework: a class library that is tuned especially for a particular category of application.

Function library: *See* Procedure.

G-base: an object-oriented LISP-based database from Graphael.

Garbage collection: a memory management routine that searches memory for program segments, data, or objects that are no longer active and reclaims the unused space.

Generic function: the message-passing mechanism in CLOS built to support the programming of simultaneous events. Also, a function whose behavior depends upon the classes of the arguments passed to it.

Gemstone: an object-oriented database from Servio-Logic, Inc.

Global variable: a variable accessible to all modules in a program.

Granularity: the level of modularity of a system. Finer granularity indicates smaller modules and provides greater flexibility.

Graphics primitive: a graphical building block, such as a line or an arc.

Handle: a system-defined 32-bit value in Presentation Manager and 16-bit value in Windows that identifies an object.

Heap: a complete binary tree whose nodes contain search keys arranged in descending order.

Hiding: *See* Information hiding.

Hierarchical: description of a system that has a structure made up of different levels with the higher levels having control or precedence over the lower levels.

Hierarchical file system: a file system that stores data in a treelike top-to-bottom organizational structure.

High-level languages: machine-independent programming languages, as opposed to assembly and machine languages, which are considered low-level.

Hypercard: an Apple Macintosh-based database program that uses an iconic representation of a paper card. A file of cards is called a stack; cards can be customized with graphic images and button icons.

IBM-compatible PC: a personal computer that is compatible with the IBM standard.

Icon: a graphical representation of an object (e.g., a data file, text document, or disk drive) on the screen. Icons are usually manipulated by the use of a mouse or other pointing device.

Iconic interface: a user interface that displays objects on the screen as tiny pictures that the user can point to and select via a mouse.

Identity-based database: a database in which entities can be referenced by their unique identities.

Information cluster: *See* Clustering.

Information hiding: a design strategy that aims at maximizing modularity by concealing as much information as possible within the components of a design.

Inheritance: a mechanism for automatically sharing methods and data types among classes, subclasses, and objects. Not found in procedural systems. Inheritance allows programmers to program only what is different from previously defined classes.

Instance: an object that is a member of a class.

Instance variable: data contained within an object that describe properties that the object possesses.

Interactive video: the use of a videodisc or CD ROM that is controlled by a computer for an interactive education or entertainment program.

Interpretive language: a programming language that requires an interpreter or translator program to run it. Interpreters translate programs on a statement-by-statement basis. Compiled languages do not require interpreters.

Join: the matching of one file in a database against another based on some condition and the creation of a third file containing data from the matching files. For example, a vendor file can be joined with a purchase order file to create a file of records of all vendors of a product.

Kernel: a fundamental part of a program, such as an operating system, that resides in memory at all times.

Kilo: one thousand.

Kilobyte: 1,000 bytes or characters.

Late binding: dynamic binding. *See* Binding.

Macintosh: a line of Motorola 6800-based 32-bit personal computers from Apple Computer. Initially introduced in 1984, the Macintosh runs a proprietary operating system that includes a simulated desktop (see Finder). The Macintosh supports medium-high-resolution graphics and has a built-in graphics language. *See* QuickDraw.

Macintosh user interface: a graphical user interface that evolved from work done in the 1970s at Xerox PARC. Common features include a pointing device or a mouse, windows, onscreen menus, icons representing files and directories, and a number of other graphical metaphors that let the user tell the computer what to do.

Macro: a small program or script commonly used to automate a series of processes or keystrokes in spreadsheet, word processor, and other application programs.

Maintainability: the ability of a program or system to be easily changed to fix newly discovered bugs and to extend functionality to meet new user requirements.

Mega: one million.

Megabyte: 1,000,000 or 1,048,576 bytes or characters.

Memory management: the way a computer deals with its memory. Includes memory protection and any virtual memory or memory swapping techniques.

Menu-driven: describes a program that is commanded by selecting options from a list displayed on screen.

Message: a request sent to an object to change its state or return a value. The same message can be sent to different objects because messages simply tell an object *what* to do. Methods, defined within the receiving object, determine *how* that object will carry out the request. *See* Method, Polymorphism.

Message-passing: a mechanism that allows objects to send messages among themselves.

Message queue: *See* Queueing.

Method: the function or procedure that implements the response when a message is sent to an object. Methods determine how an object will respond to a message that it receives. *See* Message.

Mouse: a peripheral attached to a computer and used as pointing and drawing device. As it is rolled across the desktop in any direction, the cursor moves correspondingly on the screen.

MultiFinder: a multitasking version of the Macintosh's Finder facility. *See* Macintosh.

Multiple inheritance: the ability of subclasses to inherit instance variables and methods from more than one class. Useful in building composite behavior from more than one branch of a class hierarchy.

Name clashing: a conflict that can occur in multiple inheritance, when the same method or instance variable is inherited from multiple classes.

NewWave: an operating environment from Hewlett-Packard that provides an object-management shell facility allowing data from various different applications to be merged together to create a compound document. NewWave runs with Microsoft's DOS, with Windows, and OS/2 with Presentation Manager.

Nonprocedural language: a programming language that generates the logic for the program directly from the user's description of the problem, rather than from a set of procedures based on traditional programming logic.

Normalize: the breaking down of data into record groups for efficient processing in a relational database system.

Object: the primitive element in object-oriented programming. Objects are entities that encapsulate within themselves both the data describing the object and the instructions for operating on that data.

Object identity: something about an object that remains invariant across all possible modifications of its state. Can be used to point to the object.

Object orientation: a level of computer abstraction beyond that of procedures and data. Object orientation involves thinking about the world as a set of entities or objects that are related to and communicate with one another.

Object-oriented analysis: analysis of a system's requirements in terms of real-world objects.

Object-oriented database: a database that allows data to be stored as objects.

Object-oriented design: translating the logical structure of a system into a physical structure composed of software objects.

Object-oriented graphics: generally refers to a drawing program that appears to the user to be composed of objects on the screen.

Object-oriented interface: an interface based on the direct manipulation of objects such as icons and menus.

Object-oriented language: a computer language that supports objects, classes, subclasses, methods, messages, and inheritance. Secondary features may include multiple inheritance, dynamic binding, and polymorphism.

Object-oriented programming: a methodology for creating programs using collections of self-sufficient objects that have encapsulated data and behavior and which act upon, request, and interact with each other by passing messages back and forth.

Objective-C: an object-oriented programming language from The Stepstone Corporation, formed by adding Smalltalk-inspired constructs to the C language.

Operating system: the program that runs the computer and controls the scheduling and execution of multiple programs. The operating system sets the standards for the other programs that the computer runs.

Operator overloading: a programming language feature that allows the same operator to be used with different types, such as the use of " + " with both integers and real numbers.

Package: in Ada, the term given to new data types or classes, which contain both public and private information.

Parent-child: a way of expressing the relationship between classes and subclasses. Child classes or subclasses inherit the methods and instance variables of the parent class. With multiple inheritance, a child class may have several parents.

Parent class: *See* Superclass.

Pascal: a high-level programming language originally developed by Niklaus Wirth in the early 1970s.

Passive object: an object that acts only upon request, such as Apple's Hypercard buttons, which must be pressed into action.

Paste: *See* Cut and paste.

Persistence: the permanence of an object, particularly relevant in the context of object-oriented databases, which maintain a distinction between objects created only for the duration of execution and those intended for permanent storage.

Point and click: to position the cursor over an object displayed on the screen (*point*) and press the mouse or pointing device to select it (*click*).

Polymorphism: the ability of the same message to be interpreted differently when received by different objects. The message print, for example, when sent to a figure or diagram, evokes a different method or implementation than the same print message sent to a textual document. *See* Message.

PostScript: a page description language from Adobe Corporation that allows an application program to describe text fonts and graphics images for printing.

Presentation Manager: a windowing environment from Microsoft Corporation and IBM that runs under the OS/2 operating system. It is similar to Microsoft's Windows for its DOS operating system. Both Windows and Presentation Manager are modeled after the interface developed at Xerox PARC in the 1970s.

Preprocessor: a software program that performs some preliminary processing on the input before it is processed by the main program. For example, C++ source code is commonly preprocessed or translated to C source code before it is compiled.

Procedural language: a programming language such as COBOL, FOR-TRAN, BASIC, C, and Pascal, based on using a proper order of actions and having a knowledge of data processing operations and programming techniques.

Procedure: a particular action called by another procedure. Similar to a subroutine.

Program: a collection of instructions that tell the computer what to do. A program is written in a programming language and is converted into the computer's machine language by software called assemblers and compilers.

Protocol: the set of messages to which an object can respond.

Pull-down menu: a menu that, when selected by pointing to a title on the screen, appears to be pulled downward from the point of selection.

Query: a high-level specification of a set of objects you want to access.

Query language: a generalized language that permits a user to interrogate a database.

QuickDraw: the proprietary graphics display system that is built into Apple's Macintosh computer line. It is analogous to PostScript. *See* PostScript.

Quick Pascal: a version of object-oriented Pascal from Microsoft Corporation.

Recursion: the ability of a subroutine or program module to call itself.

Relational database: a database organized physically as a set of simple tables. Any logical view of the data can be formed by joining simple tables together in different ways. Relational databases are more flexible than hierarchical and network databases, which contain records in one file that have pointers to the locations of records in other files.

Schema generation: the automatic generation of a database's schema, or description of its records and fields and how they are related, from a data definition language.

Schema modification: the process of restructuring a database.

Semaphore: a construct that provides synchronized communication between processes by sending them signal and wait messages.

Simula: a language developed in the late 1960s for programming simulations. Simula included class and inheritance mechanisms and is considered to have influenced today's object-oriented languages.

Simulation: the mathematical representation of the interaction of real-world objects.

Slots: instance variables in CLOS.

Smalltalk: the first truly object-oriented programming language and environment. Developed at Xerox PARC in the late 1970s, it was originally used to create prototypes of simpler programming languages and window-oriented graphical interfaces. Its integrated environment eliminates the distinction between programming language and operating system and allows the programmer to customize the user interface and behavior of the system.

Smalltalk / V: a version of the Smalltalk language available from Digitalk Corporation.

Static typing: the addition of types to each object at compile time. With static typing, the runtime search for the appropriate method for a message is restricted to the receiver's class and superclass, insuring that an appropriate method will always be found.

Static binding: early binding. *See* Binding.

Structured programming: a programming philosophy aimed at managing complexity by formalizing and standardizing programming methodology. Structured programming is a top-down approach: The program is abstracted into its simplest, most general form; divided into smaller, independent modules; and program components are organized into a hierarchical structure.

Subclass: the refinement of a class into a more specialized class. Sometimes referred to as a *derived* or *child* class. Common methods and data types are stored in as abstract a class as possible so they can be inherited by all relevant subclasses.

Subroutine: *See* Procedure.

Superclass: in an inheritance hierarchy, a more general class that stores variables and methods that can be inherited by other classes. Sometimes referred to as a *base* or *parent* class.

Symbolic debugger: a debugger that allows the programmer to trace the values of variables in a program by requesting a particular symbol or name from the source code.

Top-down programming: a methodology that produces a hierarchically structured, modular program. The designer first designs, codes, and tests a top-level module that represents the overall structure of the program and then proceeds in the same way to create lower-level modules that represent its subfunctions. *See* Structured programming.

Traditional programming: programming using procedural languages such as FORTRAN, COBOL, and BASIC. Such languages support program construction based on determining the sequence of procedures that act on a separate set of data. Traditional programming is done in three sequential phases: design, implementation, and testing.

Transactions: units of work that, when allowed to proceed concurrently, are guaranteed to produce results that are equivalent to the results produced by serial execution.

Triggers and assertions: concepts referring to the storage and execution of procedures as a part of an object-oriented database. An *assertion* is a property of the object with which it is associated, typically some condition that the object must satisfy. A *trigger* is a procedure that is automatically activated whenever a predefined condition arises. Triggers and assertions are like methods, but are not encapsulated along with the local data on which they operate.

Turbo Pascal: a version of object-oriented Pascal from Borland International.

Tuple: a record, or row, in relational database management.

UNIX: a multiuser, multitasking operating system from AT&T that runs on a wide variety of computer systems.

User: *See* End user.

Vbase: an object-oriented database from Servio-Logic.

Variable: a structure in memory that holds the data that have been assigned to it until a new value is assigned to it or the program is finished.

Virtual: a simulated or conceptual environment. Virtual reality, for example, is simulated reality.

Virtual function: a special member function that is invoked through a base class reference or pointer and is bound dynamically at runtime.

Visual programming: a general category of applications that make programming graphical and its effects visible to the user. In drawing packages, for example, objects can be drawn, stretched, and otherwise modified by directly manipulating the image on the screen, rather than by changing numerical data in a table of dimensions.

Widget: a predefined window element used in the X Window environment.

Windows: a separate viewing area on a display screen provided by the software. Operating systems can provide multiple windows on screen, allowing the user to keep several application programs active and visible at the same time. Individual application programs can provide multiple windows as well, providing a viewing capability into more than one document, spreadsheet, or data file.

When used as a proper name, Windows refers to a windowing program from Microsoft Corporation that runs in IBM-compatible PCs under Microsoft's DOS operating system.

Window environment: a computer that is running under an operating system that provides multiple windows on screen. DESQview, Microsoft Windows, Presentation Manager, Finder, MultiFinder, and X Window are examples of windows environments.

X Window: a windowing environment for graphics workstations developed at MIT, Digital Equipment Corporation, and IBM. X Windows differs from traditional windowing programs that work on a single computer system in that it allows graphics generated in one computer system to be displayed on another workstation in the network. X Windows is designed to run under any operating system and is supported by all major graphics workstation vendors.

Acronyms

5GL: Fifth-Generation Language.

AIX: Advanced Interactive eXecutive. IBM's version of the UNIX operating system. AIX is based on AT&T's UNIX System V with Berkeley extensions.

ANSI: American National Standards Institute. A membership organization that is devoted to the development of American industry standards and coordinates and manages American participation in the International Standards Organization (ISO) and the International Electrotechnical Commission (IEC). The standards related to data and communication codes and to programming and data management languages. ANSI was founded in 1918.

API: Application Program Interface. A language used between programs such as the application program and the operating system.

A/UX: Apple's version of the UNIX operating system, based on AT&T's UNIX System V with Berkeley extensions.

Blob: Binary Large OBject. Commonly refers to a data type useful for storing large chunks of data and is frequently used in comparing relations and object-oriented databases. A blob becomes object oriented only if methods are encapsulated with data, message handling capability exists, and the blob is part of a class hierarchy.

CAD: Computer Aided Design. CAD drawings can also provide input (in two or three dimensions) into computer aided manufacturing (CAM) systems.

CAD/CAM: Computer Aided Design/Computer Aided Manufacturing. Products designed in a CAD system and used as direct input into a CAM system. For example, after a part is designed in a CAD system, its electronic image is transferred to a numerical control (NC) programming language, which then generates the machine instructions to control the machine that fabricates the part.

CAE: Computer Aided Engineering. Software that automatically analyzes designs that have been created by CAD systems or otherwise entered into the computer.

CAM: Computer Aided Manufacturing. An extensive category of automated manufacturing systems and techniques, including numerical control, process control, robotics, and materials requirements planning (MRP).

CAP: Computer Aided Publishing. The use of software packages to facilitate the layout of text and graphics in publishing applications.

CASE: Computer Aided Software (or Systems) Engineering. The use of software packages that aid in one or more phases of the system life cycle: analysis, design, programming, or maintenance.

CD: Compact Disk. An audio disk that contains up to 72 minutes of high-fidelity stereo sound. A CD is a direct-access device, and the individual selections can be played back in any sequence.

CD-ROM: Compact Disk Read-Only Memory. A compact disc format used to hold data that include text, graphics, and motion video as well as audio. CD ROM disks hold in excess of 600 megabytes of data, which is equivalent to about 250,000 pages of text or 20,000 medium-resolution images. *See* DYI.

CIM: Computer Integrated Manufacturing. The integration of the automated factory (such as machine tool scheduling) and manufacturing accounting systems (such as bill of materials).

CLOS: Common Lisp Object System. An object-oriented version of the artificial intelligence language, LISP.

COBOL: COmmon Business-Oriented Language. A compiled high-level procedural programming language.

CUA: Common User Access. One of three categories for standard protocols that make up IBM's system application architecture.

CPU: Central Processing Unit. The part of the computer that internally performs the arithmetic and logical processing.

DBMS: DataBase Management System.

DDE: Dynamic Data Exchange. The message protocol in Microsoft Windows that allows application programs to request and exchange data automatically. It enables a program in one window to query another program in another window.

DEC: Digital Equipment Corporation.

DLL: Dynamic Link Libraries.

DOS: Disk Operating System. The operating system used in IBM compatible PCs, known as DOS, PC-DOS or MS-DOS. DOS for mainframes usually refers to the IBM DOS/VSE operating system.

DVI: Digital Video Interactive. A CD (compact disk) format that includes data, audio, and full-motion video. This format provides up to 72 minutes of full-screen video and audio or up to two and a half hours of half-screen video. DVI's proprietary compression techniques, which compress full-motion video at a ratio of 100 to 1 and still images at 10 to 1, allow the disks to hold up to 40,000 medium-resolution images or 7,000 high-resolution images.

ECAD: Electronic Computer Aided Design, i.e., CAD for electronic design.

FDDI: Fiber-Distributed Data Interface.

GOOD: General Object-Oriented Software Development. An early methodology primarily developed for use in the Ada environment.

GUI: Graphical User Interface.

HOOD: Hierarchical Object-Oriented Design. An early methodology primarily developed for use in the Ada environment.

ISDN: Integrated Service Digital Network. An international telecommunications standard that allows a communications channel to simultaneously carry voice, video, and data.

LAN: Local Area Network. A communications network that serves several users within a confined geographical area, building, or plant. Generally refers to the interconnection of personal computers functioning as distributed processing systems in which each computer, or node, in the network does its own processing and manages some of its data. Shared data are stored in a file server, which acts as a remote disk drive to all the users in the network.

LISP: List Processing Language. An artificial intelligence language that contributed dynamic binding and an interactive development environment to the evolution of object-oriented languages.

MCAD: Mechanical Computer Aided Design, i.e., CAD for mechanical design.

MIPS: Millions of Instructions Per Second. A measure of computing power. A mainframe can typically perform 10 to 50 MIPS; a microprocessor might be in the 0.05 MIPS range.

MOOD: Multiple-View Object-Oriented Design. An early methodology primarily developed for use in the Ada environment.

MPW: Macintosh Programmers' Workbench.

MS-DOS: *See* DOS.

MS-Windows: *See* Windows.

MRP: Materials Requirement Planning.

MVC: Model-View-Controller. A framework for building user interfaces associated most frequently with Smalltalk-80.

OODB: Object-Oriented DataBase.

OOP: Object-Oriented Programming.

OOSD: Object-Oriented Structural Design.

OPAL: Operational Performance Analysis Language. The proprietary data definition and manipulation language provided with Servio-Logic's object-oriented database Gemstone.

OS/2: Operating System/2. A single-user multitasking operating system from Microsoft and IBM that runs on 286 and 386-based IBM compatible personal computers.

PARC: Palo Alto Research Center. An advanced research and development arm of the Xerox corporation which developed many of the underlying techniques for Smalltalk and graphical user interfaces.

RAM: Random Access Memory. The computer's primary working memory. Called random access because each byte of memory can be accessed without regard to the adjacent byte or bytes.

RDMS: Relational Database Management System. *See* Relational Database.

SAA: System Application Architecture. SAA is a set of standards introduced by IBM in 1987 that provide consistent interconnections among all of IBM's computers. SAA includes standards for user interfaces, software interfaces, communications protocols, and other conventions.

SGML: Standard Generalized Markup Language.

SQL: Structured Query Language. A language designed to interrogate and process data in a relational database. There are many varieties of SQL incorporated into a large number of software packages.

TDL: Transaction Definition Language. Vbase's proprietary language for database schema generation.

VGA: Video Graphics Array. A high-resolution display system built into various models of IBM's PS/2 and also available for IBM PCs.

WAN: Wide Area Network.

WYSIWYG: What You See Is What You Get. The ability of a program to display on the screen the graphics and text exactly as the printer will print them.

XCMD: External Command.

Appendix B
Collected References

Alsop, S. 1989. *P.C. Letter.* 5 (7), April 16.

American Programmer. 1989. Special issue on object orientation, Vol. 2, Nos. 7–8, Summer.

Asente, P. 1988. "Simplicity and productivity." *UNIX Review,* September.

Bailin, S. 1989. "An object-oriented requirements specification method." *Communications of the Association for Computing Machinery,* Vol. 32, No. 5, May.

Beck, K., and Cunningham, W. 1989. "A laboratory for teaching object-oriented thinking." *Proceedings of Object-Oriented Programming: Systems, Languages, and Applications 1989* (OOPSLA '89). *SIGPLAN Notices,* Vol. 24, No. 10, October, pp. 1–6.

Bobrow, D., DeMichiel, L., Gabriel, R., Kiczales, G., and Moon, D. 1988. *Common Lisp Object System Specifications.* X3J13 Document 88–002R, American National Standards Institute.

Bochenski, B. 1989. "Object-oriented cells bring new life to DBMS." *Software Magazine,* June.

Booch, G. 1983. *Software Engineering with Ada.* Redwood City, Calif.: Benjamin-Cummings.

Booch, G. 1989. "What is and isn't object-oriented design." *American Programmer*, special issue on object orientation. Vol. 2, Nos. 7–8, Summer.

Borland International. 1989. *Turbo Pascal Version 5.5 Object-Oriented Programming Guide.* Scotts Valley, Calif.: Borland International.

Brooks, F. P. 1987. "No silver bullet: Essence and accidents of software engineering." *Computer,* 20 (4): pp. 10–19.

Bryan, M. 1988. *SGML: An Author's Guide to the Standardized Generalized Markup Language.* Reading, Mass.: Addison-Wesley.

Chapwick, P. 1989. "Interview: Shaku Atre." *Database Programming and Design,* August.

Coad, P. 1989. "Object-oriented analysis." *American Programmer*, special issue on object orientation, Vol. 2, Nos. 7–8, Summer.

Corbi, T. A. 1989. "Program understanding: Challenge for the 1990s." *IBM Systems Journal,* 28 (2).

Cox, B. J. 1986. *Object-Oriented Programming: An Evolutionary Approach.* Reading, Mass.: Addison-Wesley.

Dawson, J. 1989. "A family of models." *Byte,* September.

Deutsch, L.P. 1989. Comment made during a panel discussion at OOPSLA '89, October, New Orleans.

Deutsch, L. P. 1989. "The past, present and future of Smalltalk." *ECOOP '89, Proceedings of the 1989 Europe Conference.* The British Computer Society Workshop Series, Cambridge: Cambridge University Press, pp. 73–87.

Digitalk. 1989. *Smalltalk/V Mac, Tutorial and Programming Handbook.* Los Angeles, Calif.: Digitalk, Inc.

Dodani, M. H., Hughes, C. E., and Moshell, M. J. 1989. "Separation of powers." *Byte,* March.

Dyson, E. 1989. "Object-oriented database roundup." *Release 1.0,* September 22. New York: EDventure Holdings Inc.

Franz, M. 1990. *Object-Oriented Programming Featuring Actor.* Glenview, Ill.: Scott, Foresman, and Company.

Friedhoff, R., and Benzon, W. 1989. *The Second Computer Revolution: Visualization.* New York: Harry N. Abrams, Inc.

Gibson, W. 1988. *Mona Lisa Overdrive.* New York: Bantam Books.

Gilbane, F. 1989. *An Update on CALS Publishing Issues.* Seybold Computer Publishing Conference, San Francisco, Calif., September.

Goldberg, A. 1984. *Smalltalk: The Interactive Programming Environment.* Reading, Mass.: Addison-Wesley.

Goldberg, A. and Robson, D. 1983. *Smalltalk-80: The Language and Its Implementation.* Reading, Mass.: Addison-Wesley.

Gosling, J., Rosenthal, D., and Arden, M. 1989. *The NeWS book: Introduction to Network/Extensible Window System.* New York: Springer-Verlag.

Hayes, F., and Baran, N. 1989. "A Guide to GUIs." *Byte,* July.

Hewlett-Packard. 1988. *HP NewWave Environment: General Information Manual for Software Developers.* Palo Alto, Calif.: Hewlett-Packard.

Jeffcoate, J., Hales, K., and Downes, V. 1989. *Object-Oriented Systems: The Commercial Benefits.* London: Ovum Ltd.

Johnson, R. E., and Foote, B. 1988. "Designing reusable classes." *Journal of Object-Oriented Programming,* Vol. 1, No. 2.

Juniper Software Corporation. 1989. *An Introduction to the Persist Object Model.* Chelmsford, Mass.: Juniper Software Corporation.

Kapor, M. 1988. *Conference on Object-Oriented Programming: Systems, Languages, and Applications 1988* (OOPSLA '88), San Diego, CA. Dinner speech.

Keen, S. 1989. *Object-Oriented Programming in Common Lisp.* Reading, Mass.: Addison-Wesley.

Kraemer, T. 1989. "Product development using object-oriented software technology." *Hewlett-Packard Journal,* August, pp. 87–100.

Machtrone, B. 1989. "Object-oriented: Old wine, new bottles?" *PC Magazine,* May 16.

Martin, J., and McClure, C. 1988. *Structured Techniques: The Basis for CASE.* Englewood Cliffs, N.J.: Prentice Hall.

Meyer, B. 1988. *Object-Oriented Software Construction.* Englewood Cliffs, N.J.: Prentice Hall.

Miller, W. M. 1989. "Multiple inheritance in C++." *Computer Language,* August, pp. 63–71.

Miller, W. M. 1989. *What Is C++?* Sudbury, Mass.: Software Development Technologies. Videotape.

Millikin, M.D. 1988. Remark made at Patricia Seybold's Technology Forum on Object Orientation, Boston, Mass., April 5.

Millikin, M. D. 1989. "Object orientation: What it can do for you; from operating systems to user interfaces, commercial viability is near." *Computerworld,* March 13.

Neuwirth, C.M., and Ogura, A. 1988. *The Andrew System Programmer's Guide to the Andrew Toolkit, Volume 1: Theory and Examples.* Pittsburgh, Pa.: Carnegie-Mellon University.

Neuwirth, C. M., and Ogura, A. 1988. *The Andrew System Programmer's Guide to the Andrew Toolkit, Volume 2: Reference.* Pittsburgh, Pa.: Carnegie-Mellon University.

New Science Associates. 1989. *Object-Oriented Technology: Commercial Scopes and Limits.* Southport, Conn.: New Science Associates. Advanced Software Research Industry Report.

Ontologic Inc. 1989a. *Vbase.* Billerica, Mass.: Ontologic, Inc.

Ontologic Inc. 1989b. *Product Description.* Billerica, Mass.: Ontologic, Inc., March.

O'Reilly, T. 1989. "The toolkits (and politics) of X Windows." *UNIX World,* February.

Palay, A. 1989. "The Andrew toolkit: The present and the future." *Object Orientation: Defining the End-User Platform for the 1990s.* Patricia Seybold's Third Annual Technology Forum, Boston, Mass.

Parsaye, K., Chignell, M., Khoshafian, S., and Wong, H. 1989. *Intelligent Databases: Object-Oriented, Deductive, and Hypermedia Technologies.* New York: John Wiley & Sons.

Peterson, G. E., ed. 1987. *Tutorial: Object-Oriented Computing, Volume 1: Concepts.* Washington, D.C.: Computer Society Press of the IEEE.

Peterson, G. E., ed. 1987. *Tutorial: Object-Oriented Computing, Volume 2: Implementations.* Washington, D.C.: Computer Society Press of the IEEE.

Petzold, C. 1989. *Programming the OS/2 Presentation Manager.* Redmond, Wa.: Microsoft Press.

Petzold, C. 1989. "The truth about Presentation Manager." *PC Magazine,* April 11.

Poole, L. 1989. "System 7.0." *MacWorld,* August.

Pun, W., and Winder, R. 1989. "A design method for object-oriented programming." *Proceedings of the Third European Conference on Object-Oriented Programming (ECOOP).* Cambridge: Cambridge University Press.

Rettig, M., Morgan, T., Jacobs, J., and Wimberly, D. 1989. "Object-oriented programming in AI: New choices." *AI Expert,* January, pp. 53–69.

Robbins, T. 1980. *Still Life With Woodpecker.* New York: Bantam Books.

Robertson, J., Mauro, T., and Helbrig, K. A. 1988. *Guide to Andrew (X Version 11, Release 3).* Pittsburgh, Pa.: Information Technology Center, Carnegie-Mellon University.

Rymer, J.R. 1989. "Objects at floodtide: Object orientation permeates new development." *Patricia Seybold's Office Computing Report,* 12 (6), June.

Schmucker, K. J. 1986. *Object-Oriented Programming for the Macintosh.* Hasbrouck Heights, N.J.: Hayden Books.

Shlaer, S., and Mellor, S. 1988. *Object-Oriented Systems Analysis: Modeling the World in Data.* Yourdon Press Computing Series, Englewood Cliffs, N.J.: Prentice Hall.

Silicon Beach Software. 1989. *Super 3D User Manual for Macintosh.* San Diego, Calif.: Silicon Beach Software.

Southerton, A. 1989. *Programmer's Guide to Presentation Manager.* Reading, Mass.: Addison-Wesley.

Stefik, M., and Bobrow, D. 1986. "Object-oriented programming: Themes and variations." *AI Magazine,* Winter, pp. 40–62.

Stefik, M., Bobrow, D.G., Mittal, S., and Conway, L. 1983. "Knowledge programming in LOOPS: Report on an experimental course." *AI Magazine,* 4 (3).

Stein, J. 1988. "Object-oriented programming and databases." *Dr. Dobb's Journal,* March.

Stepstone Corporation. 1989. *Objective-C Language: Version 4.0.* Sandy Hook, Conn.: The Stepstone Corporation.

Stroustrup, B. 1986. *The C++ Programming Languages.* Reading, Mass.: Addison-Wesley.

Thomas, D. 1989. "What's in an object?" *Byte,* March.

Thompson, T. 1989. "The NeXTStep." *Byte,* March.

van den Bos, J., and Laffra, C. 1989. "*PROCOL: A parallel object language with protocols." *Proceedings of Object-Oriented Programming: Systems, Languages, and Applications 1989* (OOPSLA '89). *SIGPLAN Notices,* Vol. 24, No. 10, October, pp. 95–102.

Verity, J. 1987. "The OOPS revolution." *Datamation,* May 1.

Wasserman, A. I., Pircher, P. A., and Muller, R. J. 1990. "The object-oriented structured design notation for software design representation." *Computer,* Vol. 24, No. 3, March.

Watanabe, T., and Yonezawka, A. 1988. "Reflections in an object-oriented concurrent language." *Proceedings of Object-Oriented Programming: Systems, Languages, and Applications 1989* (OOPSLA '89). *SIGPLAN Notices,* Vol. 23, No. 11, pp. 306–315.

Whiting, R. 1989. "The quest for a better way to develop software." *Electronic Business,* July 10, pp. 16–17.

Whitten, G. F. 1989. "Using object-oriented programming." Comments presented at the annual Microsoft System Software Seminar, Microsoft Corporation, Redmond, Wa.

Wilson, R. 1987. "Object-oriented languages reorient programming techniques." *Computer Design,* November 1.

Young, D. A. 1989. *X Window Systems Programming Applications with Xt.* Englewood Cliffs, N.J.: Prentice Hall.

Zdonik, S., and Maier, D., eds. 1990. *Readings in Object-Oriented Databases.* Palo Alto, Calif.: Morgan Kaufmann Publishers.

Index